in

HEALTH CARE

Professional Careers Series

CAREERS in
HEALTH CARE

BARBARA M. SWANSON

FIFTH EDITION

McGraw·Hill

New York   Chicago   San Francisco   Lisbon   London   Madrid   Mexico City
Milan   New Delhi   San Juan   Seoul   Singapore   Sydney   Toronto

Library of Congress Cataloging-in-Publication Data

Swanson, Barbara Mardinly.
    Careers in health care / by Barbara M. Swanson.—5th ed.
        p.   cm. — (McGraw-Hill professional careers series)
    ISBN 0-07-143850-5 (alk. paper)
    1. Allied health personnel—Vocational guidance—United States.   2. Medical
personnel—Vocational guidance—United States.   I. Title.   II. Series.

    R697.A4S93   2005
    610.69—dc22   2004021426

This book is dedicated, with love and thanks,
to my wonderful, amazing family.

1 2 3 4 5 6 7 8 9 0   DOC/DOC   0 9 8 7 6 5

ISBN 0-07-143850-5

This book is printed on acid-free paper.

CONTENTS

PREFACE

This book was written because, today more than ever, students, parents, teachers, guidance counselors, new graduates, men and women seeking new careers, individuals reentering the workforce, and consumers of health-care services want, need, and deserve correct, complete, current, and readable information about the myriad career options that exist in the health field today. In addition to the noble profession of physician, there are dozens of other vital and challenging ways to contribute in the health field; it is on these professions that *Careers in Health Care* focuses.

For each career covered in this book, the following questions have been carefully researched and answered: What is the theory behind the work? What does the work entail? What is the workday like? How many men and women are in the profession? What education and training are necessary? What certification and licensure requirements exist? What personal qualities and abilities are important to success and satisfaction? What salaries and promotions may be anticipated? What, if any, drawbacks are inherent to the work? And, finally, what does the future of the profession look like?

To the thousands of health-care professionals I have interviewed in the course of researching the material for this and the four previous editions of this book, who so generously and graciously shared their knowledge and time, including the good people at the American Medical Association and at CAAHEP as well as to the folks at the U.S. Department of Labor, goes my sincere appreciation. Special thanks go to Roy Pollack, M.D., Celia Ores, M.D., David Ores, M.D., Youngick Lee, M.D., Lonna Yegen, M.D., James J. Pedicano, M.D., Goldie Alfasi-Siffert, Ph.D., and the late Robert H. Ringewald, M.D., for their guidance and encouragement.

The editors wish to thank Barbara Wood Donner for revising this fifth edition.

INTRODUCTION

From television, movies, or, perhaps, personal experience, we've all glimpsed the drama of the modern hospital—the fast pace of the emergency room, the methodical intensity of the operating room, the dozen pairs of educated hands setting to work to provide essential care. In a hospital, there are many educated people working together to improve lives and to save lives.

Every medical recovery and every medical discovery is the product of teamwork. There are no nonessential jobs in health and medicine. And not all of the drama in modern medicine and health care takes place in the operating room. There is drama—and challenge and satisfaction, too—in the occupational therapy room of a community rehabilitation clinic, in a rural home where a nurse-midwife is helping to deliver a baby, or in a laboratory looking through an electron microscope.

There is room in the health field for almost every ability, talent, and interest. Are you artistically inclined? Then you might consider a career as an art therapist or a medical illustrator. Are you mechanically oriented? Biomedical engineering might offer the challenges you seek. Do you enjoy working with your hands? Manual arts therapy calls for such dexterity, and so do careers in orthotics, prosthetics, and dental and ophthalmic laboratory technology. Are you interested in music? Or dance? Or gardening? Then you may find your place in music therapy or dance therapy or horticultural therapy. Do you like to write? Americans today are hungry for medical and health-related information, and opportunities in medical writing are booming. Does photography interest you? Biological photography is a fascinating field. If you have ever considered becoming a librarian, health sciences librarianship might be the perfect specialty for you. If you love working with children, a career as a child life specialist can offer very special rewards. If you would like to work in the exciting atmosphere of a hospital but do not want direct patient-care responsibility, a position as a dietitian or as a technician in the laboratory might be ideal. If you want patient contact but do not plan to become a physician, you might consider becoming a nurse or a surgical technologist, an extracorporeal perfusionist or a physician assistant. Are sports your love? The demand for certified athletic trainers is growing fast. The options go on and on—there is even a place for magicians in medicine.

The possibilities are great—and growing greater every day as new medical technologies and techniques are developed. Last year, Americans spent $2 trillion on health care—that is, 15 percent of the nation's total output of goods and services. The demand for medical services has never been greater, and the opportunities for serving are more diverse and, in most cases, more plentiful than ever before. Simultaneously, however, scrutiny of medical services has never been greater because the health-care reform movement emphasizes cost containment in addition to successful medical outcomes.

The men and women who bring their intellect, talent, and dedication to the health-care field do very important work in our society. Good luck as you seek your special place among them on the health-care team.

CHAPTER 1

ANESTHESIOLOGIST ASSISTANT (AA)

Also Known as Anesthesiology Physician Assistant, Type B, and Nurse Anesthetist

Anesthesia during surgery is one of the most critical aspects of an operation, involving the patient's pain and stress levels as well as all of the essential systems of the body. The administration of the anesthesia is controlled by the anesthesiologist or anesthetist, who is a physician with highly specialized training. Anesthesiologist assistants (AAs) are health-care professionals who have successfully completed an accredited program of academic and clinical training and are qualified to work under the supervision of an anesthesiologist. AAs assist in administering the anesthetics to patients undergoing surgery.

Anesthesiologist assistants are to anesthesiologists what primary care physician assistants are to primary care physicians (i.e., family physicians, pediatricians, and so on). They are dependent practitioners participating within a medical care team. The details of their specific responsibilities may vary from site to site depending on the particular practice guidelines in individual hospitals and individual states.

Although some AAs may participate in the preanesthetic evaluation, more commonly they assist the anesthesiologist in reviewing the data available from the surgical and medical teams. In collaboration with the anesthesiologist, they participate in inducing and maintaining the anesthesia and in monitoring the patient's status during the surgical procedure.

AAs' responsibilities may also include pretesting and calibrating anesthesia delivery systems and monitors; collecting preoperative data and performing physical examinations; inserting venous, arterial, and other invasive catheters; administering drugs for the induction and maintenance of anesthesia; administering and monitoring regional anesthesia; airway management, including intubation and fiberoptics; administering cardiovascular drugs as support therapy; providing safe transition from operating room to recovery room; performing functions in the intensive care unit and pain unit; and participating in administrative affairs, research, and clinical instruction.

The anesthesiologist is usually expected to be available in the hospital—although often not always present in the room—during all portions of the case. As a general rule, both the AA and the anesthesiologist are present at the beginning and the end of the case and at the time of any major changes in the patient's status.

SETTING, SALARIES, STATISTICS

Anesthesiologist assistants work wherever anesthesiologists work: in hospitals, clinics, outpatient surgical facilities, and academic settings. AAs currently practice in thirteen states, with other states being added as the population of AAs increases. The greatest concentration of AAs is in the two states that currently have educational programs—Georgia and Ohio. Starting salaries for anesthesiologist assistants begin in the $70,000 to $95,000 range, depending on the location and size of the hospital and the specialization of the training of the AA.

HOW TO BECOME AN ANESTHESIOLOGIST ASSISTANT

Formal educational requirements for this field are only about fifteen years old. A master's degree specializing in anesthesia is required. This degree is offered by only two universities, Emory and Case Western Reserve, both of which established their programs less than thirty years ago. Both of these programs are accredited by the Commission on Accreditation of Allied Health Education Programs (CAAHEP), an independent body that accredits most allied health education programs in the United States and that, in 1994, succeeded the American Medical Association's Committee on Allied Health Education and Accreditation (CAHEA).

Applicants to a program must have premedical undergraduate backgrounds but may have college degrees in one of several areas. Typically, they are degrees in biology or chemistry or a related allied health area, such as respiratory therapy, nursing, or medical technology. Students entering these programs range from recent college graduates to people who have been working in other areas for ten years or more. Over the years, approximately 10 to 15 percent of the graduates of the two programs have gone on for further graduate medical education, and the overwhelming majority of those who have gone to medical school have done residencies in anesthesiology.

A national certification examination for anesthesiologist assistants has been available since 1992. This examination is given by the National Commission on the Certification of Anesthesiologist Assistants (NCCAA) in collaboration with the National Board of Medical Examiners, which is the group that also assists with the national examination for primary care physician assistants.

A practicing AA who has successfully completed an educational program accredited by CAAHEP and passed this examination is designated an anesthesiologist assistant–certified, or AA-C. Thereafter, he or she must submit continuing education credits or certification renewal as well as successfully complete a Continued Demonstration of Quality exam every six years.

Anesthesiologist assistants are regulated by different legislation depending on the state in which they are practicing. In some states, AAs are qualified to be licensed as physician assistants (PAs) and, therefore, practice within mandates set forth in the legislation for regulations governing PAs (see Chapter 48). In Georgia, for example, AAs are defined as one type of physician assistant with a corresponding job description. In such states, an AA is called an anesthesiologist physician assistant, Type B, or APA. The Board of Medicine of the National Academy of Sciences (NAS) defines three categories of physician assistant—Type A, Type B, and Type C. Type A is the designation for a primary care/generalist physician assistant. A Type B assistant is distinguished by exceptional skill in one clinical specialty or, more commonly, in certain procedures within a specialty. In this area of specialty, the assistant would have a degree of skill beyond that normally possessed by a more general Type A assistant and, perhaps, beyond that normally possessed by a physician who is not engaged in the specialty.

A Type C assistant is similar to a Type A assistant in the number of areas in which he or she can perform but cannot exercise the degree of independent synthesis of information and judgment of which a Type A is capable.

Since each state's legislation, regulations, and definitions are different, consult the medical board of the state where you intend to practice or contact the American Academy of Anesthesiologist Assistants (AAAA).

THE FUTURE

As of 2004, recent graduates are much in demand, and it appears that employment growth in this still relatively new profession will remain stable through the coming decade.

For information about anesthesiologist assistants, contact:

Anesthesiologist Assistant Program
Emory University
617 Woodruff Memorial Building
P.O. Box AK
Atlanta, GA 30322
anesthesiology.emory.edu/PA_Program/index.html

Anesthesiologist Assistant Program
Case Western Reserve University
11100 Euclid Avenue, LKS 2536
Cleveland, OH 44106-5007
anesth.com

American Academy of Anesthesiology Assistants (AAAA)
P.O. Box 13978
Tallahassee, FL 32317
anesthetist.org

National Commission for the Certification of AAs (NCCAA)
P.O. Box 15519
Atlanta, GA 30033-0519

CHAPTER

2

ART THERAPIST

An art therapist uses art activities—painting, drawing, sculpting, or other media—to help patients who are being treated for physical, emotional, mental, or medical problems, whether individually or in combination. Examples could include helping an amputee to deal emotionally and physically with the loss of a hand by becoming more accustomed to using the remaining hand; helping a cancer patient cope with the physical pain of surgery and the emotional pain of the loss of a breast; or helping a child to deal with a hearing loss through the use of artwork for communication and for emotional release.

Art therapy uses art activities as a medium of nonverbal expression and communication, which can help a wide variety of mentally and physically impaired patients resolve emotional conflicts, develop greater self-understanding, and find an avenue of increased or renewed personal growth. Art therapy is used as a medium for interpretation and rehabilitation with patients who are unable or unwilling to speak as well as with those who are verbal but who may not be able to put their concerns into words. "One picture is worth a thousand words," says a well-known Chinese proverb. For psychiatric patients, art therapy sessions may help them to speak volumes.

Art therapy emerged as a profession in the 1930s. Early twentieth-century psychiatrists collected and studied the artwork they found on hospital walls and on scraps of paper in patients' rooms, hoping to gain additional insight into their patients' thoughts, feelings, and illnesses. Since then, art therapy has developed into an important and effective method of diagnosis and rehabilitation.

Similarly to the other creative arts therapies—dance therapy, music therapy, poetry therapy, and psychodrama—art therapy can be effective because patients' emotions are directly tapped and because the visual expressions of the emotions—the pictures, sculptures, and montages created—provide a medium beyond that of words and verbal language. When patients draw pictures of their homes, their families, or themselves, they may be able to be more in touch with their feelings than under the more usual circumstances of verbal discussion. Patients' artwork can also be helpful in revealing the intensity, source, or nuances of particular issues that the patients may have been unable or unwilling to discuss "in so many words."

Art therapists encourage patients in their expressions and are attuned to elements such as the colors used; degree of tension, line, mass, texture, and pattern; spatial arrangement of figures or objects; detail or lack thereof; and perspective, proportion, and technique. These elements are more than just the aesthetic elements of the drawing; they are also reflections of how the patients may be seeing the world. The patients' artwork may provide valuable insights into their subconscious feelings, desires, and fears. The patients' abilities, personalities, interests, concerns—the very nature of their emotional distress and progress—can be reflected in the artwork they create.

Art therapists are human service providers who, by virtue of their graduate-level education and extensive training in both art and psychology, are experts at involving a variety of patients in art activities to help uncover problems and bring about improvement. They may act as primary therapists or as adjuncts within a treatment team, depending on the needs of the institution and the treatment objectives of the patient.

Art therapists treat individuals, couples, family groups, and communities. Following the attacks on the World Trade Centers in New York City in September 2001, for example, art therapists were called on to help many of the city's residents cope with their feelings of horror, loss, and outrage.

Most patients—about 75 percent—who are seen by art therapists are emotionally disturbed. Individuals with physical disabilities are the second largest group, at about 6 percent. Art therapy is also used to help people who have mental disabilities, posttraumatic stress syndrome, cancer, asthma, pain, HIV/AIDS, autism, Alzheimer's Disease, learning disabilities, hearing impairment, sight impairment, brain damage, or multiple disabilities as well as individuals who are dealing with the effects of aging, sexual abuse, alcohol and drug abuse, or imprisonment. According to the American Art Therapy Association (AATA), approximately 40 percent of all art therapy patients are adults, 30 percent are adolescents, 22 percent are children, 6.5 percent are elderly, and 1.5 percent are infants.

Art therapists plan art activities, maintain and distribute arts and crafts materials, provide instruction in a variety of artistic techniques, and observe and record what takes place during the art therapy session. The emphasis is not on the quality of the artwork produced but on the patient's well-being. The art therapist will usually confer with other members of the medical health team to make the diagnosis, devise a treatment plan, and assess progress.

Other benefits are also possible through art therapy. When administered to a group of patients, such as when a group mural is being created, it provides an important social—and potentially socializing—opportunity. Creating a work of art can provide relaxation, release, pleasure, and a sense of satisfaction for anyone, and these benefits can be especially important to a patient who feels confused or victimized or who has low self-confidence or low self-esteem.

SETTINGS, SALARIES, STATISTICS

Art therapists work in private practice and in clinical, educational, and rehabilitative settings, such as psychiatric centers, clinics, community centers, nursing homes, drug and alcohol treatment centers, schools, halfway houses, group homes, women's shelters, prisons, development centers, residential treatment centers, general hospitals, colleges, and universities. Of these settings, long- and short-term psychiatric hospitals employ the most art therapists. Community mental health centers are the second-largest employer, residential treatment centers rate third, and private practice ranks fourth. The northeastern section of the United States has the highest concentration of art therapy practitioners. Both full-time and part-time opportunities are available. Between 5,000 and 6,000 art therapists are practicing today. Approximately 2,000 are registered art therapists who have satisfied the education, experience, and other requirements of the AATA for certification.

Salaries vary widely depending on the art therapist's credentials, employer, and state. Starting salaries are usually comparable to those paid to public school teachers holding a master's degree—about $28,000 to $32,000 per year. Median income is between $28,000 and $40,000. The top earning potential for salaried administrators is between $42,000 and $65,000. Art therapists who are in private practice tend to earn the most. Those with doctoral degrees can earn from $75 to $150 per hour.

HOW TO BECOME AN ART THERAPIST

Specialization in study to become an art therapist starts at the graduate level—that is, a minimum of a bachelor's degree is prerequisite—and to practice professionally, a master's degree or its equivalent is required.

Master's degree programs in art therapy usually will include courses in normal and pathological art expression, art therapy with children and adolescents, therapeutic art in special education, the nature of creativity, art therapy and the aging process, enhancing learning skills through the use of art, art therapy with stroke patients and other adults with communications problems, creative art therapy for the developmentally disabled, normal and abnormal psychological development, clinical diagnosis and treatment issues, psychological intervention and therapeutic counseling, defense mechanisms of the ego, dynamics of group process, theories of personality, and systems of psychotherapy. Studio fieldwork experience in a variety of clinical settings is also required. These programs are usually two years in length, with the first year dedicated to introductory courses and the second offering the candidate the option to specialize.

As an undergraduate, a prospective art therapist should major or minor in the creative or commercial arts or in art education. At many schools, an electronic art portfolio or slides of the student's artwork must be submitted. In addition, undergraduate courses in the behavioral and social sciences are usually required. There are approximately 130 training programs in art therapy offered by universities, clinical programs, and institutes in the United States. Twenty-four colleges and universities offer art therapy graduate training programs that are approved by the AATA. Among these programs, the name of the degree awarded and its specific curriculum varies: some award a master of art therapy degree (M.A.T. or M.A. in art therapy); others confer a master of arts in clinical art therapy, master of professional study (M.P.S.) in art therapy, or master of creative arts therapy (M.C.A.T.). The AATA has also approved two clinical training programs and one institute program.

Approximately 100 other non-AATA-approved training programs are offered by hospitals, universities, and institutes. These programs exist at every level: undergraduate, graduate-level certificate/diploma, master's degree, and doctorate.

Personal qualities that are important to success in this career include strong listening and verbal communication skills, analytical ability, patience, compassion, a degree of artistic talent, and a genuine desire to work with and help individuals who are impaired in various ways.

The AATA, the professional certifying organization for art therapy education programs and art therapists, offers registration and board certification to art therapists who satisfy their educational, internship, and paid-work-experience requirements; who provide a portfolio—in actual slides or electronic media—of acceptable-quality artwork; and who are supported by several letters of recommendation.

The AATA has assigned professional quality credit (PQC) values to the various education and experience alternatives available in art therapy; to be designated an ATR, for art therapist, registered, one must accumulate a minimum of twelve PQCs. For recertification as of 2004, 100 CEUs (Continuing Education Units) are required to be earned in a five-year period.

In the past decade, the number of art therapists applying for registration has risen dramatically, an indication both of the increasing popularity of art therapy and of the increasing demand for certification. A state license is also required if the art therapist works in a public school. The Art Therapy Credentials Board provides a copy of the Code of Professional Practice on its website, and it is important to be familiar with the code if you are considering a career in this field. The code covers the therapist's responsibility to clients; professional competence and integrity; the responsibilities to students, supervisees, research participants, and the profession; handling financial arrangements; advertising; and special ethical considerations for independent practitioners, their environment, and documentation.

The member registration list also appears on the website, along with information about special events, new developments in the field, and places and times for certification exams. Regional exams for certification are given in major cities across the country—six sites were offered in 2004.

THE FUTURE

Opportunities in art therapy are expected to grow. Recognition of this therapy and of the other creative arts therapies as valid, effective, and important primary, parallel, or adjunctive therapies for a widening patient population has resulted in the creation of more art therapy programs throughout the country. Art therapy, along with dance/movement therapy (see Chapter 11) and music therapy (see Chapter 32), was included and defined in legislation when amendments to the Older Americans Act became law in 1992.

This federal recognition has meant that more older Americans are receiving the benefits of art therapy and that federal, state, and agency grant monies are available for research. With the number of senior citizens living longer expected to grow, and the related growth in retirement and nursing home communities, the opportunities for art therapists are expected to rise also.

For more information about art therapists, contact:

American Art Therapy Association (AATA)
1202 Allanson Road
Mundelein, IL 60060-3808
info@arttherapy.org
arttherapy.org
The AATA publishes *Art Therapy: Journal of the American Art Therapy Association* as well as a number of other periodicals that contain up-to-the-minute information and source material about this profession.

Art Therapy Credentials Board (ATCB)
3 Terrace Way, Suite B
Greensboro, NC 27403
atcb@nbcc.org
atcb.org

CHAPTER

BIOLOGICAL PHOTOGRAPHER

Also Known as Medical
Photographer, Biophotographer,
Biological/Biomedical
Communicator, Forensic
Photographer, and Scientific Photographer

Biophotography is the exciting art—and science—that has brought us awe-inspiring images of living embryos in the human womb, astonishing photographs of the powerful chambers of the human heart, and mysterious pictures of the lights and darks of the winding canals of our gastrointestinal systems. Biophotography is used to capture and record a variety of medical events and subjects, such as the absence, presence, extent, and progress of a patient's condition; an entire surgical procedure, shot under sterile conditions; or the intricacies of a highly magnified tissue specimen. Biophotography is equally effective in providing views of fleeting phenomena or of events that unfold slowly.

In recent years, the combination of the availability of tremendous new camera, computer, film, and image-management technology along with the burgeoning accumulation of new medical techniques and technology has thrust biophotography to the forefront of a revolution in medical knowledge. Global awareness of medical breakthroughs and medical techniques has created a market hungry for immediate communication of medical information. Much of this is done electronically, and vivid and accurate photography is of critical importance.

Not only the field of human medicine is served, of course. In biophotography, all things that are living or that have lived are documented. Biological photographers are highly skilled scientific professionals who are responsible for the production of still and motion pictures of subjects for the health professions and the natural sciences. The prints, motion pictures, digitalized images, videotapes, and transparencies they produce are used for educational purposes, in patient records, in research, and as illustrations in publications.

Ours is a very visually oriented age. Doctors, researchers, students, patients, and the general population want to see what happens and how it happens. Today, as technologies converge and biological photographers use computers to capture, generate, and manipulate images, ever-new visual vistas are opening. The marriage of the biological photographer's artistic abilities with state-of-the-art computer hardware and software has given us "new eyes" with which to view biological form and function. Biophotography is a vital tool in health and medical education, patient treatment, and research, and biological photographers must have a thorough knowledge of photographic procedures and technology as well as a basic understanding of the biological sciences.

Biological photography is a creative, diverse, usually people-oriented profession that, increasingly, is proving invaluable in the understanding and communication of medical events. Biological photographers can specialize in one or more of several fields, such as ophthalmic photography (photographing disorders and injuries of the eye), photomicrography (photographing through a microscope), dental photography, and autopsy/specimen photography.

SETTINGS, SALARIES, STATISTICS

Biological photographers are employed by public and private hospitals, medical schools, universities, libraries, museums, federal health organizations, research institutions, dental facilities, veterinary facilities, natural science facilities, private medical and pharmaceutical companies, advertising agencies, and publishing companies. Some biological photographers freelance.

It is difficult to estimate the number of people in this field. The Bio-Communications Association (BCA)—formerly the Biological Photographic Association, or BPA—which is the professional association for biological photographers, reports a membership of approximately 1,000 men and women, but not all biological photographers are members, and a complete tally may be ten times that number. There are more men than women in this field.

It is also difficult to pinpoint salaries. The Health Careers Center states that the average annual salary for a biophotographer is $32,400, with a range of from $29,100 to $38,300. Another survey states that management and some major department heads earn as much as $85,000 annually.

In institutions that have large biocommunications departments—art, television, printing, instructional design, and photography—that employ as many as twenty-five biological photographers, advancement from an entry-level position through photography positions to management and administrative positions is possible. Government agencies that employ biological photographers usually have career ladders with steps leading to greater responsibility and authority and higher salaries.

HOW TO BECOME A BIOLOGICAL PHOTOGRAPHER

Because biophotography has become so vital and is an integral part of the health-care system, on-the-job training is no longer always adequate. Students contemplating a career in biological photography should anticipate two or four years of post–high school education. Over the last several years, there has been a trend among employers to seek qualified biological photographers from the colleges that offer associate's and bachelor's degrees in this specialty. Several schools across the country offer full or partial degree programs specifically in biological photography. Training and education are also offered by the BCA, which conducts seminars and hands-on workshops and presents a weeklong program of intensive training every June. In addition, on-the-job training is sometimes available in the photography departments of teaching hospitals.

The BCA, which has established criteria for competency, administers a certification examination through its Board of Registry and maintains a registry of certified biological photographers. Membership in the Bio-Communications Association is not required for certification by the BCA.

The certification process consists of three separate examinations: written, practical, and oral. The written part of the examination is four hours in length and is multiple choice. It is designed to test basic and specialized theoretical knowledge of photographic optics, biological terminology, planning and producing, materials and processes, photographic chemistry, applied light and filters, applied camera and lighting techniques, audiovisual technique, color, videography, cinematography, photomacrography, and photomicrography.

In the practical part of the examination, the candidate must produce to specifications a number of prints and transparencies on various assignments. In the oral examination, the candidate is expected to give a ten-minute presentation on one of four preannounced broad fields. Candidates must successfully satisfy all three parts of the examination program within five years. Upon satisfying the certification requirements, a biological photographer becomes a registered biological photographer and may use RBP after his or her name. This designation is widely accepted—and in many instances required—as a demonstration of competency.

The BCA provides a Jobs Hotline, which is a continuously updated, a prerecorded telephone message describing job openings in the United States and foreign countries for biological photographers. Listening to the often exciting job opportunities being described provides interesting and useful insight into exactly what biological photographers do.

Personal qualities that are important to a successful and satisfying career in biophotography include precision, patience, a "good eye," manual dexterity, a genuine interest in medicine, the ability to work in sometimes stressful medical settings, and the ability to develop a rapport that will help to put patients at ease when they are being photographed. Because photographic assignments may vary from day to day in subject matter, locale, and technique, biological photographers must be adaptable and able to work in physically demanding conditions, sometimes for long periods of time.

THE FUTURE

The job picture for biological photographers is very favorable. The rapid growth of the American health-care industry is causing rapid growth in biophotography. Over the past several decades, biophotography has become a vital component of the educational and research efforts of major medical, dental, and veterinary schools; various major health- and life-related activities and societies; agricultural research stations; fisheries and wildlife departments; museums and zoological societies; and health-related businesses. With that growth has come a critical demand for skilled professional biological photographers. The clarity, precision, rapid availability, and unique perspective offered by photography—and its many related special visual techniques—make it an essential tool in seeing, recording, and communicating medical subjects. As the health and medical information explosion continues and advances in photographic technique offer new possibilities, the need for the services of professional biological photographers should grow. A growth of between 10 percent and 25 percent is projected in this job market through the year 2010.

For more information about biological photographers, contact:

BioCommunications Association (BCA)
220 Southwind Lane
Hillsborough, NC 27278
bca.org

Health Sciences Communications Association (HeSCA)
One Wedgewood Drive, Suite 28
Jewett City, CT 06351-2428
hesca.org

CHAPTER

4

BIOMEDICAL COMMUNICATOR

Also Known as Medical Writer and
Health Science Communicator

The work of a biomedical communicator is a fascinating career for someone who is interested in the world of medicine and health and who also likes to write or edit. Biomedical communicators work as writers and editors for publishers, medical schools, journals, hospitals, nonprofit organizations, government agencies, pharmaceuticals, and many other organizations, both as on-staff employees and as contract or freelance writers.

Some biomedical communicators have a more formal background than others. Depending on the kind of material being written, the biomedical communicator may have an undergraduate science and writing background, hold a master's or doctorate in health communication, or be a medical professional who is also a writer and/or editor. Biomedical communications encompasses a range of publications that vary substantially in their technical depth and complexity. A biomedical communicator may edit a plain-English, question-and-answer, personal health column for the general readership of a local newspaper or write the scientifically precise lists of contraindications and side effects that are included in drug packages by pharmaceutical companies. A biomedical communicator might also write or edit highly technical scientific educational materials for medical schools, laboratories, or public education departments of government agencies or hospitals.

In between the degrees of complexity of these examples are dozens of other medical writing and/or editing opportunities: writing medical and health news for television and radio; producing public relations copy, such as informational brochures, in-house newsletters, press releases, magazine articles, and exhibits for hospitals, clinics, medical schools, and medical societies; preparing highly technical instructional manuals for the operation and maintenance of sophisticated new diagnostic and treatment equipment; developing computer software; writing advertising copy for pharmaceutical and medical/surgical equipment companies; documenting and reporting new discoveries for the medical industries; and writing scripts for public service announcements and health education films. In this wide range of medical writing opportunities, there is also the need for a wide range of competencies and talents—from proofreading for misspelled words and misplaced periods to managing all phases of the production of a new medical periodical.

It is true that many medical research reports, medical textbooks, and other very technical pieces are written by physicians, nurses, scientists, and other health-care practitioners, but much of what is read on the subjects of health and medicine by professionals in the health field as well as members of the general public is written and edited by biomedical communicators who may not have advanced training in a health-care discipline. These medical writers usually have a science background, in biology or a related science, and have shown a talent for understanding, analyzing, interpreting, and then clearly and accurately reporting what is often very complicated information. A top-quality biomedical communicator not only has the intellectual capacity to understand highly technical material, he or she has a strong interest in health and medical information.

When a medical writer writes for a medical audience—to describe a new treatment in a textbook or medical journal, for example—he or she must be comprehensive and meticulously correct. When a biomedical communicator's audience is the general population—as for a newspaper column on health or a television public service message—he or she must educate and explain, distilling that which is critical, new, and interesting from a large body of information and putting the complex medical concepts and long medical words into understandable, readable terms, all the while maintaining scientific accuracy. When a biomedical communicator writes advertising copy or public relations materials, he or she must also understand the psychology of selling.

SETTINGS, SALARIES, STATISTICS

Biomedical communicators work for newspapers, magazines, the medical press, textbook publishers, pharmaceutical and medical equipment companies, laboratories, hospitals, clinics, volunteer health agencies, medical schools, medical associations, government agencies, and in television, radio, and advertising.

Most biomedical communicators work full-time, but there are also part-time and freelance opportunities that offer the advantage of job flexibility. It is difficult to state salaries in this field because of the wide variety of employment situations involved. Annual salaries for college graduates begin around $27,000, and experienced writers/editors earn an average of $65,000 annually. More seasoned medical writers and biocommunications managers can earn up to $100,000 a year. Widely read medical columnists and authors receiving royalties from books on popular medical subjects may earn far more.

It is also difficult to estimate the number of men and women who are engaged in medical writing/editing because the work often overlaps with other forms of technical writing and so much of the writing is done on a freelance basis by medical and nonmedical personnel. The American Medical Writers Association (AMWA) is an international professional organization for biomedical communicators that offers writing and editing workshops and seminars. The AMWA also regularly compiles and publishes a job-market sheet listing job openings in the field.

The AMWA's membership in 2004 was 5,000 men and women. This figure includes copy and journal editors, advertising writers, freelance science writers and editors, pharmaceutical employees, television and film producers, abstractors, translators, public relations people, managers of medical communications departments, librarians, and medical illustrators as well as physicians, dentists, nurses, and other medical personnel who write. The total number of people engaged in biomedical communication is certainly higher.

In the advertising end of medical writing alone, there are over 1,000 job opportunities. In a recent year, the more than 200 pharmaceutical and medical/surgical equipment companies doing business in the United States spent almost $1 billion on printed advertising alone. Advertising and public education on the Internet have further increased the amount of biomedical writing and illustrating required. Creating that billion dollars' worth of copy were medical writers and medical copy editors at approximately 100 advertising agencies. In response to the public's growing interest in medical and health topics, the mass media—television, radio, magazines, and newspapers—are hiring increasing numbers of medical writers. *The New York Times*, for example, has on its staff about fourteen full-time and eight contract science writers who cover complex medical material as well as various reporters from other desks who are also equipped to cover health and science.

HOW TO BECOME A BIOMEDICAL COMMUNICATOR

To become a biomedical communicator, a bachelor's degree is usually required, and, in some cases, a graduate degree in technical writing is necessary for employment. Some employers prefer candidates who have majored in English, journalism, or the liberal arts and minored in a science, while others want writers who majored in a science, minored in English, and write effectively. In fact, of the writers presently in the field, 30 percent were English majors as undergraduates, and 18 percent were technical communications or journalism majors. Less than 10 percent majored in the sciences. In addition, it is essential that students entering the field be proficient with a computer and be familiar with the major software programs used in publishing.

In the past fifteen years, many colleges and universities have instituted undergraduate courses in medical and technical writing and scientific communication. While not always required for employment, such courses provide valuable background and teach technical competencies. There are also approximately fourteen universities that offer master's degrees in technical writing, and such additional study often enhances career advancement.

For more than thirty-five years, the AMWA has offered a continuing medical education program called the Core Curriculum, which is designed to improve skills in six major areas of biomedical communications: (1) audiovisuals, (2) editing/writing, (3) freelancing, (4) pharmaceuticals, (5) public relations/advertising, and (6) teaching. Courses in basic skills are also offered. Upon successful completion of one of these prescribed courses of study, a certificate is awarded to AMWA members.

The AMWA also offers an Advanced Curriculum to individuals who already have earned Core Curriculum certification, have taken certain qualifying core courses, or have at least five years of experience in biomedical communications. An Advanced Certificate is awarded upon the successful completion of eight in-depth advanced courses. Courses are offered at the AMWA's annual conference and at regional and chapter workshop meetings. The AMWA reports that writers with certificates from their Core Curriculum and Advanced Curriculum education programs tend to earn more and be more in demand than their peers.

Most medical writers also learn a great deal on the job, using the fundamental journalistic techniques of interviewing and researching. They visit hospitals and laboratories; interview doctors, researchers, and other scientific personnel; read textbooks, reports, and studies; analyze raw data; and then put those concepts and statistics into the most appropriate language and format for their readers. Writers should maintain a portfolio of their writing samples to present with their résumés when applying for a job or assignment.

As for the personal qualities that are important for a successful and satisfying career as a biomedical communicator, perhaps the most critical are a genuine love for writing and/or editing; the temperament to wrestle with a concept until it is in language that accurately, clearly, and appropriately communicates the message; and a genuine and abiding curiosity about medical and scientific topics. A talent for interviewing, a knack for research, the ability to relate well to others, and a healthy respect for deadlines are also essential.

THE FUTURE

This is certainly a fascinating time to be a biomedical communicator. Almost daily, new research findings and medical and surgical breakthroughs are changing health care worldwide, and there is a growing demand for medical, health, and scientific information. Our country's very sophisticated and specialized medical establishment is growing in its demands for more research literature, instructional materials, and public relations materials. The general public is also more interested in and knowledgeable of medical, health, and fitness subjects today. The thirst for more and better information is reflected in the expanding medical coverage in the mass media. Entire cable television networks are devoted to health subjects.

Technology, too, is generating new demands, and hundreds of medical and health websites provide new information daily to the worldwide Internet audience. Each new pharmaceutical or piece of equipment calls for medical writing and editing, and growth in these areas in recent years has been great. For example, the amount spent on pharmaceutical advertising has grown radically in the past ten years because so many new pharmaceuticals are being introduced annually. In addition, television advertising in the last few years has been highly developed by the pharmaceuticals as they have sought, very successfully, to educate the general public to request specific medications from their doctors.

In realistically appraising the job market for biomedical communicators, it must be noted that there is heavy competition for most openings. Therefore, it is important for students to acquire the best possible academic credentials in science and English; to develop strong interview skills and a clear, accurate, and adaptable writing style; and to pick up as much experience writing for school and local newspapers, nonprofit organizations, and the Internet as possible.

For more information about medical writing, contact:

American Medical Writers Association
410 West Gude Drive, Suite 101
Rockville, MD 20850-1192
amwa.org

Health and Science Communications Association (HeSCA)
39 Wedgewood Drive, Suite A
Jewett City, CT 06351
hesca.org

HeSCA publishes the *Journal of BioCommunication* in cooperation with the Association of Medical Illustrators and the Association of Biomedical Communications Directors.

The Society for Technical Communication
901 North Stuart Street, Suite 904
Arlington, VA 22203-1854
stc-va.org

CHAPTER 5

BIOMEDICAL ENGINEER

Also Known as Bioengineer, Medical Engineer, and Clinical Engineer

Biomedical engineers combine engineering skills with biological and medical information to design aids of all kinds to help medical patients. As the Alliance for Engineering in Medicine and Biology says in its educational literature, "The primitive man or woman who carved the first rough crutch from a stick helped to begin the development of what has become modern biomedical engineering." Biomedical engineers develop concepts and convert the ideas of physicians, rehabilitation therapists, and biologists into usable devices, instruments, materials, procedures, treatments, and techniques that improve the quality of patients' lives.

Under the broad title of biomedical engineer, there are four commonly recognized specialties: (1) bioengineering, (2) medical engineering, (3) clinical engineering, and (4) rehabilitation engineering. *Bioengineers* apply engineering principles to understanding the structure, function, and pathology of the human body. They also apply engineering concepts and technology to advance the understanding of biological nonmedical systems, such as maintaining and improving the quality of the environment and protecting human, animal, and plant life from toxicants and pollutants (sometimes referred to as bioenvironmental engineering). *Medical engineers* use engineering concepts and technologies to develop instrumentation, biomaterials, diagnostic and therapeutic devices, computer systems, artificial organs and joints, and other equipment needed in biology and medicine. *Clinical engineers* use engineering concepts and technologies to improve and manage patient-oriented health-care delivery systems in hospitals and clinics by selecting, maintaining, and testing medical instruments and machines, by training personnel in their use, and by ensuring that systems do not interact in ways that may be detrimental to patients and hospital staff. *Rehabilitation engineers* apply engineering science and design to create solutions to problems caused by disability, such as orthopedic devices, systems to electrically stimulate paralyzed muscles, and augmentative communications apparatuses.

Modern biomedical engineering formally began with a challenge more than a half century ago by the National Institutes of Health (NIH). The NIH asked, "What can engineering contribute to the biological sciences?" The answer has been a long and amazing list of lifesaving and life-enhancing inventions that have changed the way we live. The artificial heart, the heart-lung machine, the artificial kidney, nuclear magnetic resonance, respiratory and cardiac pacemakers, defibrillators, the artificial lung, surgical lasers, electrical muscle stimulators and battery powered artificial limbs, plastic heart valves, plastic and metal joints, CT scanners, digital hearing aids, and ultrasound are among the inventions that biomedical engineers have developed or helped to develop. Today, as the National Aeronautics and Space Administration (NASA) works to develop manned space stations, a major challenge for biomedical engineers is the maintenance of humans in space.

Biomedical engineering encompasses almost the full range of engineering specialties—electrical, mechanical, clinical, aerospace, chemical, computer science, agricultural, and civil—as they are applied to improving health care. Biomedical engineers work as members of health and research teams, applying the principles and technologies of these various disciplines to the understanding, defining, and solving of medical and biological problems.

Computer technology is widely employed in biomedical engineering; some biomedical engineers specialize in applying computerization to medicine. Computers are used in medical imaging, such as CT scans and MRIs. They are also used to monitor patients in the operating room and intensive care unit, to improve and expedite laboratory testing, to process medical data, and in numerous other medical situations. Future applications seem limitless.

Some biomedical engineers are engaged in analyzing and testing different materials, such as stainless steel, silicone, and various plastics, to determine whether they will be accepted or rejected by the human body when used in artificial organs and grafts. Others design and build systems to modernize laboratory, hospital, and clinical procedures. Some biomedical engineers who work in hospitals and other institutions monitor the accurate and safe performance of the instruments, devices, and machinery in use as well as teach hospital personnel how to use new equipment.

Biomedical engineering can be a very challenging and satisfying profession for men and women who are interested and talented in engineering as well as medicine and who want to contribute to the improvement of health care without necessarily having direct contact with and responsibility for patients. Although a biomedical engineer may never actually meet the patients he or she helps, the ideas and the inventions he or she develops touch those patients' lives in very important ways.

SETTINGS, SALARIES, STATISTICS

Biomedical engineers are employed in a wide variety of settings: hospitals; research foundations; medical, industrial, academic, and government laboratories; undersea and space programs; industry—more than 4,600 companies make medical devices; universities; and private consulting firms. The Department of Veterans Affairs, NIH, NASA, the Department of Defense, and the Environmental Protection Agency all employ biomedical engineers. Most job opportunities are in or near major cities.

Approximately 7,600 biomedical engineers had jobs in the United States in 2002. Of these, approximately 40 percent were employed in manufacturing, primarily of pharmaceuticals and medical equipment. Although the majority of them are men, a steadily increasing number of women are entering this profession.

Because of the wide range of work settings available to biomedical engineers and the variety of credentials encompassed by this job title, there is significant variation in salaries. According to a 2003 survey by the National Association of Colleges and Employers, annual starting salaries for biomedical engineers holding bachelor of science degrees averaged $39,126 in 2003, and those with master's degrees averaged $61,000. Median annual earnings for bioengineers were $60,410 in 2002, with the lowest salaries at less than $48,450 and the highest at more than $107,520, according to the U.S. Department of Labor.

Biomedical engineers work hours that can be highly variable. Those who work in research or on the production side, especially, may put in long, irregular hours as projects reach critical phases. Biomedical engineers who install and calibrate biomedical equipment and medical engineers who act as sales representatives for companies that manufacture biomedical equipment usually must travel to some extent.

HOW TO BECOME A BIOMEDICAL ENGINEER

A bachelor's degree in biomedical engineering from one of the twenty-nine programs accredited (as of November 2003) by the Accreditation Board for Engineering and Technology (ABET) is considered as entry-level in this profession. However, a graduate degree in biomedical engineering—a master's or preferably a doctorate—is highly recommended and in most settings is necessary for employment. A doctorate is almost always necessary for university and college teaching positions and for top research positions in industry and government laboratories. Among the courses typically offered by a four-year undergraduate program are biomedical engineering systems and design, biomedical computers, engineering biophysics, bioinstrumentation, biomechanics, biomaterials, biothermodynamics, biotransport, and artificial organs. For graduate study there are currently eighty-eight university programs in the United States.

Another route to a career in biomedical engineering is to concentrate only on the traditional engineering disciplines as an undergraduate and then to go on to do biomedical engineering work at the graduate level. Many universities offer ABET-accredited degrees in traditional engineering disciplines, such as mechanical or chemical, with specialties or options in biomedical engineering.

Prospective biomedical engineering students should concentrate in high school on mathematics—advanced algebra and trigonometry or precalculus are usually the minimum requirements for acceptance into an engineering discipline, with high school calculus preferred; chemistry; biology; physics; and English. Computer science proficiency is also essential, and proficiency in more than one language is strongly recommended.

Engineering schools look for a good scholastic average, and while solid college entrance examination scores are important for acceptance to many of these schools, some do not rely exclusively on these tests. In addition to the aptitudes necessary for this career—mathematical ability, analytic thinking, inventiveness, logic in thought process (which is learnable), and science ability—there are other, personal qualities that can contribute to success and satisfaction as a biomedical engineer. These include patience, perseverance, and, because biomedical projects are almost always team efforts, the ability to communicate verbally and in writing and to cooperate with a wide variety of coworkers.

Biomedical engineers must have or learn that very special kind of creativity that can cross disciplines to come up with the best answers. From the various physical and medical sciences, biomedical engineers adopt, adapt, merge, and synthesize theories, principles, technologies, and materials in their efforts to analyze situations and solve problems. A career in biomedical engineering can offer very stimulating, exciting challenges that entail a minimum of repetition and a maximum of innovative thinking.

Licensing as a professional engineer (PE) is encouraged for all biomedical engineers; for some employment situations, it is required by law.

THE FUTURE

The demand for qualified biomedical engineers currently far exceeds the supply, and a huge shortfall of biomedical engineers, as well as other types of engineers, is expected in coming years. Biomedical engineers play an important role in tissue engineering, in nanotechnology, and in mapping the human genome, and work in these fields is rapidly expanding. In addition, demand for rehabilitation engineers is increasing as more types of disabilities caused by illness and accident can be helped and as the population expands and lives longer.

There is a solid awareness of the value of this work. The National Institutes of Health has created the National Institute for Biomedical Imaging and Bioengineering (NIBIB). This new institute coordinates with the programs of other institutions and the NIH to facilitate use of research and new technologies for medical applications. The Whitaker Foundation of Arlington, Virginia, in an extraordinary expression of support, has funded more than thirty-eight new biomedical engineering academic departments in the field. Many undergraduate programs of biomedical engineering are seriously recruiting at the junior high and high school levels to ensure that the United States will have the workforce to continue this important work.

For more information about what biomedical engineers do, the various educational options in this field, and a list of colleges and universities offering biomedical engineering degree programs, contact:

Association for the Advancement of Medical Instrumentation (AAMI)
3330 Washington Boulevard, Suite 400
Arlington, VA 22201-4598
aami.org

Accreditation Board for Engineering and Technology (ABET)
111 Market Place, Suite 1050
Baltimore, MD 21202-4012
abet.org

C H A P T E R

6

BIOMEDICAL EQUIPMENT TECHNICIAN (BMET)

Also Known as Biomedical Engineering Technician and Biomedical Electronic Technician, Including BMET I (or Junior BMET), BMET II, BMET III (or Senior BMET), and BMET Supervisor

The health-care professionals responsible for the safe use of high-tech biomedical equipment are called biomedical equipment technicians (BMETs).

Breakthroughs in biomedical engineering are radically improving the ways disease and injury are diagnosed and treated. The application of the various engineering disciplines and technologies to health and medical problems has resulted in thousands of pieces of biomedical equipment that save lives; alleviate discomfort; and diagnose medical conditions earlier, more accurately, less painfully, and less dangerously. CT scanners, dialysis machines, x-ray machinery, transducers, magnetic resonance imagers (MRIs), electrocardiographs (EKGs), electroencephalographs (EEGs), incubators, and inhalators are but a few of those important pieces of sophisticated biomedical equipment to which doctors, nurses, and other health-care personnel can turn when diagnosing and treating patients.

The number of new biomedical inventions, their complexity, and their success seems to be increasing each year. But modern medicine's sophisticated biomedical equipment is life-enhancing or life-extending only if it is available, accurate, safe, and correctly used.

A biomedical equipment technician is knowledgeable in the theory of operation; the underlying physiologic principles; and the practical, safe, clinical application of biomedical equipment. His or her capabilities may include the installation, calibration, inspection, preventative maintenance, and repair of general biomedical and related technical equipment. He or she might also be involved in the operation or supervision of equipment and in equipment control, safety, and maintenance.

When a piece of biomedical equipment fails, the biomedical equipment technician is responsible for correcting the problem as quickly as possible. Biomedical equipment technicians also teach hospital personnel how to operate the various pieces of biomedical equipment. They assist doctors, nurses, and researchers in conducting experiments and procedures. Their work is crucial to the safety and correct treatment of the patient as well as to the safety of the health-care personnel handling the equipment.

There are four levels of expertise in the job category of biomedical equipment technician. A BMET I (or Junior BMET) works at the entry level, performing skilled work of routine difficulty under close supervision. He or she primarily carries out preventive maintenance, repair, and safety testing and has the minimum of education and experience required. A BMET II (or BMET) has at least several years of related education or experience and works independently in repair and maintenance programs. A BMET III (or Senior BMET) has a significant amount of education and/or training, can perform highly skilled work of considerable difficulty, and works with little supervision. The highest level in this occupation, the BMET supervisor, has a significant amount of preparation and supervises others. He or she reports to a department head or to the hospital administration. It should be noted that these definitions are general. In reality, the lines between levels are defined by each hospital and tend to be somewhat blurred, depending on the needs and structure of each institution's work environment.

SETTINGS, SALARIES, STATISTICS

BMETs in the United States are employed by large hospitals and clinics; university, government, and industrial laboratories; research institutions; biomedical equipment maintenance services; and specific medical instrument manufacturers. Most job openings are in cities, as hospitals with budgets large enough to permit the hiring of full-time biomedical equipment technicians are usually located in high-population areas.

Some hospitals do not hire their own biomedical equipment technicians, relying instead on technicians who are employed by the manufacturers or distributors of their various pieces of biomedical equipment. Bowing to cost constraints, however, more are now hiring in-house biomedical equipment technicians, which is usually much more cost-effective.

There are also a substantial number of biomedical equipment technicians on active duty with the armed forces.

Overall, salaries vary with the BMET's education and experience, the location, and the type of employer. A two-year associate's degree is required. The median annual salary for a biomedical technician in 2002 was $36,380, according to the Center for Health Careers. In other surveys, starting pay in 2002–2003 was stated at approximately $18,000 to $30,000 annually, with higher salaries in the larger cities and larger medical centers. Certified biomedical equipment technicians and those with four years of experience averaged between $31,000 and $38,000 yearly. Well-established and top technicians averaged $48,000 to $65,000 annually.

Working conditions for biomedical equipment technicians are usually pleasant. Hours are mostly predictable—forty hours per workweek, with evening, weekend, and holiday "on call" duty rotated in for hospital workers. The nature of the work, however, means that emergency situations can and do arise, and longer, erratic, and more stressful hours may be required when emergencies occur.

Biomedical equipment technicians who work for manufacturers must travel to some degree and, when emergencies develop, this traveling may have to be done without notice. Biomedical equipment technicians who are employed by hospitals, clinics, and similar institutions may advance from beginning technician to positions of greater responsibility and independence and then on to supervisory positions. A biomedical equipment technician who works for a manufacturer can progress from field service trainee to field service technician and, with experience and success, to customer service representative and regional service manager. In either case, certification enhances the prospects for promotion.

The majority of biomedical equipment technicians are male, but the number of women entering the field is gradually increasing.

HOW TO BECOME A BIOMEDICAL EQUIPMENT TECHNICIAN

Biomedical equipment technicians train for between one and four years after high school. Nationwide, there are approximately sixty formal biomedical engineering—also called electronic or equipment—technician programs, located in colleges, universities, community colleges, junior colleges, and vocational/technical institutes. Most of these programs offer associate's degrees, but some award bachelor's degrees. In most cases, associate's degree course work can automatically be transferred to a bachelor's program for credit. Almost all of the associate's programs provide field-work experience in laboratories or hospitals as part of the training.

The curriculum for a biomedical equipment technician educational program typically includes courses in electronics, computer technology, mathematics, biology, chemistry, anatomy, physiology, and medical terminology.

An alternative educational route to the training needed for this career is to attend one of the many two-year colleges offering general programs leading to an associate's in applied science degree in electronics, then to train on the job in a laboratory or hospital. However, with the growing number of biomedical equipment technicians in the field, it is less likely that someone without a BMET degree will be employed in a health-care setting.

To prepare in high school, interested students should take algebra, trigonometry, physics, biology, chemistry, electronics, and shop courses. Because good communication skills are necessary for quality performance as a biomedical equipment technician, students also need to emphasize English and communication courses.

Like biomedical engineers, biomedical equipment technicians must possess both mechanical aptitude and an interest in mechanical, electronic, electrical, and other technical matters. Excellent manual dexterity, vision, eye-hand coordination, and facility with numbers are also essential.

Career-long success and satisfaction in this field require personal qualities of appreciation for precision; the ability to handle emergency situations calmly, quickly, and correctly; and, in the case of biomedical equipment technicians who work in hospitals and other health-care settings, the ability to work well among patients.

The biomedical equipment technician must know how to speak, write, and listen accurately. BMETs must write as well as read correspondence containing crucial detailed information, write operating manuals for hospital staffers, and routinely give verbal instructions to and receive feedback from a wide variety of hospital personnel. It is equally important that biomedical equipment technicians know how to relate well to their various coworkers.

Certification in this field is voluntary, but it does enhance earnings, especially at the entry level. Candidates can earn certification as a certified biomedical equipment technician—a CBET—by passing a national exam and meeting the educational and experience requirements. The International Certification Commission (ICC) administers the certification process. ICC offers two levels of certification: candidate, which is a step toward full certification, and full certification. In both of these levels, there are three options: (1) general biomedical equipment, (2) radiological equipment, and (3) clinical equipment. A competency examination is administered for each option.

To be eligible to take the candidacy certification examination, an individual must have (1) an associate's degree in biomedical equipment technology, (2) an associate's degree in electronic technology, plus one year of biomedical equipment technician experience, (3) two years of biomedical equipment technician experience, *or* (4) successfully completed a U.S. military biomedical equipment technician course.

To be eligible to take the General Biomedical Equipment Certification Examination (CBET) for full certification, a person must have a minimum of (1) two years of biomedical equipment technician experience plus an associate's degree in biomedical equipment technology, (2) four years of biomedical engineering technician experience, *or* (3) three years of biomedical equipment technician experience and an associate's degree in electronics technology.

To sit for a certification examination in a limited specialty area, the requirements are the same as those for the general equipment technician, except that applicants must show that at least 40 percent of their work time over the last two years, or 25 percent over the last five years, has been spent in their specialty.

The CBET exam contains questions on anatomy and physiology, electric and electronic fundamentals, medical equipment function and operation, safety in health-care facilities, and medical equipment problem solving.

The Clinical Radiological Equipment Specialist Examination (CRES) covers anatomy and physiology, electric and electronic fundamentals, radiographic instrumentation, safety, and radiographic troubleshooting and management. There are currently several hundred BMETs certified in radiological equipment.

The Clinical Laboratory Equipment Specialist Examination (CLES) covers anatomy and physiology, electric and electronic fundamentals, safety in the health-care facility and the clinical laboratory, and clinical laboratory equipment fundamentals.

THE FUTURE

The rapid growth of computerized technology has created a need for biomedical engineers and technicians. As the number of biomedical inventions and their complexity grow so will the demand for qualified technicians.

With more and more medical institutions recognizing the cost-effectiveness of regularly maintaining their much-used, extremely expensive equipment, the hiring of staff biomedical technicians has become more common. Biomedical equipment technicians with the best academic credentials and work experience will be most in demand, but at all levels, opportunities in this profession are expected to grow at least as fast as the average occupation through 2012.

For more information about biomedical equipment technicians, a list of educational programs, and information about certification, contact:

Association for the Advancement of Medical Instrumentation (AAMI)
1110 Glebe Road, Suite 220
Arlington, VA 22201
aami.org

At the same address as the AAMI in Arlington, Virginia, are the International Certification Commission (ICC), the U.S. Board of Examiners for Biomedical Equipment Technology, and The Society for Biomedical Equipment Technicians (SBET).

Junior Engineering Technology Society
    (JETS)
1420 King Street, Suite 405
Alexandria, VA 22314
jets.org

CHAPTER 7

CARDIOVASCULAR TECHNOLOGY PERSONNEL

Also Known as EKG Technician or Technologist and ECG Technician or Technologist, Including Electrocardiograph Technician and Cardiovascular Technologist

Electrocardiograph technician is the entry-level position in the field of cardiovascular technology, which is the scientific field devoted to recording and studying the function of the heart (cardio) and circulatory (vascular) system. Cardiovascular technology personnel provide supportive services to the physician by gathering and reducing the data necessary to establish a diagnosis and by developing appropriate patient management plans. EKG technicians work in a laboratory or at a patient's bedside using an electrocardiograph machine to record electromotive variations in the action of the heart muscles. An electrocardiograph picks up minute electrical changes that occur during and between heartbeats.

The EKG technician prepares the equipment and explains the procedure to the patient; applies a layer of gel to the patient's skin to facilitate the passage of electrical impulses; attaches between three and twelve electrodes or leads from the EKG machine to the patient's chest, arms, and legs; and then, with the machine recording, moves the chest electrodes to specific monitoring positions across the patient's chest. A stylus responds to the electrical impulses, creating a permanent visual record of the heart muscle's action. The electrocardiogram that is produced is then used by the patient's physician in making an evaluation of the patient's heart and circulatory function.

Electrocardiograms are routinely ordered before surgery and are often part of physical examinations for insurance reasons and for individuals over a certain age. Cardiovascular technology provides crucial diagnostic information about the heart's action, the condition of the vascular system, and how certain activities and medications affect these systems.

With additional training and course work, an EKG technician may become a cardiovascular technologist, specializing in invasive, noninvasive, or noninvasive vascular technology. An invasive cardiovascular technologist is a highly specialized diagnostician who, using physiologic analytic equipment and working in an invasive cardiovascular laboratory, hospital coronary care unit, or medical/surgical intensive care unit, carries out tests that require the introduction of various dyes, probes, and medical instruments into the patient's body. Such procedures include cardiac output studies, vessel and chamber pressure recording, cardiac catheterization, arterial angiography, drug response tests, implantation of temporary and permanent pacemakers, and balloon angioplasty.

In some settings, the title cardiovascular technologist is used to describe the individuals who carry out these various procedures. In others, more specific titles are used. For example, the technologists who assist cardiovascular surgeons in performing delicate catheterizations, in which a fine tube is inserted through a patient's blood vessel and then snaked through to the heart to determine if obstructions exist, may be called *cardiac catheterization assistants* or *technologists*.

Job titles for cardiovascular personnel who carry out the various noninvasive procedures may also reflect the specialized nature of the work they perform and the special training it entails. Technologists who conduct echocardiogram tests, in which computerized echocardiograph equipment that uses high-frequency sound waves examines the structure and function of certain portions of the heart, may be called *echocardiographers* or *cardiac sonographers*. Technologists who use ultrasound to visualize the blood vessels and organs of the body are referred to as *vascular technologists*. Personnel who conduct twelve- to twenty-four-hour-long ambulatory electrocardiogram tests using a Holter monitoring machine are often called *Holter monitor technicians*. *Stress-testing technicians* conduct exercise tests. *Phonocardiograph technicians*, *vectocardiograph technicians*, and *cardiac Doppler technicians* are other noninvasive cardiovascular technologists.

Because their patients are often individuals who are at high risk for cardiopulmonary arrest, all cardiovascular personnel are trained in advanced life-support techniques, including CPR, defibrillation, airway management, bag-mask ventilation, and the preparation and delivery of emergency and support medications.

Among the physicians who typically request cardiovascular function evaluations are adult and pediatric cardiologists, cardiovascular surgeons, internal medicine specialists, and family physicians. Cardiovascular technology personnel also interface with other health personnel who have related functions: nurses, extracorporeal perfusionists, diagnostic medical sonographers, radiologic technologists, and nuclear medicine technologists, all of whom may work with components of a diagnostic workup or provide therapeutic care to cardiac patients.

SETTINGS, SALARIES, STATISTICS

In 2003, about three out of four jobs for EKG technicians were in hospitals. Most cardiovascular technology personnel work in the invasive and/or non-invasive cardiac testing laboratories of hospitals, in the emergency room, or at the patient's bedside, performing cardiac catheterization and cardiac and vascular ultrasound. A forty-hour workweek, with evening and weekend hours "on call" or rotated in, is routine. Technologists and technicians need stamina because they are on their feet a great deal of the time and a calm temperament because their patients are frequently in life-or-death situations.

Opportunities for cardiovascular technology personnel also exist in outpatient clinics, comprehensive health centers, health maintenance organizations, health-care facilities, and physicians' offices.

There were approximately 43,000 cardiovascular technology personnel in the United States as of 2002. The majority of these are women.

Salaries vary widely depending on specific responsibilities, years of experience, educational background, and the geographic location. Median annual earnings for cardiovascular technicians and technologists in 2002 were $36,430. Entry-level jobs began at about $21,000, and the best-paying jobs for more seasoned workers in the highest-paying areas of the country were offering more than $56,080.

HOW TO BECOME AN EKG TECHNICIAN OR CARDIOVASCULAR TECHNOLOGIST

To become an EKG technician, a student must have a high school diploma or its equivalent. In high school, courses in health, biology, and mathematics are helpful. Most EKG technicians are trained on the job, and this training, typically provided by an EKG supervisor or a cardiologist, usually takes six weeks.

Formal training for EKG technicians is also available. Hospitals, vocational/technical schools, and junior and community colleges offer programs lasting from one semester to two years. Formal classroom programs range from six to eight months for basic EKG procedures. Longer programs, which have both clinical and academic components, prepare technologists to assist with complex procedures such as cardiac catheterization, echocardiography, and vascular ultrasound. An associate's degree is awarded upon successful completion of these two-year programs.

For technicians who cannot or choose not to return to the classroom, twelve to twenty-four months of on-the-job training is usually sufficient to prepare them to perform the more specialized functions.

Education programs in cardiovascular technology are accredited by the Commission on Accreditation of Allied Health Education Programs (CAAHEP), an independent body that in 1994 succeeded the American Medical Association's Committee on Allied Health Education and Accreditation (CAHEA). There are no licensing requirements for EKG technicians and other cardiovascular personnel, and credentialing, which is available through Cardiovascular Credentialing International (CCI), is voluntary. CCI offers certification for several levels of cardiovascular technologist: invasive, noninvasive, noninvasive vascular, and cardiographic exams—EKG, stress, Holter.

Cardiovascular technology personnel work directly with the patient and must be able to relate well to all kinds of people, knowing how to allay their fears and elicit cooperation so that optimal test results can be obtained. Personal qualities and aptitudes important to effective performance and satisfaction in this occupation include mechanical aptitude; mathematical aptitude, to compute calculations from which diagnostic and treatment determinations are made by the physician; presence of mind in emergencies; patience; reliability; and strong written and verbal communication skills.

THE FUTURE

Jobs in this area are expected to grow faster than the average through the year 2012. Heart disease, stroke, and other blood vessel disorders account for more than 11 million physician visits each year. Despite decreased death rates from strokes and heart attacks in the past decade, cardiovascular disease is still the number one killer and cause of disability in the United States.

The American Heart Association estimates that Americans will suffer as many as 1.8 million heart attacks this year. Eighty percent of patients in hospital settings and 75 percent of those in nonhospital settings who are being seen for suspected heart problems need the evaluative diagnostic testing services that are provided by cardiovascular technology personnel. In addition, the noninvasive cardiology procedures that cardiovascular technology personnel conduct or assist in are gaining in popularity because they are so accurate and provide new and more specific cardiac information with less discomfort, risk, cost, and time lost to the patient. And because middle-aged and elderly people are much more likely than young people to have heart and/or blood vessel disease, the rapid increase in these population groups is also heightening demand for cardiac care and, in turn, for cardiovascular personnel.

Despite these factors that strongly suggest growth in this profession, the increasing cost-containment efforts and financial pressures on all sides of the medical field may result in less demand for EKG technicians in some areas. As hospitals train their on-staff registered nurses, respiratory therapists, and other personnel to perform EKG procedures, some hospitals and clinics may cut back on technician jobs. Nevertheless, employment prospects should be stable for those technicians with specialized training, especially in Holter monitoring and stress testing.

Three professional organizations have served cardiovascular personnel. The American Cardiology Technologists Association, the National Alliance of Cardiovascular Technologists, and the National Society for Cardiovascular and Pulmonary Technology merged in 1993 to form the American Society of Cardiovascular Professionals. Until the fall of 1997, this organization was known as the American Society of Cardiovascular Professionals/Society for Cardiovascular Management. It now goes by the name Alliance for Cardiovascular Professionals.

For more information about cardiovascular technologists, contact:

Alliance for Cardiovascular Professionals
Building Suite 103
4356 Bonney Road

Virginia Beach, VA 23452-1200

acp-online.org

Certification information can be obtained from:

Cardiovascular Credentialing International (CCI)

4456 Corporation Lane, Suite 120

Virginia Beach, VA 23452-1200

cci-online.org

C H A P T E R

8

CERTIFIED ATHLETIC TRAINER (ATC)

Certified athletic trainers (ATCs) are health-care specialists who are professionally trained and educated to (1) recognize and evaluate injuries associated with competitive sports; (2) provide immediate treatment and determine if an injury requires further, specialized care; (3) implement injury-prevention programs; (4) plan and implement regimens for rehabilitation of injuries; (5) educate and counsel athletes concerning health care; and (6) organize and administer athletic training programs. In most situations, an athletic trainer works under the supervision of a physician.

Athletic training was recognized by the American Medical Association in 1990 as an allied health profession. An ATC takes care of athletic trauma, such as sprains, strains, and contusions; makes protective devices, such as injury pads and mouthpieces; wraps and pads athletes' injuries; uses a wide range of contemporary therapeutic modalities and rehabilitation equipment; plans and helps athletes with corrective exercise techniques, conditioning, and rehabilitation; and counsels athletes on general health, including nutrition.

Sound knowledge of anatomy, physiology, psychology, hygiene, nutrition, taping, conditioning, injury-prevention methodology, and protective equipment is essential. After the team physician makes a diagnosis of an athlete's injury and prescribes the treatment, the athletic trainer carries out that treatment and informs the coach of the athlete's physical and emotional progress. Some athletic trainers also purchase and fit the equipment and make travel arrangements for them. Many athletic trainers who work

DANCE/ MOVEMENT THERAPIST

Also Known as Dance Therapist, Movement Therapist, and Psychomotor Therapist

For many years the American Dance Therapy Association used as its logo the drawing of the figure of a person with arms gracefully stretched skyward and head raised, reaching out of an egg-shaped outline. This simple symbol effectively conveyed a feeling of what dance therapy is all about, the physically and psychologically therapeutic use of movement as a process that furthers emotional, cognitive, social, and physical integration of the individual.

Dance and movement are used in the diagnosis and treatment of patients suffering from schizophrenia, psychotic depression, personality disorders, brain injury, and learning disabilities. It is also used for the visually impaired, the hearing impaired, individuals with physical disabilities, the elderly, adult survivors of violence, sexually and physically abused children, substance abusers, individuals with eating disorders, autistic children, the homeless, and others who experience psychological and/or physical limitations. Dance/movement therapy can be a powerful tool for stress management and for the care and prevention of physical and mental health problems.

Fundamental to dance/movement therapy is the concept that the human mind and body constantly interact. Pain or pleasure felt on the skin registers emotionally, and we feel frightened or happy. Likewise, pain—or anxiety, depression, or disorganization—felt within can involuntarily be reflected outwardly in posture, movements, muscle tension, and breathing patterns.

For centuries, the therapeutic value of dance and other forms of body movement has been recognized in many cultures. To dance makes one "feel good." It provides a diversion, which, in turn, provides a respite from worries; it eases tensions, recharges energy, and, in general, renews emotional well-being. Most important, dancing and other body movements can communicate feelings that perhaps otherwise would be left unexpressed.

Dance/movement therapy formally began in the United States during World War II. A dancer/choreographer by the name of Marian Chace worked with psychiatrists to create the first program, at St. Elizabeth's Hospital in Washington, D.C. Its purpose was to gain insight to and treat the 1.5 million men who were rejected for or discharged from military service because of emotional problems as well as to help treat the scores of veterans who were returning home traumatized by the war.

Dance/movement therapists are trained in both dance and psychology. The dance/movement therapist reads the outward physical indicators in a patient that might suggest inward disorder, then uses this same mind/body dynamic to make contact with the patient, working with him or her toward the attainment of greater emotional and/or physical freedom.

Dance/movement therapists' goals for their patients are communication; improved self-image; greater confidence in dealing with their surroundings and with other individuals; and, in general, better integration of the physical, mental, and emotional aspects of the individual; all leading to a better ability to enjoy life. Ideally, the body is exercised to heal the mind. The mind, in turn, heals the body.

Schizophrenics and individuals who suffer from extreme depression are among the most severely emotionally disturbed patients whom dance therapists treat in institutions. A schizophrenic may manifest the severe personality disorganization he or she is feeling inside with abrupt, fragmented, and disconnected movements. A depressed patient's movements may become limp and slow, or he or she may become altogether immobile. Dance/movement therapy can help to draw these patients out of their psychoses. Group activities that call for touching and rhythmic motion can promote the patients' renewed contact with their surroundings and interactions with others, thereby breaking the isolation and rebuilding the damaged self-image that often accompany these illnesses. Gradually, mind/body integration can be restored.

Drawing on a repertoire of movements led by a dance/movement therapist, a patient may be willing to express nonverbally the fears and impulses he or she is feeling but can not talk about. Emotional pain that has been locked up can sometimes be communicated gradually through movement experiences. With time, after repeated safe and successful expressions of these highly charged emotions, the patient may progress to the point where verbalization can take place. In some cases, the communication achieved in the dance/movement therapy session is the patient's first step toward recovery.

Children who suffer from various forms of autism are often unable to form relationships or to interact with their environment in meaningful ways. They may shut out the world and retreat within themselves. Their psychological isolation is sometimes expressed in repetitive movements, such as rhythmic rocking or twirling, that draw their attention further inward and away from their environment. Some autistic children may seem lost even to themselves—sitting silently and expressionlessly and rocking for hours. By working one to one, a dance/movement therapist may try to establish contact with an autistic child nonverbally by mirroring the repetitive movements—creating for him or her a sort of "dance" that is familiar and, therefore, reassuring. It is hoped that an important acknowledgment of another individual—the dance/movement therapist—will take place and that, with time, a relationship that allows the autistic child to explore his or her emotions and the environment will be forged.

Persons who are developmentally disabled often experience problems with coordination, mobility, communication, and social interaction. A dance/movement therapist can initiate activities that teach them size, direction, and time and spatial relationships that will improve their attention span, focus, and motor skills so that they can better care for themselves and eventually become employable.

Children with brain damage or learning disabilities are also helped by dance/movement therapy. The perceptual and behavioral problems; poor balance and coordination; and disoriented, incomplete body images exhibited by these children can often be relieved through movement activities that stimulate kinesthetic and tactile senses and that teach organization.

For the elderly, who often experience social isolation, loss of mobility, and inactivity, a dance/movement therapy session can provide an atmosphere of physical and psychological safety in which a measure of self-worth and revitalization can be restored.

The visually impaired can also be helped by dance/movement therapists in a variety of ways. The dance therapy studio can become a safe and familiar space to explore, where they can develop the ability to move with assertiveness and confidence. Postural misalignment and accompanying tensions created by habitually tentative movement can also be relieved. Dance/movement therapy can provide visually impaired patients with a secure and protected opportunity in which to express feelings. Feelings of isolation are experienced by many patients with hearing impairment, and they can expand their communicative skills with the "vocabulary" of symbolic movements that a dance therapist can teach. For individuals with physical disabilities, a dance therapist can teach exercises that improve coordination, focus, and endurance.

SETTINGS, SALARIES, STATISTICS

The settings for dance/movement therapy vary, and dance therapists may work in psychiatric hospitals, community mental health centers, substance abuse treatment programs, special education settings, nursing homes and senior citizen centers, day-care facilities, rehabilitation settings, correctional facilities, crisis centers, private and group practices, research centers, and wellness and alternative health-care centers.

Because knowledge of the benefits of this work is relatively limited and there are so few dance/movement therapists at this time and because of recent budget constraints, most dance/movement therapists work in hospitals and long-term health-care facilities in metropolitan areas.

Dance/movement therapists work in locations throughout the world—in the United States as well as in Africa, Asia, Canada, Europe, the Middle East, and South America.

At this time, there are approximately 1,250 dance/movement therapists certified by the American Dance Therapy Association (ADTA), which is the professional organization for dance/movement therapists. Another approximately 300 men and women are currently providing dance/movement therapy as they work toward certification.

Salaries for dance/movement therapists range from $27,000 to $65,000 per year, depending on the therapists' training and experience, the region of the country, and the type of facility. Recent government jobs in Health and Human Services departments in various states offered pay ranges of from $27,500 to $42,500 for a Dance Therapist I and from $31,500 to $48,250 for a Dance Therapist II, whose duties would include supervision.

HOW TO BECOME A DANCE/MOVEMENT THERAPIST

To work as a dance/movement therapist, a minimum of a master's degree is necessary. At the graduate level, studies include courses in dance/movement therapy theory and practice, psychopathology, human development, and movement observation and research skills as well as a supervised internship in a clinical setting. As an undergraduate, a student interested in becoming a dance/movement therapist should pursue a broad liberal arts background with emphases in psychology and dance. Extensive training in a variety of dance forms, with courses in theory, improvisation, choreography, and kinesiology—the science of human muscular movement—plus experience teaching dance to children and adults who are not patients are recommended.

There are only a few institutions that offer graduate degree programs in dance/movement therapy. Master's degree programs in dance/movement therapy typically entail two years of study. The specific degree awarded varies from program to program—some award a master of arts in movement therapy (M.M.T.); others award a master's in dance therapy; still others confer a master of arts in creative arts therapy (M.C.A.T.).

The American Dance Therapy Association (ADTA) registers dance/movement therapists and has established specific criteria for two different levels of registration. A DTR, for dance therapist registered, is a therapist who has a master's degree, which includes 700 hours of supervised clinical internship, and who is deemed by the ADTA to be fully qualified to work in a professional treatment system. An ADTR, for Academy of Dance Therapists registered, is a therapist who has met additional requirements, including approximately 3,600 hours of supervised clinical work, and is considered fully qualified to teach, supervise, and engage in private practice.

Registration is not always required for employment. However, increasingly this credential is recognized as the standard of competency and proficiency in dance/movement therapy. Registration tends to enhance the quality and quantity of employment opportunities open to a dance/

movement therapist. The ADTR also approves graduate programs of dance/movement therapy.

To become a dance/movement therapist, a student should love both dance and people; a strong commitment to both is necessary to function in this profession. Strength, flexibility, stamina, and a strong desire to relate to and help others are essential.

At this time, licensing requirements for dance/movement therapists vary from state to state. Some states—Pennsylvania, for example—have creative arts therapist licensing regulations; in other states—such as Texas—dance/movement therapy falls under the jurisdiction of the Licensed Professional Counselors Board; and yet other states have no licensing requirement. The National Board for Certified Counselors now offers the National Certified Counselor (NCC) credential to qualified ADTRs who pass its certification exam.

THE FUTURE

Dance/movement therapy is still a small health-care field, and the number of job openings is limited. The economy may play the biggest role in determining the employment outlook for this field. Both the validity and the importance of dance/movement therapy are well recognized. Today, larger numbers of emotionally and physically impaired Americans are in public and private health-care settings that can support the costs and needs of the creative arts therapies. The American population is both increasing and aging, and the number of people who could benefit from dance/movement therapy is likely to grow. In 1992, dance/movement therapy (along with art therapy [see Chapter 2] and music therapy [see Chapter 32]) was included and defined in federal legislation as part of the amendments to the Older Americans Act. This federal recognition means that more older Americans are receiving the benefits of dance/movement therapy and that dance/movement therapists can obtain state funds to provide their services. In 1993, the ADTA received a national grant to study dance/movement therapy's applications with head-injury patients, and the National Institutes of Health (NIH) Office of Alternative Medicine awarded the ADTA a study grant as well. In 1996, Medicare coverage for therapy in certain hospitalization programs was extended. Opportunities do exist, and there will be future growth. Exactly how much growth will in large part be determined by budget considerations and any health-care and/or health insurance reform.

Dance/movement therapy is important and potentially satisfying work. For students who are interested in dance and who would like to apply their talents to serving others, dance therapy is a very special career.

For more information about dance/movement therapy and a list of dance/movement therapy educational programs, contact:

American Dance Therapy Association (ADTA)
2000 Century Plaza, Suite 108
10632 Little Patuxent Parkway
Columbia, MD 21044-3263
adta.org

For information on scholarships and other educational support, contact:

Marian Chase Foundation
ADTA
2000 Century Plaza, Suite 108
10632 Little Patuxent Parkway
Columbia, MD 21044-3263
adta.org/chace

12

DENTAL ASSISTANT

Dr. C. Edmund Kells, who practiced dentistry in New Orleans in the late 1800s, is generally credited with hiring the first dental assistant, whose name, unfortunately, has been lost to time. We do know quite a bit about her, though, because of an article entitled "Management of Dental Practice," which Dr. Kells wrote in 1893. In it, he described his ideal "lady assistant":

> To be a successful assistant, a young lady must be quick, quiet, gentle, attentive without being obtrusive, and intelligent. In your office her duties will be systematically arranged. . . . While the engine is being used for excavating, she should keep the cavity free from chips with the chip-blower, which will allow the wall to be always in plain sight, and that step in the operation will be much more rapidly completed. Just before being ready for it, she should prepare the filling material, whether it be gold, amalgam or cement, that all will be ready and no delay met with when the same is called for. It should be her duty to see that supplies of all kinds are always on hand; a small stock of everything that is used should be kept in a cabinet reserved for that purpose. The rubber dam should be cut in the sizes used, silk cut into proper lengths and waxed, spunk torn up into various sizes desired, and placed, according to size, into the several compartments reserved for it. . . . In a little while she will learn to anticipate your wants, and a look or semi-gesture may be frequently used instead of a sentence.

That during a protracted sitting she will rapidly perform one duty after another, with scarcely a word from yourself, will be frequently a source of surprise to the patient. . . . It should be her duty to receive all patients, make appointments, attend to your correspondence, look after the linen, and take a general interest in the welfare of the office.

Although more than 100 years old, this description of dental assisting is remarkably appropriate today. Modern dental assistants assist in the direct care of dental patients under the supervision of a dentist and perform other auxiliary responsibilities in the dentist's office. The specifics of a dental assistant's work are a function of the size of the dental practice, the state in which she or he works, and the number of other auxiliary dental personnel working with her or him. Usually, the more dental auxiliaries (hygienists and other assistants) there are in an office, the more closely defined a particular dental assistant's responsibilities will be.

The dental assistant and the dentist work as a team to treat the patient's dental needs efficiently and comfortably. Dental assistants may provide support to the dentist on several levels. They provide chairside support, which includes taking and exposing radiographs, recording vital signs, making preliminary impressions for study casts, and participating in "four-hand procedures," where they serve as the dentist's other set of hands. When assisting chairside, the dental assistant must anticipate both the dentist's and the patient's needs, quickly and deftly handing the dentist the necessary instruments, preparing filling materials and cements, taking impressions, keeping the patient's mouth comfortable, and clearing the area being worked on of debris.

Dental assistants may also provide clinical support by preparing and dismissing patients, sterilizing and disinfecting instruments and equipment, explaining postoperative and oral hygiene instructions to patients, preparing tray setups for dental procedures, assisting in the prevention and management of medical and dental emergencies, and maintaining accurate patient treatment records. They may offer laboratory support: pouring, trimming, and polishing study casts; fabricating custom impression trays from preliminary impressions; cleaning, repairing, and polishing removable appliances; and fabricating temporary restorations. And depending on the size and arrangement of the dentist's practice, dental assistants may also provide business office support: answering telephones, coordinating appointment schedules, organizing supply controls, setting up payment plans, and processing insurance payment claims (though almost half of all dentists employ full-time personnel who handle only business- and insurance-related matters and who are referred to as dental business assistants or practice managers).

Each state has its own laws governing the expanded functions of dental assistants. For example, in some states, dental assistants may independently take impressions, apply medications, place restorations, polish teeth, and remove oral sutures.

A dental assistant may work for a general dentist or for a dentist who concentrates on one specific type of dentistry, such as endodontics, or the treatment of the dental pulp, usually with root canal therapy; orthodontics, or bite correction; oral surgery; pedodontics, or children's dentistry; or periodontics, or the treatment of gums. The nature of the specialty will determine the specific functions that a dental assistant must perform.

Dr. Kell's 1893 description of his ideal dental assistant missed the mark in one big area. He wrote, "She should realize that her duties do not include entertaining the patients, and should understand that the less she has to say the better satisfaction she will give." Today's dental assistant plays an important role in personalizing the dental experience for patients. The best dental assistants offer understanding, comfort, and information that can allay a patient's apprehension about a pending dental treatment. Many patients feel more comfortable talking to their dental assistant than to their dentist.

SETTINGS, SALARIES, STATISTICS

Most dental assistants work in the private offices of dentists who are in solo or group practice. Dental assistants also work in hospital dental departments, state and local departments of public health, mobile dental units, nursing homes, the Public Health Service, the Department of Veterans Affairs, the military, clinics, and dental schools. Many teach dental assisting or are representatives for dental practice products. Although dental assistants typically work thirty-two to forty hours per week, Saturday office hours and evening hours are often required. At least 30 percent of all dental assistants work part-time, and some work in more than one office.

In 2002, there were approximately 256,000 dental assistants in the United States, and this number was expected to increase by 43.4 percent by 2012.

Salaries depend largely on the type of practice, the specific responsibilities assigned, the assistant's experience, and the geographic location. Students with on-the-job training start at about $16,000 annually, and students with formal training begin at approximately $18,000 per year. Average annual earnings for experienced dental assistants who worked for private dentists were $25,168—or $17.79 per hour—in 2002. The average workweek in the private dental offices was just over twenty-seven hours.

Advancement as a dental assistant in a private practice is limited, but many dental assistants who want additional challenges go on to enter other allied health professions, such as dental hygiene, or acquire the education necessary to become an educator. Some dental assistants also become sales representatives for companies that manufacture dental equipment and dental products.

HOW TO BECOME A DENTAL ASSISTANT

Many dental assistants are still trained on the job by the dentists who hire them. In recent years, however, there has been a steady trend toward formal dental assistant educational programs that are offered by community and junior colleges, trade schools, and vocational/technical schools.

There are basically two formal accredited educational routes to becoming a dental assistant: one-year study and training programs offered by vocational/technical institutes that award a certificate or diploma and two-year associate's degree programs offered by community and junior colleges. Either educational route usually requires a high school diploma or its equivalent, above-average grades in science and English, and a high school grade point average of C or better. Some programs also require a certain standard of performance on a college entrance examination as a prerequisite for admission.

There are also nonaccredited, four- to six-month dental assistant courses offered by private vocational schools. Some dental assistants learn their skills in the armed forces.

The curriculum of an approved dental assistant program typically consists of classroom, laboratory, and preclinical instruction. Subjects taught include chairside assisting, dental anatomy and pathology, dental terminology, sterilization and bacteriology, laboratory techniques, local and general anesthesia for oral surgery, preventive dentistry, pharmacology, dental radiology, first aid, ethics, the care of dental equipment, and office management practices. Practical experience is acquired during work assignments in dentists' offices, hospital dental departments, dental laboratories, and other dental settings.

In high school, students who are interested in dental assisting should take courses in biology, chemistry, mathematics, health, English, typing, bookkeeping, and other business subjects.

Personal qualities that are important to effective performance and enjoyment as a dental assistant include manual dexterity, a friendly personality, a neat appearance, common sense, the ability to think quickly, and a willingness to follow instructions.

Graduates of accredited dental assisting programs who pass a competency examination administered by the Dental Assisting National Board and satisfy other requirements become certified dental assistants and may use the letters CDA after their names. Individuals who have two years of dental assisting experience but have not completed an accredited dental assistant program may also become eligible for certification by passing an examination.

Although not required for employment, certification is generally accepted as evidence of a high level of preparation. The Dental Assisting National Board also offers examinations in dental radiology, infection control, orthodontics, and practice management.

THE FUTURE

Employment opportunities for dental assistants should be excellent for the next several years, according to the U.S. Bureau of Labor Statistics. As many as 111,000 new positions should be added in the next twelve years, bringing the number of dental assistants in the United States to 367,000.

The greatest contributor to this growth is the increased use of dental assistants by dentists. Most dentists find that hiring one or more assistants is essential to providing the dental services patients expect and to enlarging their practices.

A number of other factors should create a greater demand for dental services and, therefore, for more dental assistants. The general population is increasing, and more people today are able to pay for dental care because of dental insurance plans. There is also an increased awareness of the importance of regular dental care. In addition, the percentage of Americans over sixty-five years of age is increasing, and senior citizens tend to require more dental care. Finally, a shortage of dentists appears to be developing, which could lead to more expanded functions being performed by assistants and, therefore, more demand.

For more information about dental assistants, contact:

American Dental Assistants Association
203 LaSalle Street, Suite 1320
Chicago, IL 60601
members.aol.com/adaal/index.htm

Dental Assisting National Board (DANB)
676 N. St. Clair, Suite 1880
Chicago, IL 60611
www.dentalassisting.com

CHAPTER

13

DENTAL HYGIENIST

Dental hygienists are skilled health-care workers who are responsible for patient care of certain kinds, for patient education and instruction, and for occasional chairside assistance for the dentist. They perform prophylactic dental treatments and provide other direct patient care.

Specific legal definitions of how dental hygienists may provide services are provided in laws and regulations called Practice Acts, which vary from state to state. Typically, however, all dental hygienists clean and polish teeth, removing calculus and plaque (hard and soft deposits) from above and below the gum line using various handheld instruments called curettes and often a machine that removes calculus with ultrasonic vibrations. They also examine teeth and gums; take medical and dental histories, charting the condition of decay and disease for the dentist's analysis; expose, process, and interpret dental x-rays; screen patients for oral cancer; and take blood pressure readings. Dental hygienists often record blood pressure readings because high blood pressure—the silent killer—can easily be detected by taking a patient's blood pressure with a sphygmomanometer, and some patients' blood pressure may rise dangerously during treatment, due to stress.

Other duties of the dental hygienist include making impressions of teeth for study models; instructing patients in home oral health-care procedures, such as proper brushing and flossing and selecting the proper toothbrush; putting temporary fillings in teeth; analyzing and counseling patients on diet as it pertains to good dental and gum health; educating patients regarding the negative impact of tobacco on oral health; applying topical, cavity-preventive agents such as fluoride and sealants; and designing and implementing community and school dental health programs. Another responsibility of the dental hygienist is to ensure that appropriate protocols and procedures are followed so that both patient and hygienist are protected from infectious disease and other hazards. In many states, dental hygienists may perform certain pain control and restorative procedures as well.

Until recently dental hygienists worked under supervision. Today, supervision levels vary from state to state. Also, in some settings, such as nursing homes and other institutions, they do not require supervision.

SETTING, SALARIES, STATISTICS

Most dental hygienists practice as clinicians in the private offices of dentists who are in single or group practice. Dental hygienists are also employed in the dental departments of hospitals, health maintenance organizations, private and state institutions, dental and dental hygiene schools, community agencies, primary and secondary schools, private industry, and the military.

The Peace Corps and the World Health Organization offer dental hygienists opportunities abroad. Dental hygienists with the appropriate experience and educational background may assume additional roles, such as researcher, educator, consultant, or administrator of dental programs or as a representative of a company that manufactures dental products. Dental hygienists who work in private offices usually work thirty to thirty-five hours per week, including Saturday and evening office hours. In 2002, more than half of all dental hygienists worked part-time, less than thirty-five hours a week. Flexible time arrangements are often available, and some dental hygienists work for more than one dentist.

Median hourly wages for dental hygienists in 2002, according to the U.S. Bureau of Labor Statistics, was $26.59 per hour. The lowest-paid 10 percent earned less than $17.34, and the highest-paid 10 percent earned more than $39.24 an hour. Compensation may be based on a weekly salary, wage, or commission basis.

In 2002, there were approximately 148,000 dental hygienist jobs in the United States. The majority of these were in dental offices.

HOW TO BECOME A DENTAL HYGIENIST

Dental hygienists must have specific training and pass certain examinations before they can practice. Dental hygiene is also a licensed profession in all 50 states and the District of Columbia.

To be eligible for licensure, a candidate must complete at least two years of college in a dental hygiene program that is accredited by the Commission on Dental Accreditation of the American Dental Association. There are more than 280 such programs offered by community colleges, dental schools, colleges, universities, and technical schools. Most of these award an associate's degree, which is usually sufficient for employment in a private practice. Other programs lead to a bachelor's degree in dental hygiene. To work in a public or school health program, a minimum of a bachelor's degree is necessary. A master's degree in dental hygiene is also offered by a number of universities, and such graduate work is usually necessary for research, administrative, and teaching positions in dental hygiene.

Dental hygiene educational programs offer laboratory, clinical, and classroom instruction. The curriculum typically includes course work in anatomy, physiology, chemistry, microbiology, oral pathology, oral anatomy and histology, nutrition, periodontology, pharmacology, dental materials, medical emergencies, psychology, sociology, and public health. In high school, students considering a career as a dental hygienist should take courses in biology, mathematics, chemistry, health, and, if offered, speech.

Upon graduation from an accredited educational program, a dental hygienist is eligible to sit for the day-long written National Board Dental Hygiene Examination, which is administered by the American Dental Association Joint Commission on National Dental Examinations, and a state or regional practical/clinical examination. The candidate must pass both examinations and be licensed by the state board of dental examiners in the state or states in which he or she intends to practice.

For the clinical part of the examination, the candidate is required to perform specific dental hygiene procedures. Candidates may satisfy the written part of the licensing examination by passing the National Board Dental Hygiene Examination, which is recognized in all fifty states. Some states require additional exams.

Personal qualities that can contribute to success and satisfaction as a dental hygienist include manual dexterity, appreciation for detail, personal neatness and cleanliness, good health, and good communication skills. A dental hygienist should be able to understand a patient's apprehensions and preferences so that he or she can institute an effective dental-care regimen that the patient will follow. A dental hygienist also interacts with the other dental-care providers in the workplace as well as other health-care workers, so the ability to work as part of a team is crucial. A dental hygienist must enjoy working with people, as dental hygiene is a very people-oriented profession.

THE FUTURE

Job opportunities for dental hygienists are expected to grow much more rapidly than other jobs areas through 2012. Although the demand for dental hygienists varies according to geographic area, for the next decade or so, at least, the nationwide demand for dental hygienists is expected to be one of the fastest-growing job fields in the country.

Spurring this growth are several factors: greater retention of natural teeth, due to fluorides and other factors of better dental care; increased awareness of the importance of preventative dental care; the proliferation of dental insurance plans; and increases in both the general population and the number of senior citizens. Another factor is the greater number of medically complex patients—individuals with long-term illnesses, multiple disabilities, and other situations—who are living longer and may be able to benefit from dental hygiene procedures or who, because of the effects of their medical treatment, often require them.

For more information about dental hygienists, contact:

American Dental Hygienists' Association (ADHA)
Professional Development Division
444 North Michigan Avenue, Suite 3400
Chicago, IL 60611
adha.org

CHAPTER 14

DENTAL-LABORATORY TECHNICIAN

Also Known as Dental Technician

Dental-laboratory technicians work primarily with models of teeth and gums, at the direction of dentists and orthodontists. They seldom work directly with the dental patients themselves.

Dental-laboratory technicians make and repair single and whole sets of prosthetic teeth, crowns, inlays, fixed bridges, partial removable bridges, and corrective orthodontic appliances according to the specifications and instructions provided by dentists. Working from models made from impressions of the patient's teeth or mouth and the dentist's prescription, they fabricate these various dental prostheses out of the appropriate materials by choosing from, and sometimes combining, gold, silver, platinum, stainless steel, various plastics, porcelain, and other ceramics. They use small hand tools, such as wax carvers, heated spatulas, scrapers, and knives; precision measuring instruments, such as micrometers and articulators; bench fabricating machines, such as fine electric drills, electric lathes, and buffing wheels; metal melting torches; high-heat furnaces; and other specialized laboratory equipment and electrical devices. The end product is a dental prosthesis that fits perfectly, is strong enough to do its job, and satisfies the patient's aesthetic expectations as much as possible.

There are five dental-laboratory technician specialists who carry out certain specific functions in the dental laboratory. *Orthodontic technicians* use metal and plastics to construct and repair appliances for straightening teeth, such as retainers, tooth bands, and positioners, according to an orthodontist's prescription. *Dental ceramists* apply layers of carefully color-matched porcelain paste or acrylic resin over a metal framework to form crowns, bridges, and tooth facings. The prosthesis is placed in an oven to harden, more layers of ceramic material are added and baked on until the denture exactly conforms to specifications. *Complete denture specialists* set teeth in a denture base for complete upper and/or lower restoration. *Partial denture technicians* fabricate removable partial dentures from acrylic or a combination of metal framework and acrylic teeth for patients who have lost one or more of their natural teeth. *Crown and bridge technicians* design fixed restorations for one or more adjacent teeth from metal and porcelain, which are cemented into the patient's mouth.

Although dental-laboratory technicians rarely work directly with patients, their contributions to the patient's comfort, appearance, and health are significant.

SETTINGS, SALARIES, STATISTICS

Most dental-laboratory technicians are employed by commercial dental laboratories. These laboratories are usually small, privately owned businesses, although there are a few dental laboratories employing fifty or more technicians. Some dental-laboratory technicians own their own laboratories. About 20 percent of all dental-laboratory technicians work directly in dentists' offices, usually in group practices.

Dental-laboratory technicians are also employed in the dental departments of hospitals and by various governmental agencies, including veterans' hospitals and clinics and the armed forces. Opportunities also exist in sales, research, and education. Salaried dental technicians usually work a standard forty-hour week.

There were approximately 47,000 dental-laboratory technicians in the United States in 2002, down from 60,000 just four years before, probably due to job cuts during the economic recession. Men and women are equally represented in the profession. Traditionally this field has offered excellent opportunities for older students and those reentering the job market.

Median hourly earnings in 2002 were $13.700 or $24,734 annually. The lowest 10 percent of wages were less than $8.16 per hour, and the highest 10 percent were more than $23.65 per hour. Supervisors and managers in private laboratories earn higher salaries, and self-employed dental technicians who work alone or who own their own laboratories and employ other dental technicians can earn significantly more.

HOW TO BECOME A DENTAL-LABORATORY TECHNICIAN

In Florida, Kentucky, South Carolina, and Texas, the basic educational requirement for a dental-laboratory technician is a high school diploma or its equivalent; in the other states, a high school diploma or its equivalent is necessary only if the dental-laboratory technician intends to become certified. In high school, prospective dental-laboratory technicians should take courses in art, various sciences, metal shop, and metallurgy. After high school, a student interested in dental technology may be trained on the job or in one of the many two-year formal training programs offered by community colleges, vocational/technical institutes, and dental schools around the country.

Formal training programs are designed to provide instruction in both the principles and the technology of the five dental technology specialties: complete dentures, partial dentures, crowns and bridges, ceramics, and orthodontics. Formal programs are usually broken into two segments. The curriculum for the first year typically includes course work in anatomy, chemistry, metallurgy, dental law and ethics, and laboratory techniques; in the second year, students are given supervised practical experience. Following the completion of a formal two-year classroom program, prosthetic students perfect their skills by working under an experienced dental-laboratory technician. Approximately forty of these formal programs, all of which award an associate's degree, are accredited by the Commission on Dental Accreditation in conjunction with the American Dental Association; the other formal programs offer a certificate or diploma.

On-the-job training in a commercial dental laboratory is also a valid route to the education necessary to become a dental-laboratory technician. Apprenticeships usually last five years, during which time the technician is paid for his or her work.

Certification for dental-laboratory technicians is available through the National Board for Certification, a trust established by the National Association of Dental Laboratories. Dental-laboratory technicians who have completed formal accredited training programs may sit for the RG (Recognized Graduate) exam. When they have completed two years of employ-ment experience, they are eligible to take the examination for the higher level of certification. By successfully passing this second examination, which tests both skills and knowledge, a dental-laboratory technician becomes a certified dental technician and may use the designation CDT after his or her name. Technicians who are trained in apprenticeship pro-grams are not eligible to take the certification examination until they have completed five years of employment experience and have successfully passed a comprehensive examination covering all five dental technology specialty areas.

Although not usually required for employment, certification is a respected credential that is growing in importance.

Personal qualifications for a career in dental-laboratory technology include a high degree of manual dexterity, a well-developed sense of color perception, the ability to follow instructions, and an appreciation for accu-racy. In this field, precision is extremely important.

THE FUTURE

The outlook is expected to be favorable, but less actual job growth is expected through 2012 than for other industries, according to the U.S. Department of Labor.

For more information about dental-laboratory technicians contact:

National Board for Certification in Dental Laboratory Technology
1530 Metropolitan Boulevard
Tallahassee, FL 323088
nadl.org

CHAPTER

15

DIAGNOSTIC MEDICAL SONOGRAPHER

Also Known as
Ultrasound Technologist

Diagnostic images of all kinds are an important part of modern medical procedures, providing doctors with powerful tools as they examine and diagnose patient's problems. X-rays, MRIs, CAT scans, and sonography are the most important of these technologies.

Sonography, or ultrasonography, is the use of high-frequency sound waves, or ultrasound, to obtain visual information about various health conditions within the human body. The sound wave frequencies used are thousands of times higher than the human ear can detect. These waves are directed into the body from a transducer, which is a device capable of converting electrical energy into mechanical energy or sound waves. In most applications, the transducer is moved over the patient's skin. A gel is first applied to the skin so that the transducer and the skin will be in direct contact without interference from air between the two.

The sound waves produced are directed into the patient's body. As they pass through the patient's body, reflections, or echoes, are received back from the body to the transducer and electronically converted into an image that reveals the contours and composition of the organs and structures within the body. These images are displayed on a monitor, giving health-care professionals a clear, immediate, easily obtainable, and often otherwise unavailable view of various situations, such as tumors, cysts, blockages, and even developing fetuses, deep within the patient's body.

Ultrasound is generally considered safe, and in many cases its use spares the patient more complicated, uncomfortable, invasive procedures. Sonography is a relatively noninvasive procedure. It is also a nonionizing modality—that is, it does not involve the use of radiation. It is a relatively new and very important diagnostic tool. With it, doctors can study the contours and inner structures of the brain (neurosonology), the structure and action of the heart (echocardiography), the study of blood vessels (vascular sonography), various organs, the eyes, lymph nodes, and other parts and systems of the body to determine if there is disease or malfunction.

The use of sonography in obstetrics is well known and commonplace. Using ultrasound, an obstetrician can see an outline of the unborn child and predict multiple births, detect many abnormalities in utero, determine more accurately the specific state of prenatal development, and locate the exact position of the fetus before amniocentesis or a Cesarean-section delivery is performed.

Diagnostic medical sonographers are the specially educated and trained health-care professionals who, working under the supervision of a doctor of medicine or osteopathy, perform diagnostic medical sonographic examinations. They select the appropriate equipment for the tests ordered, explain the procedure to the patient, position the patient to facilitate optimum image making, position and operate the transducer and other equipment, and then, while moving the scanner, view the oscilloscope screen and record the images produced. Prior to the testing, the sonographer will review the results of any other diagnostic procedures already performed on the patient and take any additional medical history needed to supplement the images produced during the ultrasound scanning.

Because the sonographer's role is to obtain information for a diagnosis, he or she must be able to recognize obstructions, abnormalities of function and shape, and subtle differences between healthy and pathological tissues or areas of concern. A sonographer must exercise discretion and judgment and have a high degree of technical skill and a thorough knowledge of anatomy and physiology.

SETTINGS, SALARIES, STATISTICS

Diagnostic medical sonographers held about 37,000 jobs in 2002. Half of these work in hospitals, and about three out of every four work in urban areas. They also work in medical centers, clinics, doctors' offices, and research facilities as well as for commercial companies.

Nationwide, diagnostic medical sonographers earned annual salaries ranging between $35,800 and $66,680 in 2002. These figures vary with the position's responsibility, the sonographer's experience, and the type of employer. Annual earnings were somewhat higher in private physicians' offices than in hospitals. Advancement to administrative and supervisory positions and teaching positions can bring higher pay levels. Sonographers typically work forty-hour weeks, but night hours and emergency calls are common. Much of this time is spent standing or sitting, producing and reading the ultrasound printouts.

HOW TO BECOME A DIAGNOSTIC MEDICAL SONOGRAPHER

A student may receive the education and experience necessary to carry out the responsibilities of a diagnostic medical sonographer in a formal educational program or sometimes through on-the-job training. Some diagnostic medical sonographers are registered nurses (RNs), radiologic technologists, respiratory therapists, medical technologists, or other allied health professionals who have received special on-the-job instruction in sonography.

Diagnostic medical sonography educational programs are approved by the Commission on Accreditation of Allied Health Education Programs (CAAHEP). These are between one and four years in length and award one-year certificates, two-year associate's degrees, or four-year baccalaureate degrees, depending on the candidate's preparation and the length of the program. Programs are offered by hospitals, medical centers, community colleges, and universities. These programs accept small numbers of students each year.

Formal sonography programs consist of classroom education plus supervised clinical education in an actual clinical environment. All of these programs require a high school diploma or its equivalent and previous training in a clinically related health field or its equivalent. Some programs specifically accept only RNs and radiologic technologists.

The curriculum typically contains course work in acoustical physics and the physical principles of ultrasound; imaging and display techniques;

equipment standards, such as calibration, operational standards, and quality control; the biological effects of ultrasound; human anatomy and physiology; histology; organ and system relationships; certain clinical diseases; the effects of pathological conditions on anatomy; ultrasound characteristics of abnormal tissues; clinical medicine; medical ethics; patient psychology; emergency care; the applications and limitations of ultrasound; image evaluation; and administration, such as record keeping, coding, indexing, and laboratory management.

Approved programs that teach echocardiography also include courses in circulatory anatomy and physiology, cardiac anatomy, symptomatic impairment in congenital and acquired cardiac diseases, alterations in hemodynamics, the fundamentals of cardiac physical examinations and history taking, nuclear cardiology, pulse recording, and such diagnostic techniques as phonocardiography, apex cardiography, exercise stress testing, Doppler echocardiography, cardiac cineangiography, and catheterization.

Personal qualities important to successful and satisfying performance in this career include patience; attention to detail; and the ability to work well and communicate well with patients, their families, physicians, and other health-care personnel. Good vision is needed for observing and studying ultrasound images. A sonographer must also be strong enough to lift and position patients.

The American Registry of Diagnostic Medical Sonographers (ARDMS) administers comprehensive, qualifying examinations in various sonographic specialties—abdomen, adult echocardiography, neurosonology, obstetrics and gynecology, ophthalmology, pediatric echocardiography, and peripheral vascular Doppler. The examinations cover the specialties plus general ultrasound physics and instrumentation concepts. Certification is voluntary, but increasingly it is enhancing employment opportunities.

To sit for the ARDMS registry exams, a candidate must (1) have completed training in a two-year, CAAHEP-recognized, allied health occupation, such as RN, radiologic technologist, respiratory therapist, physical therapist, occupational therapist, medical technologist, plus have a minimum of twelve months of full-time clinical ultrasound experience; (2) have completed an accredited ultrasound educational program; (3) be enrolled in a bachelor's degree program in ultrasound or radiology with a minor in ultrasound and have at least twelve months of full-time clinical ultrasound experience; (4) have two years of formal education past high school plus a minimum of twenty-four months of full-time clinical ultrasound experience; *or* (5) have two years of on-the-job training in any recognized allied health occupation plus two years of full-time clinical ultrasound experience.

After successfully completing the certifying examination, candidates may use the title registered diagnostic medical sonographer and use RDMS after their names. To maintain certification, a registered diagnostic medical sonographer must obtain thirty hours of continuing education every three years. Most registered sonographers are certified in more than one specialty. As of 2003, no states required diagnostic medical sonographers to be licensed.

THE FUTURE

Currently, the demand for sonographers exceeds the supply, and the long-range job outlook for this field appears to be excellent. It is expected to grow faster than average through 2012.

Educators, researchers, and administrators in this field are also very much in demand. New technologies and new applications of sonography plus the constant expansion in hospital health services and the expanding and aging American population should, over the coming ten years, together contribute to as much as a tenfold increase in the number of sonographers needed.

Developments in this profession are unfolding rapidly. Obstetric sonograms and echocardiograms were rarely performed twenty years ago; today they are commonplace. "Real-time" devices, which use multiple transducers, record pictures in a way that resembles a motion picture, thereby enabling the sonographer to observe motion within the body as well as the internal functioning of organs and structures. They are called real-time devices because they are used to observe and record functions as they occur. Such important advances in the use and application of sonography should make the coming decade an exciting and challenging time to work as a sonographer. With the benefits of sonography clearly established, more small and rural hospitals as well as private offices are instituting sonography services, and this trend should make the coming ten years a very good time for sonographers to find well-paying positions.

For more information about diagnostic medical sonographers, contact:

Society of Diagnostic Medical Sonographers (SDMS)
2745 Dallas Parkway, Suite 350
Plano, TX 75093-8730
sdms.org

For a list of accredited educational programs, contact:

Joint Review Committee on Education in Diagnostic Medical
    Sonography
2025 Woodlane Drive
St. Paul, MN 55125-2998
jrcdms.org

For information about certification, contact:

American Registry of Diagnostic Medical Sonographers (ARDMS)
51 Monroe Street, Plaza East 1
Rockville, MD 20850-2400
ardms.org

DIETETICS PROFESSIONS

Including Registered Dietitian, Dietetic Technician, and Dietary Manager, Formerly Known as Dietetic Assistant

Whether formally or informally, dieticians and nutritionists of various kinds and under different names have been a recognized part of the health-care team for more than 100 years. Since the 1980s, however, an unprecedented wave of public and medical interest has arisen in nutrition. From a time when most doctors and nurses did not even have one nutrition course in their professional preparation, we have arrived today at a time of broad new awareness and concern about the role of diet in health and illness and its importance in medical concerns in general.

REGISTERED DIETITIAN

Registered dietitians (RDs) are food and nutrition experts who counsel individual patients and groups in health-care institutions, the community, and the food industry on the principles of sound nutrition; design and supervise food service systems in hospitals, nursing homes, schools, and other facilities; and carry out educational and research programs that promote good health through proper diet. Dietitians know what foods are essential for the maintenance of good health and the prevention of disease at each stage of life, what foods or nutritional deficiencies are suspected of contributing to illness, and what modifications in diet can correct or alleviate certain health conditions.

There are many areas of practice in dietetics: clinical, management, business, consultation, community, and education/research. *Clinical dietitians*, or therapeutic dietitians, specialize in the nutritional care of patients in hospitals, clinics, nursing homes, and other health-care institutions. Their job is to assess the patient's nutritional needs to determine what foods must be eliminated, added, or restricted to improve the patient's health or maximize the effects of therapy; plan and implement an appropriate nutrition plan; follow up on the patient's progress; and instruct the patient and his or her family on the importance of the diet and on how to maintain it after leaving the hospital or clinic. They work with hospital pharmacists, physicians, and nurses in nutrition support units or teams to build up seriously undernourished patients and to tackle other complicated nutritional conditions that may threaten the life or affect the treatment of a patient.

Food service management dietitians, or administrative dietitians, are experts in applying the principles of nutrition and food management to the large-scale food requirements of hospitals, long-term health-care facilities, schools, universities, restaurants, hotels, company cafeterias, prisons, and other institutions. Their job is to manage all aspects of what are often multimillion-dollar-a-year food service systems—from menu development and evaluation, food preparation, and enforcement of safety and sanitary standards to hiring and training food personnel, procuring food and equipment, and budgeting.

Consultant dietitians offer a variety of services to health-care facilities as well as counsel patients on an inpatient, outpatient, or private practice basis.

Community dietitians are sometimes called nutritionists, although this term is often used generically to refer to anyone trained in nutrition. They engage in nutrition counseling and research at the community level. Most community dietitians work for public and private health and social service agencies, such as prenatal and child government nutrition or meals on wheels programs. They teach individuals and groups how to maintain general good health, prevent or alleviate the effects of certain diseases, rehabilitate by eating healthy foods, plan and prepare meals, shop prudently, and budget.

Research dietitians usually have advanced degrees and work in medical centers, educational facilities, government agencies, private companies, or community health programs. They direct experiments to explore new nutritional approaches to preventing, curing, and alleviating certain diseases; to improve health at every stage of life; and to meet the nutritional needs of the expanding populations of the future. Dietetic educators teach the principles of dietetics and new developments in the field of nutrition to members of the health-care team in hospitals and in educational settings.

A *business dietitian* advises companies in the food/product development, purchasing, marketing, advertising, sales, and public relations fields. They may also work in consumer affairs providing product nutrition information to the public.

SETTINGS, SALARIES, STATISTICS

Dietitians held about 49,000 jobs in 2002. RDs worked at numerous functions in a wide variety of settings. About 10,000 worked for government agencies and institutions. More than 7,000 dietitians were in part-time or full-time private practice, providing individual client counseling, or in consultation to health-care facilities or industry. Some dietitians work with physicians whose patients need careful guidance.

Dietitians work in local, state, and federal health agencies; in the military; in school systems; in day-care centers; in hotels; at colleges and universities; for industrial food services and restaurants; and in research institutions. The vast majority of dietitians, however, work in hospitals, clinics, and extended-care facilities. Surveys show that 97 percent are female.

The salaries earned vary significantly. The dietician's education and experience and the region are factors. In its 2002 survey, the U.S. Department of Labor Statistics stated the median annual salary to be $41,170, with the lowest salaries being less than $25,520 and the highest being more than $58,700 per year.

Advancement is possible in all fields of dietetics. With experience, a dietitian may be promoted to a supervisory capacity as assistant director or director of an institution's dietetics department. A graduate degree opens the door to teaching, business, management, and research. In all facets of dietetics, graduate study enhances the prospects for promotion, and approximately 40 percent of all dietitians have advanced degrees in related areas.

HOW TO BECOME A REGISTERED DIETITIAN

The basic educational requirement for a career in dietetics is a bachelor's degree in dietetics, nutrition, home economics, food science, or food service management. Approximately 286 colleges and universities offer course work approved by the Commission on Accreditation/Approval for Dietetics Education (CAADE) of the American Dietetic Association (ADA). Areas of studies covered in ADA-approved or accredited educational programs include biology, organic and inorganic chemistry, biochemistry, anatomy, physiology, microbiology, diet therapy, advanced nutrition, community nutrition, food service basic management, food service systems management, quantity food production, accounting, statistics, and data processing. A high school student who is interested in becoming a dietitian should study chemistry, biology, health, mathematics, business administration, and home economics.

Most jobs in dietetics are very people-oriented; therefore, in addition to an aptitude for and interest in food science and nutrition, the personal qualities that are important to effective and satisfying performance in this career include the ability to relate well with people and to communicate with them in effective ways. In some settings, dietitians instruct patients, other health professionals, businesses, and clients on nutrition and diet modification, so they should like and be comfortable in the role of teacher.

Most dietitians are registered dietitians, which means that they have satisfied the classroom, clinical, and examination requirements established by the Commission on Dietetic Registration. Being credentialed provides evidence that certain high standards of education and training have been met and is required for employment in most positions in dietetics.

To become registered, one of two routes must be completed, each of which calls for a combination of classroom education and experience. The first requires a student to supplement his or her bachelor's degree and ADA-approved course work with an ADA-accredited dietetic internship or ADA-approved preprofessional practice program. These programs provide a minimum of 900 hours of supervised practice and are usually eight months to one year in length. Many of these programs offer graduate credit.

The second education/experience route to becoming an RD is to enroll in an ADA-accredited coordinated program. These four- to five-year programs combine academic work with experience, so that upon successful completion of the curriculum, a student is awarded a bachelor's or master's degree while having simultaneously fulfilled the ADA's experience requirements.

On successful completion of either of these two plans, a candidate is eligible to take the registration examination for dietitians, which is offered by the Commission on Dietetic Registration. This half-day-long test is given nationwide in April and October, and it covers six major areas of study: normal nutrition, clinical nutrition, community nutrition, management, food service systems, and food science. On passing this examination, a person becomes a registered dietitian and is eligible to use the letters RD after his or her name.

To maintain registration, an RD must accumulate seventy-five hours of approved continuing education every five years. If this requirement is not satisfied or if for any other reason the credential lapses, the ADA examination must be passed again to be reinstated as an RD.

Legislation requiring licensure or certification to practice as a dietitian has been enacted or is pending in thirty states.

THE FUTURE

Employment opportunities for dietitians, especially for RDs, are expected to grow as fast as the average for other occupations through the year 2012. Openings for additional dietitians are anticipated to meet the demands of hospitals, long-term health-care institutions, and industries serving an expanding, aging, and more health-conscious American population.

As the job market improves, public and private health insurance plans should do much to make better health care available to many more individuals, thereby enhancing the job picture for dietitians. And as awareness of good nutrition and its preventive potential continue to increase, many more opportunities at the community, public, and health clinic levels should open up. Careers in research, consulting, and business should also expand.

For more information about registered dietitians and ADA-approved/ accredited educational programs, contact:

The American Dietetic Association Affiliate/Management Team (ADD)
216 West Jackson Boulevard, Suite 800
Chicago, IL 60606-6995
eatright.org/careers.html

In addition to registered dietitians, there are two other levels of employment in the field of dietetics: dietetic technicians and dietary managers. The nature of the work, the variety of work settings, the personal qualifications, and the job outlook are basically the same for all three types of dietetics professionals. However, there are differences in the scope of responsibility, the education required, and the salaries for each position.

DIETETIC TECHNICIAN, REGISTERED

The specific functions that a dietetic technician may perform depend on the nature and size of the employer. In smaller institutions, dietetic technicians tend to assume supervisory positions and, working under the supervision of a consultant dietitian, are responsible for the food service operation. In medical centers and large hospitals, dietetic technicians usually work directly under the supervision of a registered dietitian, managing cafeterias, training and managing personnel, handling budget responsibilities, developing and standardizing recipes, and enforcing sanitation and safety standards.

SETTINGS, SALARIES, STATISTICS

Approximately 100,000 men and women work as dietetic technicians. Annual salaries range from $22,000 to $43,000 for full-time registered dietetic technicians with at least five years of experience.

Advancement in this career comes in the form of promotion to supervisory positions. There is little "career laddering" in dietetics—that is, not much, if any, of the classroom work and practical training necessary to become a dietetic technician is applicable toward the educational requirements for becoming a dietitian. If there is any integration between the two educational programs, it is where they are both offered by the same educational institution. When a dietetic technician is trained in one institution and then applies to enter a dietitian educational program offered by a different school, usually little credit is given for the technician's training. For this reason, it is prudent to inquire in advance about a school's policy on credit transfer and acceptance.

HOW TO BECOME A DIETETIC TECHNICIAN

Many junior and community colleges offer basic educational programs for the training of dietetic technicians. Approximately seventy of these programs are approved by the Commission on Accreditation/Approval for Dietetics Education (CAADE) of the American Dietetic Association (ADA). A high school diploma or its equivalent is the minimum prerequisite for acceptance.

Upon graduation from an ADA-approved dietetic technician program, students are awarded an associate's degree and are eligible to take the National Registration Examination for Dietetic Technicians, which is offered by the Commission on Dietetic Registration. Dietetic technicians who pass this exam are then eligible to use the credential DTR, for dietetic technician, registered, to signify professional competence. DTRs must accumulate fifty hours of approved continuing education every five years in order to maintain their registration.

For more information about dietetic technicians, contact:

American Dietetic Association (ADA)
ADA Student Operations
120 South Riverside Plaza, Suite 2000
Chicago, IL 60606-6995
eatright.org/careers.html

DIETARY MANAGER

A dietary manager, also known as a dietetic service supervisor or food service supervisor, carries out various activities in the food service operation of a hospital, long-term health-care facility, school, correctional facility, or other institutional setting. Specific job responsibilities vary depending on the size, locale, and nature of the institution, but dietary managers are trained in understanding the basic nutritional needs of their clientele.

Dietary managers work in partnership with registered dietitians. The dietary manager is responsible for purchasing, storing, preparing, and delivering balanced meals, in most cases three times a day, 365 days a year.

They are charged with providing menu variety and appetizing entrees while maintaining nutritional requirements within cost/profit objectives.

SETTINGS, SALARIES, STATISTICS

In their 2003 Salary and Benefits Survey, the Dietary Managers Association found that some important developing trends were indicated. First, salaries were up by about 7 percent, and second, the respondents were putting in more work hours—forty-five hours per week—with only 21 percent of them being eligible for overtime.

The average annual wage in the survey was reported as $34,640. Nearly half of the survey respondents work in nursing homes, and almost two-thirds work in small towns or rural areas. More than 90 percent reported having earned their certified dietary manager, certified food protection professional (CMD, CFPP) credentials, and the average experience level reported was eighteen years.

Salaries in the western states, including Alaska and Hawaii, and the northeastern states were the highest, close to $40,800. In the United States in general, retirement facilities and assisted-living facilities also paid higher than average, at almost $43,000 and $39,000, respectively.

HOW TO BECOME A DIETARY MANAGER

Many postsecondary vocational/technical schools and community colleges around the country offer dietary manager training programs, which are typically one year long. Graduates of these programs are eligible for certification from the Dietary Managers Association (DMA) upon passing an exam, whereupon they may use CDM following their name.

For more information about dietary managers, contact:

Dietary Managers Association (DMA)
406 Surrey Woods Drive
St. Charles, IL 60174
dmaonline.org

ELECTRONEURO-DIAGNOSTIC TECHNOLOGIST (END)

Also Known as EEG Technologist, END Technologist, Evoked Potential Technologist, Nerve Conduction Technologist, Polysomnographic (Sleep) Technologist, and Intraoperative Neurophysiologic Monitoring Technologist

The electrical activity in the brain and the nervous system governs all of the body's systems; to diagnose any problem within it, doctors must have accurate observations of the activity, along with other images and measurements. EEG techs or, more currently, electroneurodiagnostic technologists are the specially educated and trained health-care professionals who carry out the sophisticated electronic tests and studies used for observation and diagnosis of problems of the brain and spinal cord.

Electroneurodiagnostic (END) technology is the scientific field devoted to the monitoring, recording, interpretation, and study of the full nervous system, focusing on the use of highly technical tests and instruments. Until the late 1980s, the name for this profession was electroencephalic technology, but as the field expanded and new technologies and applications developed, it became more comprehensively known as electroneurodiagnostic technology.

Electroencephalography (EEG) remains the primary diagnostic tool in this field, however, and an electroneurodiagnostic technologist who specializes in basic electroencephalography may be called an electroencephalographic technologist, or EEG technologist.

Electroencephalography is the recording and study of the brain's electrical activity (*encephalo* is from the Greek word *enkephalos*, meaning "of the brain"). This electrical activity reflects the functional state of the brain at any given waking or sleeping moment. The instrument used to collect, record, and amplify these millionth-of-a-volt electrical impulses is an electroencephalograph, and the written tracing this machine produces is called an electroencephalogram, or brain wave record. Neurologists and other physicians use electroencephalograms in diagnosing and evaluating head trauma, stroke, infectious diseases, brain tumors, Alzheimer's disease, epilepsy, and other medical conditions.

In the case of testing for epilepsy, for example, a new offshoot of EEG, the Epilepsy Monitoring Unit, entails monitoring for seizure activity around the clock for up to ten consecutive days. In cases where a patient experiences severe adjustment or learning difficulties, EEG is used to determine if the source of the problem is organic. Electroencephalograms are also used to determine when a person is medically dead, an issue of increasing significance in light of advances in the field of organ transplants.

The EEG technologist, or electroencephalographic technologist, is the health-care worker responsible for recording a patient's EEG activity. After briefing the patient and taking a medical history, the EEG technologist applies to the patient's scalp small electrodes that are connected to the electroencephalograph. The EEG technologist is trained to understand the optimal use of the electroencephalograph and how to apply EEG procedures to a patient's specific problem. EEG technologists must know what normal and abnormal brain activity look like on an electroencephalogram, what combinations of electrodes and instrument controls are necessary to obtain the required information, and how to record that information in a meaningful way. A fundamental understanding of EEG equipment and of the diseases and conditions that are commonly encountered is essential.

Additional tests that END technologists perform today include "evoked potential" studies, which monitor and evaluate the pathways of the visual, auditory, and somatosensory systems; nerve conduction studies, which stimulate peripheral nerves and record their ability to conduct the response; polysomnography, which is the monitoring of the patient's nighttime sleep patterns and any other physiologic changes that might occur; and intraoperative neurophysiologic monitoring, which is the monitoring of the brain, spinal cord, and other nervous system functions during surgical cases.

Throughout the recording period, the electroneurodiagnostic technologist monitors the patient's neurological, cardiac, and respiratory data and keeps a careful record of the patient's behavior. END technologists are also trained to respond appropriately to medical emergencies that may arise during the session.

When the testing is completed, the END technologist debriefs the patient and writes a descriptive report of the tracing for the electroencephalographer or other physician. The responsibilities of an END technologist may also include management of the END laboratory, and senior technologists are often responsible for supervising and training END students.

SETTINGS, SALARIES, STATISTICS

Electroneurodiagnostic technologists work primarily in the neurology department of hospitals. The work is usually a full-time, forty-hour week with little overtime, although some hospitals require the electroneurodiagnostic staff to rotate and be on call. If sleep studies are being conducted, night hours may be necessary. Some END technologists work in clinics, and there are also openings in the private offices of neurologists and neurosurgeons. Some of the electroneurodiagnostic technologists employed by the federal government are called medical machine technicians.

Salaries vary from area to area in the United States and depend on the technologist's training, experience, and initiative. According to a survey conducted by the American Society of Electroneurodiagnostic Technologists, in 2003, the most common salary range was $30,000 for recent graduates to $70,000 for the highest-paid, most experienced specialists. The average salary for all END technologists in the United States was approximately $45,000.

Progression in this career may come in the form of promotion to a supervisory position, such as chief END technologist. An experienced electroneurodiagnostic technologist may work with a highly specialized neurosurgery team or teach in an END training program at a university. There are also often positions at medical teaching centers for experienced technologists who are interested in doing medical research.

HOW TO BECOME AN ELECTRONEURODIAGNOSTIC TECHNOLOGIST

There are two educational routes to a career as an electroneurodiagnostic technologist. One entails on-the-job training at a hospital, while the other route entails graduation from a formal electroneurodiagnostic training program. Both types of preparation require that a student have a high school diploma or its equivalent and a good academic record. Successful END technologists usually are in the upper one-third of their high school graduating classes. High school courses in health, biology, human anatomy, and mathematics are recommended. Further education at the college level tends to strengthen a candidate's application. On-the-job training to become an END technologist usually consists of six months of instruction followed by six months of supervised practice. Most on-the-job trainees are paid during this learning period.

Formal educational programs are one to two years in length and are offered by hospitals, medical schools, community colleges, senior colleges, universities, and vocational/technical institutes, but they are not yet available in all states. Formal training programs in the United States are approved by the Commission on Accreditation of Allied Health Education Programs (CAAHEP), an independent body that accredits this and seventeen other allied health programs. These formal programs usually include laboratory experience plus classroom instruction in neurology, anatomy, neuroanatomy, physiology, neurophysiology, electronics, and instrumentation. Upon successful completion of a formal END technologist educational program, depending on the institution, a graduate will receive either an associate's degree or a certificate. Starting in 2005, the standard for entry-level education will be the associate's degree.

An END technologist must be tactful, patient, compassionate, dedicated, and able to handle patients who are very ill. In addition, he or she must possess good communication skills, manual dexterity, good vision, an aptitude for working with electronic equipment, the ability to deal with visual concepts, and the ability to take the initiative.

None of the fifty states require licensing in this field. END personnel who have one year of training and laboratory experience and who successfully complete an examination administered by the American Board of Registration for Electroencephalographic and Evoked Potential Technologists (ABRET), are designated registered electroencephalographic technologists (or R. EEG T.). ABRET also offers an examination in evoked potentials and intraoperative neurophysiologic monitoring.

Until very recently, an additional, separate professional designation, the electroencephalographic technician, or EEG technician, existed in this field. EEG technicians performed duties similar to those carried out by END technologists, but the training required was shorter and less in-depth and the work was supervised by both a physician and an END technologist. Today a clear distinction is not always made between technologist and technician in this profession—a "technician" is usually simply someone who has yet to pass their registry board exams.

THE FUTURE

The outlook for this career is positive. Growth is expected in this career field, but it may be slow. On the one hand, a significant factor is the increased concern over cost containment, both by hospitals and the insurance industry. Many hospitals are relying upon cross-training to have fewer technicians and technologists manage a variety of diagnostic instruments and areas. On the other hand, however, the use of END monitoring—in surgery and in diagnosing and monitoring patients suffering from brain diseases—is steadily increasing. END is also playing an ever-greater role in research of the brain. Recent advances in clinical neurophysiology have created more kinds of electrophysiological examinations for END personnel to perform.

In addition, the increasing needs caused by the size and age of the American population and the greater access to health care being urged by the public may make the job outlook more favorable for END technologists. At this time this field is understaffed and there is need—though not yet the funds to finance job openings—for several hundred technologists.

For more information about END technologists, contact:

American Society of Electroneurodiagnostic Technologists (ASET)
204 West 7th Street
Carroll, IA 51401
aset.org

American Board of Registration for Electroencephalographic and
   Evoked Potential Technologists (ABRET)
P.O. Box 916633
Longwood, FL 32791-6633
abret.org

EMERGENCY MEDICAL TECHNICIAN (EMT)

Including Emergency Medical Technician–Basic, Emergency Medical Technician–Intermediate, and Emergency Medical Technician–Paramedic

EMTs, or emergency medical technicians, are called out to work at all hours of the day or night and are often the first medical specialists that a patient will call upon in an emergency. They are the first health-care personnel on the scene at accidents, such as car, truck, boat, and plane crashes; at natural disasters, such as hurricanes, floods, tornadoes; and, in recent years, all too often at the site of terrorist attacks and acts of violence. Their work is often fast-paced, hard, and dangerous. They provide instantaneous help, often in life-or-death situations.

EMTs are trained to give lifesaving prehospital care to individuals in emergency situations such as heart attacks, emergency childbirth situations, psychiatric crises, drownings, poisonings, fires, explosions, athletic injuries, environmental injuries, industrial accidents, radiation accidents, child abuse cases, rapes, gunshot wounds, and automobile accidents, to name only a few.

Emergency medical technicians are alerted to emergencies by a police, fire department, hospital, or emergency medical service dispatcher who provides the exact location of the victim and any preliminary information available regarding the nature of the emergency. The EMTs, working in an ambulance corps or in advanced life-support units, respond to the emergency and immediately set to work assessing the victim's illness or injuries, taking vital sign readings (pulse, respiration, and blood pressure), and initiating the appropriate lifesaving measures. Depending on the situation, they may open and maintain airways, restore breathing, control bleeding, treat for shock, immobilize the victim's neck and spine, splint fractures, and dress wounds. They are also trained to manage mentally disturbed patients, begin emergency burn treatments, assist in childbirth, apply an automatic defibrillator to shock the heart and restore the pulse, and provide whatever other prehospital medical care and comfort are indicated.

As the condition is being assessed, the emergency medical technicians will look for any identification indicating preexisting medical conditions, such as allergies, diseases, or medications taken, in the victim that might affect treatment. As the assessment proceeds, the EMTs will radio or telephone the emergency department physician at the hospital to which the patient will be transported regarding the nature and assessment of the patient's illness or injury, the treatment that has been given, and an estimated time of arrival at the receiving facility.

While prehospital-care professionals provide care based on their training and standing orders, they are also in constant communication with the receiving facility's emergency physician. Intravenous therapy may be initiated, medications administered, electrocardiograms may be taken, oxygen administered, cardiopulmonary resuscitation initiated, or electrical defibrillation may be applied. Working within the limits of their training, the laws of the jurisdiction in which the emergency is taking place, and the directions of the hospital physician, EMTs may provide a wide spectrum of prehospital medical procedures to save patients and prevent further damage.

The EMTs then move the patient to the ambulance—whether it is a van, truck, plane, helicopter, or boat—and transport the patient to the hospital. During the ride, they constantly monitor the patient and provide additional treatment as needed. If necessary, radio or telephone communication with the emergency room physician is maintained.

At the hospital, the EMTs transfer the patient from the ambulance to the emergency department and report their observations and care of the patient to the emergency department staff. The emergency medical technicians are part of a health-care team, and their assessments and treatment interventions help the emergency room physicians and nurses as they treat the patient.

When patient care has been transferred to the emergency physician or receiving facility, the EMTs make a written account of the patient's condition, the treatment given, and the patient's response to the treatment. This written legal document becomes part of the patient's permanent records.

After the conclusion of the run, the emergency medical technicians clean and decontaminate their vehicle, restock it with linens and supplies, check all of the medical equipment aboard, and refuel and check the vehicle itself so that it is prepared for the next call.

With almost 15 million calls for emergency medical services coming in every year in the U.S., the role of the emergency medical technician is vital.

SETTINGS, SALARIES, STATISTICS

Emergency medical services evolved gradually in towns and cities across the country, responding to different geographic, social, and economic demands. As a result, many different types and levels of prehospital, emergency medical personnel and services exist in the United States today.

From state to state and community to community, emergency medical services are organized differently and are operated and managed by different agencies. In some towns, emergency medical personnel work for the fire department; in others, they work for the police department. Some emergency medical services are operated by the county. In urban areas, ambulance service is often provided by private companies. Some geographic areas are served by hospital-dispatched ambulances.

Emergency medical personnel may be full-time paid professionals or part-time community volunteers. EMTs come from many backgrounds, such as emergency ambulance crews, rescue teams, military field service, and military independent-duty-personnel groups; they may be health-care personnel such as RNs, LPNs, surgical technicians, lab technicians, x-ray technicians, and orderlies; or they may be law enforcement officers or industrial safety workers.

The National Registry of Emergency Medical Technicians recognizes three separate levels of emergency medical technician. An Emergency Medical Technician–Basic (EMT-B) carries out basic life-support skills such as cardiovascular resuscitation, bleeding control techniques, fracture care, treatment of shock, and assistance in childbirth. An Emergency Medical Technician–Intermediate (EMT-I) performs all of the functions of an

EMT-B, but may also establish intravenous lifelines, perform trauma patient assessment, use antishock garments, and carry out other, more advanced prehospital procedures. An Emergency Medical Technician–Paramedic (EMT-P) is trained to perform the most advanced emergency medical service care, including applying defibrillation, interpreting electrocardiograms, administering medications, and carrying out advanced airway maintenance techniques.

The median level salary for EMTs and paramedics in 2002 was $24,030. The lowest pay levels were less than $15,550, and the highest were more than $41,980. There were approximately 202,000 paid emergency medical technicians in the United States, and many volunteers as well. Unpaid emergency medical technicians earn—and deserve—the heartfelt appreciation and admiration of the communities they serve so well without financial reward.

Median earnings varied by industry, and the average median annual salary for EMTs employed by local governments was $27,440; for those employed by general medical and surgical hospitals, it was $24,760, and for those working for other ambulatory health services, it was $22,180.

HOW TO BECOME AN EMERGENCY MEDICAL TECHNICIAN

Only in the last thirty years has formal education for EMTs been mandatory. The basic educational requirement is a minimum 110- to 120-hour program of instruction and practice in dealing with such emergencies as bleeding, shock, fractures, soft tissue injuries, airway obstruction, chest and abdominal injuries, environmental injuries, extrication of trapped victims, cardiac arrest, and emergency births as well as in the legal aspects of prehospital care; the use of common emergency equipment, such as backboards, suction machines, splints, and oxygen apparatus; vehicle operation and maintenance; communications; and documentation. Basic EMT programs are available in all fifty states and the District of Columbia and are offered by police, fire, and health departments; hospitals; colleges; universities; and medical schools.

The standard training course designed by the U.S. Department of Transportation is commonly followed by accredited programs. This basic training prepares the student to qualify as an EMT-B. An applicant for entry into a basic program must be a minimum of eighteen years old, have a high school diploma or its equivalent and a valid driver's license, read at the high school level, and meet certain criteria of emotional and physical ability.

If a technician wishes to advance from the basic EMT level, he or she may acquire the additional training and experience necessary to progress to the EMT-I level, or he or she may skip this level and proceed directly to a paramedic program of training. EMT-Is usually supplement the basic program with courses and experience in patient assessment, shock management, utilization of intravenous lifelines, fluid administration, use of antishock garments, more advanced methods of airway maintenance, and medication administration.

To qualify for paramedic training, a candidate must be eighteen years old, a high school graduate, and a certified or licensed EMT-B or EMT-I. Some paramedic programs combine EMT-I and EMT-P training. EMT-P training entails an average of 800 to 2,000 hours of intensive didactic instruction, in-house hospital clinical practice, and supervised field internship, during which time the student gains a more in-depth knowledge of physiology and of psychological and clinical symptoms as well as perfects such skills as patient assessment, cardiac monitoring, intravenous fluid administration, defibrillation, medication administration, and endotracheal intubation.

Registration for EMT-Bs, EMT-Is, and EMT-Ps is available from a credentialing body, the National Registry of Emergency Medical Technicians (NREMT). The NREMT has established specific training, field experience, and examination criteria at each level and offers a standardized national licensing examination that in many cases offers state-to-state reciprocity. Technicians who satisfy these requirements earn the title Registered EMT-Basic, Registered EMT-Intermediate, and Registered EMT-Paramedic, respectively. Most states require registration.

In all fifty states and the District of Columbia, some form of certification procedure for emergency medical technicians exists. In most states, registration with the National Registry is necessary, and in several other states, the candidate is offered the choice of taking a state certification examination or the National Registry exam. Most states accept National Registry as the basis for reciprocity. Several states have specific licensing of EMT-Ps.

Personal qualifications necessary to carry out this important work include good mental and physical health, the ability to lift and carry up to 100 pounds, good vision or good corrected vision, accurate color discrimination—for example, blue lips might indicate oxygen deprivation—manual dexterity and good motor coordination, the ability to give and receive accurate verbal directions, emotional stability, compassion, and the all-important ability to react correctly, efficiently, and calmly in extremely stressful situations. It is important to note that stress is a major cause of turnover in this field.

THE FUTURE

Emergency medical technicians held approximately 179,000 jobs in 2002, down from more than 200,000 just a few years earlier. The decline was due primarily to falling budgets in all areas of employment because of the overall economic recession.

Growth in this profession should be rapid through 2012. Opportunities are expected to be most plentiful in hospital, municipal, and private ambulance services. Because of the job security, benefits, and good pay, employment with fire, police, and rescue squads should remain attractive. As the American population ages, demand for EMT services will increase, and this demand should translate into larger appropriations for emergency services.

For more information about emergency medical technicians, contact:

National Association of Emergency Medical Technicians (NAEMT)
P.O. Box 1400
Clinton, MS 39060-1400
naemt.org

National Registry of Emergency Medical Technicians (NREMT)
Rocco Morando Building
6610 Busch Boulevard
P.O. Box 29233
Columbus, OH 43229
nremt.org

CHAPTER 19

FOOD TECHNOLOGIST

Also Known as Food Engineer and Food Scientist, Including Food Technician

Frozen concentrated orange juice, freeze-dried coffee, dehydrated soups and eggs, precooked sausages, granola bars, low-fat or fat-free products, and juices in "juice boxes" are among the thousands of improved and new foods that food technologists have helped to develop.

Food technologists are scientists who apply the principles of the biological and physical sciences and engineering to the selection, preservation, processing, packaging, distribution, and use of safe, nutritious, and wholesome food. Working in the laboratory, in the test kitchen, and on the production line, food technologists seek ways to improve the nutritional value, purity, taste, appearance, shelf life, convenience, safety, and cost of foods.

Some food technologists apply their scientific and engineering talents to increasing the nutritional level of diets in underdeveloped nations. They seek methods to improve and preserve the quality of harvests and to convert low-cost food sources, such as soybeans, grains, and nutrients reclaimed from wastes, into foods that will be both nutritious and palatable.

The majority of all food technologists are employed by industry and work in food processing plants, food ingredient plants, and food manufacturing plants. Food processing plants convert raw foods into beverages, cereals, dairy products, meats, poultry, game, fish and seafood products, fruit and vegetable products, snack and convenience foods, and animal foods.

Food manufacturers differ from food processors in that they build entirely new kinds of foods from new, previously unthought-of, or unusual sources, such as powdered artificial cream made from soy protein. Food ingredient plants process and manufacture salt, pepper, spices, flavors, preservatives, antioxidants, vitamins, minerals, and stabilizers.

In all of these industrial settings, there are numerous points at which the expertise of the food technologist is needed—in the research, development, and testing of a new food, process, piece of equipment, or packaging system; in the chemical analysis of food composition and ingredients; and in the supervision of quality control, plant safety, sanitary standards, and waste management. Often food technologists are among the top executives of food companies, and some even own their own food companies.

Many food technologists work at the federal and state levels of government in education or research. In government, food technologists work for the Food and Drug Administration, the Environmental Protection Agency, and other regulatory agencies and in the Departments of State, Defense, Commerce, and Agriculture, carrying out much the same work in chemistry, microbiology, food safety and quality, inspection, and research as food technologists in industry do.

Some food technologists work for NASA in Houston, developing foods for space travel. The United Nations employs food technologists in its Food and Agriculture Organization and in the World Health Organization. Food technologists who work in basic research study the structure and composition of food and the changes that occur during processing and storage. Food technologists who are in education and/or research usually work for major colleges, universities, or education and health foundations. Still other food technologists work in private testing labs or in the business end of the field—sales, marketing, technical service, advertising, private consulting, technical writing, and patent law.

Rapid advances in the field of biotechnology in the past twenty-five years have affected the foods industry in many ways, and some food scientists use this new technology to manipulate the genetic makeup of plants to try to make crop plants larger and more flavorful, more plentiful, and more resistant to disease. A variety of new research job opportunities have opened up in this type of work in the food industry.

Food and agricultural scientists held approximately 18,000 jobs in 2002, according to the U.S. Department of Labor Statistics. Several thousand more held jobs as agricultural science faculty members in colleges and universities. There were approximately 68,000 food technologists in 2003, of which 25,500 were members of the Institute of Food Technologists (IFT), the international professional organization of food technologists. Nearly half of these are women.

Food technologists can be found working in all fifty states and in other countries throughout the world. The foods and products with which the food technologist works are often defined by region—potatoes in Idaho and Maine, cereals and meat products in the Midwest, and citrus and vegetables in California and Florida. Two-thirds of all food technologists work in private industry, and the remaining third work in government, education, and research.

Salaries for food technologists vary because of the great variety of work situations in this field. In 2002, median annual income was $48,670, according to the U.S. Bureau of Labor Statistics, with the lowest levels being less than $28,750 and the highest being more than $85,460.

Food technologists usually work thirty-five to forty-hour weeks. Some of the food processing industry work is seasonal, however, and some jobs may require overtime hours during peak periods.

HOW TO BECOME A FOOD TECHNOLOGIST

Prospective food technologists should plan on a minimum of four years of college study. A bachelor's degree in food technology, food service, or a related science such as chemistry, biochemistry, agriculture, microbiology, nutrition, or food engineering is the minimum educational requirement for entrance into the food technology profession.

Approximately sixty colleges and universities around the country offer programs that provide the necessary course work, and fifty of these have been approved by the Institute of Food Technologists. Most of the schools with undergraduate food technology programs also offer advanced degrees in the field, and almost half of all food technologists have master's or doctorate degrees. Food technologists holding master's and doctorate degrees have more job opportunities available to them—a Ph.D. is generally required for teaching, for example—tend to be in greater demand, and earn higher salaries.

In general, the course work in a food technology program will include courses in food science, including processing, microbiology, chemistry, food analysis, engineering; humanities and social sciences; physics; mathematics/statistics; biosciences; communications; and electives—with economics and business administration strongly recommended for students planning to work in the management aspects of the business. Courses that develop computer skills and critical thinking may also be required.

Personal qualities important to the successful execution of jobs in this field include a love of science; an orderly, inquisitive mind; honesty; perseverance; and good communications skills. The ability to work on a team is also essential.

For men and women who are interested in entering this field at the technical level, numerous junior colleges and vocational/technical schools offer two-year programs that prepare students to become food technicians. Associate certificates are awarded upon satisfactory completion of these programs. Food industries on the West Coast employ food technicians extensively.

At this time there are no state certification or licensure requirements for food technologists or food technicians. The Institute of Food Technologists offers member status to individuals in the field or related fields. Members with a bachelor of science or an advanced degree in food technology, plus five years of professional experience, may apply for professional member status.

THE FUTURE

Employment for food technologists and food technicians should remain steady or grow slightly through 2012. The ever-pressing need to feed populations in poor and underdeveloped nations and the ever-present consumer demand in the United States and other developed nations for new, healthier, and more convenient foods may generate more jobs if the United States and other countries experience a strong economic recovery.

For more information about food technologists and food science and technology, contact:

Institute of Food Technologists
525 West Van Buren Street, Suite 1000
Chicago, IL 60607
ift.org

American Society of Agronomy
Crop Science Society of America
677 South Segoe Road
Madison, WI 53711-1086
agronomy.org

Food and Agricultural Careers for Tomorrow
Purdue University
1140 Agricultural Administration Building
West Lafayette, IN 47907-1140

GENETIC COUNSELOR

The Human Genome Project is a major force in the field of genetics today, and it is driving enormous change in all areas. From the world-renowned discoveries made by James Watson and Francis Crick a half-century ago to the stunning revelations of the Human Genome Project at the turn of the twenty-first century, genetics has become one of the most dazzling of scientific fields in our lifetimes.

Watson and Crick won a Nobel Prize for their work, which gave the world its first glimpse of DNA's double-helix structure and explained how DNA stores and passes on hereditary information. The field of genetics research has progressed so rapidly since then that today, through a variety of diagnostic procedures, parents can actually get a genetic "glimpse" of their offspring even before they are born.

The medical community has developed technologies and techniques that are capable of detecting hundreds of genetically transmitted diseases and conditions in the unborn. In amniocentesis, for example, samples of the amniotic fluid that surrounds the developing unborn child are withdrawn with a fine needle. Amniotic fluid contains cells that have been shed by the fetus. These cells are cultured so that the chromosomes in them can be studied microscopically for abnormalities, which suggest genetic disease and/or genetic anomaly.

Amniotic fluid also has waste materials containing proteins that come from the fetus. Analysis of these proteins can reveal other genetic disorders. Another technique, chorionic villus sampling (CVS), similarly samples fetal chromosomes. For the common alpha-fetoprotein (AFP) test, a small sample of the mother's blood is tested for abnormally high or low levels of a protein that the fetus produces, and there are other similar maternal serum tests to detect other potential conditions. In ultrasound testing, sound waves are sent through the amniotic fluid, producing on a screen an image of the developing fetus that parents and physician can see.

Together, the results from these prenatal diagnostic tests create a "genetic picture" of the unborn child. Among the hundreds of genetic conditions that can be tested for are Down's syndrome, hemophilia, Tay-Sachs disease, certain forms of mental retardation, muscular dystrophy, cystic fibrosis, and sickle-cell disease. Ultrasound scans can reveal malformations of the spine and various organs, such as the heart, kidneys, and lungs, and the size of the baby. One baby in fifty is born with a congenital condition. Many of these conditions are not devastating or life-threatening, but many require treatment. New ground is being broken in the surgical correction or alleviation of certain conditions while the baby is still in utero.

Human genetics is one of the fastest-changing fields in medical science, and with such rapid and drastic change has come a myriad of medical, ethical, and emotional considerations. In an increasing number of hospitals, genetic counselors are helping parents and prospective parents understand their genetic situation and options.

A genetic counselor is a health-care professional who, by virtue of extensive education and training, is particularly equipped to communicate technical genetic information to individuals and families who want to know more about a suspected or actual genetic disorder. The genetic counselor is a member of the medical genetics team. While it is the physician who often orders the prenatal screening tests and presents their results to the patient, the genetic counselor's job is to explain those tests and their results and then to devote as much time as necessary to one-to-one patient counseling. The counselor uses specially developed communications skills to explain test results, short- and long-range consequences of a genetic disease or anomaly, and options to parents. Some counselors specialize in a particular genetic disease or group of related diseases. Genetic counselors not only provide crucial information, they also provide important emotional support and critically needed coping skills to parents and prospective parents going through what is a very personal and often bewildering and highly emotional experience.

Genetic counselors also work with prospective parents who are concerned about possible genetic conditions in their offspring because they suspect that they are in a high-risk group, such as persons with a family history of childhood deaths or a pattern of genetic anomaly, members of certain nationalities in which there is a high incidence of certain defects, or individuals who have been exposed to certain potentially harmful materials.

As a result of the genetic information emerging from the Human Genome Project, the scope of the genetic counselor's expertise is expanding to include adult conditions such as cancer, neurogenetics, and certain psychiatric disorders. Genetic counselors also participate in clinical research projects, as well as teach other members of the health-care community, such as general practitioners, nurses, social workers, and consumers about genetic disorders.

SETTINGS, SALARIES, STATISTICS

About 70 percent of all genetic counselors work in university medical centers where genetic screening and prenatal diagnosis are offered, most commonly in departments of obstetrics and pediatrics; in private hospitals; and in specialty clinics where children and adults with genetic disorders are treated. They also work in health maintenance organizations, federal and state government departments of health, and private diagnostic laboratories. In addition, a growing number of genetic counselors are in private practice and in outreach clinics.

Genetic counseling is still a relatively new profession, and programs and salaries vary greatly. The National Society of Genetic Counselors (NSGC) does a status survey every two years and posts the findings on its website. Their 2001 survey found that annual salaries ranged from $18,000 to $80,000 per year, depending on qualifications, experience, level of job responsibility, region of the country, and so on. The mean salary with up to five years of experience ranged from $18,000 to $57,876; for twenty to twenty-five years of experience, the range was $41,477 to $75,000. Government jobs in general paid better than those in any other category.

These findings show mean annual salaries in six regions of the United States to vary by several thousand dollars per year. The mean salaries by region were: Region 1 (the Northeast, including parts of Eastern Canada),

$42,166; Region 2 (roughly the Appalachian and Mid-Atlantic states and Quebec), $45,092; Region 3 (the Southeast and Gulf states), $40,638; Region 4 (the Midwest and Central states and Ontario), $40,264; Region 5 (the Rocky Mountain states, Manitoba, Saskatchewan, and Alberta), $41,888; and Region 6 (the West Coast, Alaska, Hawaii, and western Canada), $48,483.

The NSGC also shows mean annual salary variation by primary specialization: Teratogens, $40,137; Pediatrics, $40,924; Specialty Diseases, $41,489; Cancer Genetics, $42,808; Prenatal, $42,994; Neurogenetics, $44,760; Public Health/Newborn, $44,795; and Molecular Genetics, $46,976.

HOW TO BECOME A GENETIC COUNSELOR

To practice as a professional genetic counselor, two years of postbaccalaureate study, usually leading to a master's degree in human genetics, is necessary. The first master's-level program in this specialty was established in 1969 at Sarah Lawrence College in Bronxville, New York. Today, there are twenty-nine master's degree genetic counseling training programs in the nation. Most of the programs require applicants to have taken the following courses as undergraduates: general biology, developmental biology (vertebrate embryology), Mendelian and molecular genetics, basic chemistry, psychology, and probability and statistics. Recommended prerequisites may include organic chemistry, the psychology of personality, and fluency in a foreign language, preferably Spanish.

The master's program of study typically entails two years of full-time enrollment. Some schools offer part-time programs. Courses include biochemistry, human anatomy and physiology, clinical medicine, human genetics laboratory, bioethics, issues in clinical genetics, client-centered counseling, medical genetics, and delivery of genetic services. There also may be group sensitivity workshops. At Sarah Lawrence, 600 hours of field training experience are required. Students are placed in clinical settings and in a cytogenetics laboratory for this fieldwork.

Personal qualities important for satisfaction and effectiveness as a genetic counselor include extremely strong communication and counseling skills. A counselor deals with individuals and families coping with very personal, often very emotional issues. One might expect a high rate of burnout among women and men doing this work, but, in fact, no higher level is reported for genetic counselors than for persons in other helping professions. Ideally, a genetic counselor has that special blend of objectivity and sensitivity so crucial to the successful practice of so many health-care professions.

Graduates of the master's degree programs in genetic counseling are eligible to sit for the certification examination given every three years by the American Board of Genetic Counseling (ABGC). This board was formed in 1993 and certifies only genetic counselors. Until 1991, certification was awarded by the American Board of Medical Genetics, but this organization now certifies only individuals working in the field of genetics who hold M.D.s or Ph.D.s.

THE FUTURE

Genetic counseling is still a relatively new field, and it is expected to grow rapidly over the next decade, due especially to the broad new frontier of knowledge that is being opened up by the Human Genome Project. That 100 percent of the available graduates of genetic counseling programs are employed in the field of human genetics demonstrates both acceptance of this health profession and strong demand for the services of these health professionals, even during a time of economic downturn.

For more information on genetic counselors, contact:

National Society of Genetic Counselors (NSGC)
233 Canterbury Drive
Wallingford, PA 19086-6617
nsgc.org

For information about certification, contact:

American Board of Genetic Counseling (ABGC)
9650 Rockville Pike
Bethesda, MD 20814-3998
abgc.net

HEALTH ADVOCATE

Also Known as Patient Representative, Patient Advocate, and Ombudsman

Worries, confusions, and concerns often plague medical patients—adding to their primary needs, which are to overcome their injuries and diseases and get well. In many hospitals and other organizations, there is help and comfort in the form of a health advocate.

The word *advocate* means "a person to speak up for you," and in the specific context of health care, it means someone to listen patiently, to understand your needs, to organize potential solutions, and to help you make decisions based on the best choices available.

Traditionally, health advocates have helped individuals and their families to deal with specific medical and health situations, usually in a hospital setting. In recent years, the definition of the health advocate's work has expanded even further. Today, health advocates work to advance the interests of the patient/consumer and of the population in general in hospitals, nonprofit organizations, and government agencies.

In their original role, health advocates help patients understand hospital procedures, services, and policies; obtain solutions to patients' problems and address their concerns; and sensitize hospital personnel to patients' perceptions of the hospital experience. A health advocate is a listener, a communicator, and a catalyst for change from within the system. He or she is an open line between the patient—and often the patient's family—and the institution and is there to help the patient deal not only with his or her health problem but with the personnel, procedures, and policies working to resolve that health problem. Health advocates are also known as patient representatives, patient advocates, ombudsmen, and a dozen other similar titles that denote the liaison nature of the work.

More choices are available in health care than ever before. Age-old illnesses are being cured, infirmities once thought hopeless are being corrected, and life spans are lengthening. Yet sometimes the very things that enable our modern hospitals to deliver an ever-improving level of health care—the huge, rotating staffs of specialized professionals; the myriad sophisticated diagnostic and therapeutic procedures; the complicated and expensive care options available because of new technology—can confuse and distress a patient in pain who is already feeling disoriented, worried, and vulnerable. If that patient is also economically and socially disadvantaged, elderly, or not fluent in English, the confusion and distress may be compounded.

Although the patient physically benefits from all of the new advancements in modern medicine, he or she may feel victimized by the very complexity and fragmentation that make them possible. The personal, individual needs of the patient may be overshadowed or perceived to be forgotten. The patient may be neglected, and sometimes, amidst all that complexity and fragmentation, may not receive the proper health care.

The health advocate's job is to humanize and individualize health care for the patient—assisting him or her by acting on his or her behalf in securing appropriate medical care, evaluating problem areas in patient care, and serving as a catalyst for improvement. By displaying a personal interest in the patient and by working to resolve that patient's problems, a health advocate can bring that vast, busy medical staff in that huge, impersonal hospital down to a one-to-one level. The health advocate is a caring constant in a fast-changing scene; an unhurried listener to the patient's concerns; an articulate—and heard—voice for the patient's needs, wishes, and complaints; a sensitive and compassionate translator of the medical team's treatment plans, goals, concerns, and the hospital's policies; and a defender of the patient's legal, social, and human rights.

Many states and health-care institutions have established their own "Patient's Bill of Rights" or adopted the American Hospital Association's "Patient's Bill of Rights." These rights are given to and/or read and explained to each patient upon admission. Some typical rights are: considerate and respectful care at all times; complete and current information concerning diagnosis, treatment, and outcomes, presented in understandable terms; every consideration of privacy; an interpreter if a language barrier or hearing impairment presents a continuing problem to the patient's understanding of care and treatment; confidentiality; continuity of care; notification if the institution proposes to engage in or perform human experimentation affecting the patient's care or treatment; and refusal of treatment to the extent permitted by law. Health advocates also work to sensitize other health-care professionals to the need for humanizing patients' hospital experiences by conducting new-employee orientation programs and ongoing training programs.

This is still a relatively new health career, and specific duties, education and training requirements, criteria for employment, and even the name are not sharply defined. Exact responsibilities of the health advocate differ from hospital to hospital. The National Society for Patient Representation and Consumer Affairs (formerly the National Society of Patient Representatives) has developed a list of functions and goals for health advocates, which it calls "Elements of Patient Representatives Programs in Hospitals." This list is available to guide hospitals as they initiate such programs.

Depending on the institution and the situation, a health advocate will be an advocate, working for change on behalf of an individual patient or for changes in the health-care delivery system; a facilitator; a bilingual translator; an ombudsman; an educator; a troubleshooter; a negotiator; a spokesperson; and—always—someone ready to listen, care, and work for the patient's safety and well-being.

In their expanded role, health advocates develop and run outreach programs, such as cancer, child-care, or geriatric programs. They educate the population in general, and they provide consulting and information to all levels of government and industry on issues of disease prevention, health care, and health insurance. They are policy analysts and lobbyists, and they monitor the integrity of medical research. They champion the cause of good health and the fair delivery of good health services for all people, from prenatal screening to end-of-life decisions, and further this goal from the bedside of each patient to the decision-making arenas of Congress and the White House.

SETTINGS, SALARIES, STATISTICS

Experienced health advocates employed by hospitals, doctors' groups, and corporations earn between $40,000 and $60,000 per year, according to The University of Texas Career Center's 2001 publication. Entry-level and new health advocates, who may have been working in related areas, can expect to earn approximately $20,000 to $28,000. Independent contractor consultants or advocates working for a consulting firm usually charge for their services by the hour, with fees varying greatly in different areas.

Approximately 70 percent of U.S. hospitals have health advocacy services. Small and average-size hospitals often employ one part-time patient representative, while a large teaching hospital may have several health advocates on its staff. In addition, health maintenance organizations, government and private programs for the elderly, nursing homes, schools, programs for the physically and mentally disabled, community and rural health centers, disease-related foundations, and industry employ health advocates.

HOW TO BECOME A HEALTH ADVOCATE

Criteria for employment in this field have been flexible, and there have been no official, specific requirements. Instead, hospitals and other employers have established their own educational and work experience requirements to meet the specific needs of their institution and community. Health advocates have come from a variety of backgrounds, with educations ranging from high school diplomas to graduate degrees. A significant number of people now entering the profession, however, have backgrounds specifically in the health field, and many employers now require a bachelor's degree for employment.

The schools of human services at several universities across the country offer undergraduate courses in health advocacy, and since 1980, one school, Sarah Lawrence College in Bronxville, New York, has offered a unique master's degree in health advocacy. The curriculum for this program can be completed in eighteen or twenty-four months, or part-time in three years, and includes courses in the history of health care in the United States, health-care organization and concepts for change, human anatomy and physiological systems, the language of patient care, the psychology of stress and the coping process, health law, and the economics of health and health advocacy. It also includes 600 hours of practical fieldwork.

Prerequisites for admission to the Sarah Lawrence Health Advocacy Program include a bachelor's degree, course work in introductory biology and microeconomics, and intermediate-level work in the social sciences. Facility in a second language, especially Spanish, is considered advantageous.

The Society for Healthcare Consumer Advocacy (SHCA) and Cleveland State University have instituted an online Patient Advocate Certification Program. SHCA also provides a code of ethics to its members on its website.

In its guidelines, the National Society for Patient Representation and Consumer Affairs suggests that persons selected to coordinate patient representative programs understand the health-care system and have education or experience in human relations, communications, supervision, management, conflict negotiation, and medical terminology.

Personal qualities that are important to effective and satisfying performance in this job include empathy, tact, objectivity, maturity, the ability to cope with stress and pressure, tenacity, a sense of humor, and sound judgment. A health advocate must be able to understand and interpret state and national legislation; effect change at the highest levels of their institutions through the collection and examination of data; and possess excellent writing and marketing skills. In addition, a health advocate must be able to relate to a wide variety of patients as well as to the hospital staff and be the type of person in whom a patient can quickly and justifiably place his or her trust.

No certification or licensing requirements exist for health advocates at present.

THE FUTURE

Predicting the future for health advocates is difficult. Certain important trends may work against each other. Cost-containment efforts may inhibit some institutions from inaugurating health advocacy programs. At the same time, however, patient consumerism is increasing. As results from these programs come in, more and more health-care institutions, health-care personnel, and patients are becoming aware of the important benefits of health advocacy. It is estimated that the proactive approach to health issues saves Americans many hundreds of millions of dollars annually.

Also affecting the job outlook will be the increasing American population and the increasing percentage of elderly persons in that population.

Weighing these factors, it is expected that the number of job opportunities for health advocates should grow steadily through 2012.

For more information about patient representatives, contact:

Society for Healthcare Consumer Advocacy
The American Hospital Association (AHA)
One North Franklin, 31 North
Chicago, IL 60606

For more information about a master's degree in health advocacy, contact:

Health Advocacy Program
Sarah Lawrence College
1 Mead Way
Bronxville, NY 10708
slc.edu/health/_advocacy

CHAPTER

HEALTH INFORMATION MANAGEMENT (HIM) PERSONNEL

Including Health Information Administrator, Health Information Specialist, Health Information Technician, Coding Specialist, Registered Records Administrator (RRA), Accredited Records Technician (ART), and Certified Coding Specialist (CCS)

Continuity of patient care and compliance with medical, administrative, ethical, and legal requirements in patient care would be completely impossible without reliable information and records management.

The information explosion of the past twenty-five years has not spared the health-care industry. If we expected a paperless society as a result of the computer revolution, we were wrong—and nowhere is this as evident as it is in health care. In the course of diagnosing and treating a patient's illness or injury, an enormous amount of detailed information is generated, and all of it is potentially significant.

Every patient and patient's family is astonished at the amount of paperwork they must complete—and their portion is dwarfed by the records of the medical institutions, insurance companies, and other third-party organizations involved.

To make a diagnosis, for example, a doctor will examine and observe the patient, interview the patient about symptoms and his or her medical history, and, often, order one or more laboratory, radiologic, and/or other diagnostic tests and evaluate the results. Diagnosing is putting together all of the pieces of information gathered to identify and assess the patient's health condition. It is, therefore, important that none of this information be lost.

Over the course of the subsequent treatment, additional important information comes in. What medications is the patient taking? How much?

When? With what results? What is the patient's fluid intake? Output? Blood pressure? Temperature? Blood count? How many stitches were used to close the incision? What anesthesia was used? How was it tolerated? What treatments are being administered? For how long? With what results? What dietary restrictions are being imposed? What did the x-rays show? The amount of information grows with the nature, complexity, and duration of the patient's condition, and any part of it can have important bearing on the patient's subsequent treatment, the assessment of his or her progress, and the handling of any future medical problems. Sometimes, this information can have bearing on the health of the patient's family members or coworkers. It is, therefore, vitally important that all of this information be collected, recorded, organized, and preserved so that all of the details of the patient's situation can be communicated clearly and quickly to other medical personnel handling the case, thereby maximizing the value of what has already been learned about the patient and reducing the chance of error. A patient's health or medical record is that important communicator.

The health record is a permanent document of the history and progress of a patient's illness or injury, made by the patient's physician(s) and any other health professionals who come in contact with the patient. It contains information about when and how the condition first came to medical attention; how the diagnosis was arrived at; the patient's medical history, including his or her age, sex, height, weight, occupation, habits, family illnesses, allergies, information about chronic health conditions and previous injuries, treatments, and medications, plus the physicians' observations; the findings of the patient's physical examination; the doctors' orders and progress reports; the nurses' notes; diet orders; medications and doses prescribed; treatments administered; laboratory test results; x-rays; electrocardiogram tracings; and a report of any surgery performed. Ideally, it is a complete, clear, objective, and readily available profile of the patient's medical history.

In addition to helping the medical team in diagnosing and treating the patient expeditiously, accurate and complete health records are important for several other reasons. Public health officials depend on health records to provide data that indicate disease patterns and trends, and researchers use them to uncover, correlate, and compare data that may lead to new methods of diagnosis and treatment. Hospitals and health-care facilities often use the information in health records to facilitate planning and to substantiate performance for accreditation purposes. Health records are also used for the evaluation of treatments and medications, as case studies for the training of medical personnel, and for legal actions.

Most recently, health records provide the primary source documents for the complicated procedures necessary for current insurance claim policies. Hospitals and other health-care facilities, as well as patients, depend on health information coding for reimbursement purposes.

The amount of information that accumulates in the course of one patient's illness or injury can be substantial. Multiply that by the number of patients treated in a health-care facility over a many-year period, and the volume of information that must be processed and maintained can be astronomical. Microfiche and computers have revolutionized the handling and storage of all this information. Still, fundamental to the recording, organization, and retrieval of this data are the health-care personnel who are experts on medical information. Health information administrators and health information technicians are the specially trained and educated members of the medical team who are responsible for the processing, organization, and maintenance of these important health records.

HEALTH INFORMATION ADMINISTRATOR

Health information administrators plan, develop, and supervise systems for the acquisition, analysis, retention, and retrieval of health records that are consistent with the medical, administrative, ethical, and legal requirements of the particular health-care delivery system.

They develop, analyze, and technically evaluate health records and indexes; supervise personnel who are engaged in coding the health records; collect and analyze patient and institutional data for health-care and health-care–related programs and research; develop in-service educational materials for the health-care personnel; assist the medical staff in evaluating the quality of patient care; develop and implement policies and procedures for processing medical legal documents and insurance and correspondence requests that conform to professional ethics and to federal, state, and local statutes; safeguard the confidentiality of the health records; and, when necessary, testify in court about records and record procedures.

The specific scope of the health information administrator's responsibilities depends on the size and type of the institution. The nature of this work has changed in recent years, becoming far more technical. Health information administrators with the greatest expertise in both the traditional and technical aspects of the work can today find positions at the hospital executive level.

SETTINGS, SALARIES, STATISTICS

Most health information administrators work in general, specialized, and/or teaching hospitals. They also work in ambulatory-care centers; outpatient clinics; nursing homes; rehabilitation centers; health maintenance organizations; group practices; insurance companies, where they determine liability for payment of clients' medical fees; professional services review organizations; local, state, and federal government research centers; private industry; and on the teaching staffs of colleges and universities.

Most large hospitals have chief health information administrators who supervise other health information administrators, health information technicians, and clerks. A smaller hospital may need only two or three personnel to run its health information management (HIM) department. In certain small health-care facilities, sometimes only one or even one part-time health information administrator is employed.

Working conditions are generally pleasant, and a typical workweek is forty hours long. There are also part-time opportunities available. In larger institutions, there may be three shifts a day, seven days a week, so overtime and shift work may be involved.

Health information administrators on average earn approximately $30,000 to $80,000, depending upon the position, the administrator's education level and years of experience, the type of employer, and the region. At the highest levels, the health information administrators who are part of the executive administrative staffs of major hospitals earn well over $100,000 per year.

HOW TO BECOME A HEALTH INFORMATION ADMINISTRATOR

Preparation for this career entails a minimum of four years of study after high school, leading to a bachelor's degree in medical record administration or health information management.

Three categories of HIM personnel are certified through the American Medical Records Association, in Chicago, Illinois.

- *The registered records administrator (RRA)* is a manager as well as a records specialist. He or she manages a department, sets policies and procedures, supervises and trains records technicians, and works with the medical staff and other personnel in hospitals and medical centers.
- *The accredited records technician (ART)* organizes and evaluates health information, compiles statistics, assigns medical code numbers, maintains various health record indexes, supervises information staff members, and manages the use, storage, and release of the health information.
- *The certified coding specialist (CCS)* is a specialist in analyzing health records and assigning the numerical codes used for reporting diagnoses and information for bill payment, Medicare and Medicaid categories, and more. The CCS can prepare with a solid high school record plus courses in medical record technology programs. The American Health Information Management Association (AHIMA) also provides an Independent Study Program in ISP/Coding.

The Commission on Accreditation of Allied Health Programs (CAAHEP) in an independent body that succeeded the American Medical Association's Committee on Allied Health Care Education and Accreditation in accrediting education programs for many allied health professions. The CAAHEP-accredited programs for HIM offer several educational options. More than half of them require applicants to have completed at least two years of college. These programs are typically two years in length and award a bachelor of science in health information management. Almost one-quarter of the programs require a minimum of only a high school diploma or its equivalent and are four years in length. They, too, award a bachelor's degree.

Several programs are approximately one year in length and are for undergraduates who have completed three years of college. This alternative also leads to a bachelor of science in health information administration. For individuals who are already college graduates and have taken required courses in the liberal arts, biology, and statistics, a small number of accredited postgraduate certificate programs in health information administration are available. It should be noted that health information administrators working at executive levels increasingly bring additional advanced degrees—a master's in business administration, information management, or public health administration—to their careers.

In addition to liberal arts and sciences, a student health information administrator will study fundamentals of medical science, anatomy, physiology, medical terminology, disease classification, health information administration, statistics, research methods, medical law, and computer science. He or she will also have carefully supervised practice in accredited health-care institutions.

High school students considering a career in health information administration should elect the general college preparatory course, including classes in biology, chemistry, mathematics, English, health, computer science, business administration, anatomy, and physiology.

Personal qualities that are important to success and satisfaction in this career include the ability to plan and organize well, facility with numbers and details, strong communication skills, integrity, the ability to teach others, sensitivity, flexibility, alertness, competence, and good vision.

Upon graduation from an approved health information administrator educational program, a student is eligible to take the national registration examination, a one-day test given yearly in October by AHIMA. Passing this examination entitles the candidate to use RHIA, which stands for registered health information administrator, after his or her name. Registration is voluntary, but it is a widely accepted standard of proficiency in this field and can significantly enhance job opportunities and salary. Many employers require this credential. To maintain registration, an RHIA must fulfill certain continuing education requirements and must be a member of AHIMA.

THE FUTURE

Job prospects should be good, and this field is expected to grow faster than average through 2012. Growth in the number of medical tests, treatments, and procedures is expected to create enormous quantities of records that will be needed by patients and their families, doctors, hospitals, nursing homes, rehabilitation centers, third-party payers, Veterans' Administration and other government agencies, researchers, regulators, and the courts, to name a few. All of these demands for medical records should result in increasing employment opportunities for health information administrators, especially for those who are certified.

HEALTH INFORMATION TECHNICIAN

Health information technicians serve as technical assistants to health information administrators. In large hospitals and health-care facilities, they are usually responsible for supervising many of the HIM department's day-to-day functions and for carrying out many of the more demanding technical functions.

Health information technicians code diseases, operations, and therapies according to recognized classification systems (these codes are used to abbreviate the medical facts of the case to facilitate review). They enter these codes in patients' medical records; maintain registries; analyze records; cross-index medical information; abstract records; review records for accuracy and consistency; and from these records, gather statistics that may be needed by insurance companies, law firms, government agencies, and researchers for studies of bed utilization, operating room use, disease, and other aspects of health-care delivery.

Like health information administrators, health information technicians may be called upon to take records to court. Health information technicians also supervise health information personnel—the health information clerks, health information transcriptionists, and coding specialists who provide support for technicians and administrators.

SETTINGS, SALARIES, STATISTICS

Health information technicians work in the same settings as health information administrators. Most work in hospitals, but an increasing number are finding opportunities in ambulatory-care facilities, industrial clinics, state and federal health agencies, group practices, medical research organizations, health maintenance organizations, and insurance companies.

Some are self-employed consultants. In addition, health information technicians are often employed as directors of health information management departments in small hospitals and some nursing homes. A forty-hour workweek is typical, and work conditions are usually pleasant.

Salaries will vary greatly depending on the type of institution, scope of responsibility, and region. Recently graduated health information technicians working in hospitals average approximately $22,000 annually, and experienced technicians with an associate's degree average about $30,000 annually.

Advancement in this field is available in the form of promotion to positions of greater authority within the HIM department. Health information technicians holding bachelor's degrees may also become health information administrators by supplementing their educations and passing the AHIMA competency examination.

HOW TO BECOME A HEALTH INFORMATION TECHNICIAN

Increasingly, health information technology students are receiving their educations and training in the two-year associate's degree programs that are accredited by CAAHEP in collaboration with AHIMA. Because these programs must maintain certain high standards in preparing students, most employers prefer their graduates.

Educational programs for health information technicians include theoretical instruction plus practical hospital experience. Required courses include medical terminology, medical law, anatomy, physiology, processing of health data, medical transcription, and hospital procedures.

Upon successful completion of an approved health information technician educational program, a candidate is eligible to take the national accredited health information technician examination, which is administered once a year in the fall. Those who pass this examination are entitled to use the letters AHIT, for accredited health information technician after their names. While having this credential is not required for employment, it often results in greater career opportunities, positions of greater responsibility, and higher starting salaries.

The American Health Information Management Association also offers certification for a third classification of health information management personnel—the coding specialist. Coding specialists are trained through a combination of on-the-job experience and coding education workshops, seminars, and health information technology programs offered by AHIMA to analyze medical records and then to assign and sequence numerical classification codes to diagnoses and procedures. A high school diploma or its equivalent is prerequisite, but today most credentialed coding specialists have at least an associate's degree. Upon completing this training, a candidate may sit for the AHIMA certification examination, and upon passing it may use the designation CCS, for certified coding specialist, after his or her name. On average, CCSs earn $15.00 per hour.

Personal qualities important to the satisfactory execution of this job include mental acuity; good vision; manual dexterity for data entry, transcribing, and filing; an analytical mind; maturity; and respect for the important and sensitive nature of the material being handled.

THE FUTURE

As is the case with health information administrators, the job outlook is favorable, especially for health information technicians who are accredited. The American population is growing larger and living longer and thus generating more and more health information. In addition, with the creation of each new diagnosis, treatment, and therapy, more types of information are being created. Add to these factors the dramatic increase in demand from researchers and insurers for this information, and a positive job picture emerges. Employment of health information technicians is expected to grow faster than average for all occupations through 2012. Demand for coding specialists should be particularly strong.

For more information about health information technicians and accredited schools and also about other health information management personnel, contact:

American Health Information Management Association (AHIMA)
233 North Michigan Avenue, Suite 2150
Chicago, IL 60605
ahima.org

HEALTH SCIENCES LIBRARIAN

Also Known as Medical Librarian, Hospital Librarian, and Health Information Professional

The volume of new medical information is so great and increasing so rapidly that it has been estimated that more medical and health literature has been published in the last ten years than in all previous years together. An information explosion is taking place in the health sciences. New medical tests, treatments, pharmaceuticals, equipment, procedures, research results, data, and theories emerge almost daily, affecting the way illness and injury are handled and adding to the already huge body of knowledge for which health-care professionals must be responsible.

Last year alone, more than 3,800 new books and 1,250 new audiovisual programs on medical and health subjects were made available to the American medical community. There are also more than 8,000 different journals serving the various health sciences fields, each generating numerous issues per year. According to a survey by the Association of Academic Health Science Library Directors (AAHSLD), there are approximately 230,000 bound volumes in the average health sciences library in the United States.

The health sciences libraries of a major teaching hospital may contain more than 500,000 bound volumes, subscribe to 4,000 journals, maintain thousands of audiovisual programs, and provide access to thousands of indexes via online searching. This tremendous amount of incoming information must be cataloged, organized, and maintained in a way that will allow effective and efficient dissemination to all of the various kinds of health sciences practitioners, students, educators, researchers, and administrators who depend on them.

Health sciences librarians are specially trained information specialists who are responsible for the collection, compilation, and dissemination of this essential biomedical information. Using knowledge of both library science and the health sciences, they select and purchase books, journals, and other materials on the health sciences; classify and catalog acquisitions for easy access; instruct health-care students and professionals in the use of information resources; prepare guides to reference materials; compile bibliographies; answer mail and telephone requests for information; help health-care personnel track down elusive information; translate or find a translator for biomedical pieces written in foreign languages; and manage the operation of the library, including budgeting, long-range planning, and supervising health sciences library technicians and other library personnel.

Using computerized databases, health sciences librarians can quickly produce complete and current bibliographies on almost any medical or health-related subject, and, through participation in national networks of information resources, they can locate specific books and journals in libraries around the world. Computerization and interlibrary cooperation have revolutionized the health sciences library. With the push of the right buttons, for example, MEDLINE, a worldwide online bibliographic retrieval system, initiated by the National Library of Medicine, can lead the health sciences librarian to more than 11 million citations within seconds. In October of 1998, the National Library of Medicine launched MEDLINEplus, a Web-based consumer health information resource. Other databases on specific aspects of medicine and health care also exist:

- CANCERPROJ provides access to bibliographies on cancer research projects.
- BIOETHICSLINE contains information about ethics and related public policy issues in health-care and biomedical research.
- DENTALPROJ covers dental research projects.
- GENE-TOX is a chemical mutagenicity database.
- POPLINE houses population information.
- HISTLINE is a bibliography retrieval system for information on the history of medicine.
- TDB is a toxicology data bank.
- AIDSLINE contains information on Acquired Immune Deficiency Syndrome (AIDS).

There are hundreds more biomedical databases, and new ones are constantly being developed.

Some health sciences librarians who work in hospitals are also responsible for providing book-cart services and programs for patients who are ambulatory as well as for those who are confined to bed.

SETTINGS, SALARIES, STATISTICS

Health sciences librarians work in medical, nursing, pharmacy, veterinary medicine, and allied health schools; hospitals; pharmaceutical companies; professional associations; federal and state agencies; research centers; health maintenance organizations; and health planning organizations. Two-thirds of all health sciences libraries are located in hospitals. Approximately 12 percent are in medical, professional, and vocational schools. There are approximately 3,700 health sciences librarians in the United States, of whom 95 percent are female.

Salary levels in this field range from $32,000 to $58,000, with an average annual salary of $45,000. Advancement in this career can come in the form of promotions up the administrative ladder or in the form of specialization in a single area of responsibility. Administrators of large medical libraries can earn salaries that are much higher.

HOW TO BECOME A HEALTH SCIENCES LIBRARIAN

A master's degree in library science, preferably from a college or university accredited by the American Library Association (ALA), is the usual and preferable preparation for professional librarians. There are approximately sixty ALA-accredited, one- or two-year graduate librarian education programs in the United States and several in Canada. Of these, more than forty offer one or more specific courses in health sciences librarianship, such as science literature; biomedical communications; the evaluation, selection, and use of bibliographic and informational resources in medicine and the allied health sciences; introduction to the organization and administration of the medical library; standard informational systems;

budgeting; personnel; and book selection. Many of these schools also offer postgraduate programs leading to a doctor of philosophy or doctor of library science.

As an undergraduate working toward a bachelor of arts or bachelor of science, a prospective health sciences librarian should consider courses in the physical and biological sciences, including chemistry, physics, mathematics, biology, zoology, and anatomy; the life sciences, including psychology, sociology, and anthropology; computer science; and management. Health sciences librarians with undergraduate majors in these fields are usually in greater demand. Applicants to master's programs must have a good reading knowledge of at least one foreign language.

Personal qualities essential to success as a health sciences librarian include highly developed literary skills, intelligence, patience, imagination, intellectual curiosity, strong communication and organizational skills, friendliness, the ability to handle details, and a genuine interest in the subject matter.

While not compulsory, membership in the Academy of Health Information Professionals (AHIP) of the Medical Library Association (MLA) is a useful credential that can enhance job opportunities and salaries. The MLA offers four levels of certification.

Entry-level certification requires a post-baccalaureate degree from an ALA-accredited program or a post-baccalaureate degree in a related field, such as informatics, information science, or computer programming, from a program accredited by the appropriate agency, as well as demonstration of competency in seven areas of health librarianship that have been designed by the MLA (library schools, library associations, and other institutions offer courses in these areas of knowledge). Combinations of additional course work, research, published papers, and service to the MLA qualify candidates for higher certification status.

THE FUTURE

Employment prospects for health sciences librarians in the coming decade are expected to be average, but very qualified health sciences librarians will continue to be in demand to manage the biomedical information explosion. The numbers of jobs that will become available through 2012 will depend greatly upon the economic condition of the country and the pressures upon medical libraries to further contain costs.

For more information about health sciences librarians and for a list of accredited educational programs in this field, contact:

Medical Library Association (MLA)
Professional Development Department
65 East Wacker Place, Suite 1900
Chicago, IL 60601-7298
mlanet.org

American Library Association (ALA)
50 East Huron Street
Chicago, IL 60611
ala.org

CHAPTER 24

HEALTH SOCIOLOGIST

Also Known as Medical Sociologist

International programs of research on HIV/AIDS and problems of populations that suffer from high levels of malnutrition or exposure to environmental toxins are often the substance of the work of health sociologists.

Health sociologists identify and explain the influence of social factors on health and health care. They conduct research on how social factors affect the incidence and course of disease, called social epidemiology; on patients' and the general population's responses to various health conditions and health-care settings; and on the acceptance or rejection of specific treatments. They gather data and then look for common social values and behavioral and attitudinal orientations in an attempt to discover trends in what prompts patients to seek medical attention, how patients cope with terminal illness, how patients and health-care practitioners behave, how members of the health profession interact, and how communities will react to a new medical technology. Health sociologists then share this information with medical personnel to help them identify and deal with health trends and deliver health care more ideally suited to the varied needs of the community.

A good way to understand the work of health sociologists is to look at the research that the people in this field have done on the medical and social crisis, Acquired Immune Deficiency Syndrome (AIDS). Health sociologists were part of the research team at the Centers for Disease Control (of the U.S. Public Health Service) that discovered the first cluster of sexually transmitted cases of AIDS. They documented the spread of AIDS and for the past twenty years have studied changing behavior patterns in the population, focusing on mental health and sexual conduct. Populations considered to be high risk are being studied for the answers to questions such as: How do persons with AIDS and those close to them cope with the anger, isolation, despair, loss of self-esteem, and legal and economic consequences that may accompany this disease? Who gets AIDS, and who does not? Why do some individuals expose themselves to AIDS, while others do not? What motivates some AIDS patients to expose other people while others do not? How does society respond to AIDS and persons with AIDS? How can a community and its resources cope with AIDS and all that it means? Health sociologists are also studying and analyzing the effectiveness and acceptability of various methods of avoiding AIDS exposure as well as of various methods of educating not only the public about AIDS, but also the health-care management community. Because of their special and thorough work on AIDS, the National Academy of Sciences recently asked health sociologists to design strategies for improving healthcare and social services for those afflicted with the illness and for allaying the public's fear of AIDS. A number of sociologists have organized the Sociologists' AIDS Network, which acts as a clearinghouse for sociological research and activity on AIDS.

SETTINGS, SALARIES, STATISTICS

Health sociologists work in universities, for federal health agencies, in state and local health departments, in major hospital and research institutes, and for medical, nursing, and other professional schools.

The exact number of health sociologists is difficult to determine. The medical sociology section of the American Sociological Association (ASA) in Washington, D.C., lists 1,100 members. A total figure in excess of 3,000 men and women with doctorates is probably close; many more bachelor's- and master's-level sociologists work in medical and health-related occupations and/or have built upon their sociology training with other professional degrees, such as epidemiology, public health, or counseling.

Salaries range greatly depending on the type of employer, the position, and the region. In general, however, health sociologists who are employed by the government earn the highest salaries. Research tends to pay the second highest salaries, and teaching positions at universities pay the least, but university salaries are based on a nine-month contract. Recent starting salaries for health sociologists with bachelor's degrees have ranged from approximately $20,000 to $43,000. For those holding doctorates, it is much higher, at approximately $47,000 annually, while health sociologists with Ph.D.s who work for the federal government earn an average of $58,000 per year. The average annual income of all sociologists in government jobs is $53,000.

HOW TO BECOME A HEALTH SOCIOLOGIST

Most health sociologists have Ph.D.s, which means that after four years of college with a major in sociology or an allied field, they have successfully completed the course work, thesis, and examination requirements for the master's degree in sociology and then gone on to satisfy the requirements for a doctorate in sociology, including the writing of a doctoral thesis based on advanced research. While a master's degree is sufficient for employment in this field, a doctorate greatly enhances the range of employment and advancement opportunities. About seventy-five universities in the United States offer specific health or medical sociology educational programs. Many more sociology departments offer a significant number of courses in health or medical sociology and often link these courses with other programs in the university. In this competitive field, acquiring the best credentials—that is, the best grades from the best schools and learning from the best minds in health sociology—is extremely important.

In high school, interested students should take as much English and mathematics as possible, and as an undergraduate majoring in sociology or an allied field, students should take courses in biology, health, and environmental science. Good computer skills are also necessary.

Personal qualifications for success in this field include inquisitiveness; strong speaking, writing, and analytic skills; objectivity; and perseverance.

There is no licensing for health sociologists by the states and no certification by the profession itself. Certification as a clinical sociologist is offered by the ASA, which requires a doctorate in sociology, a minimum of two years of practice, letters of recommendation from colleagues, course work in medical sociology, and membership in the ASA. Certification is also offered by the Sociological Practice Association, which confers the designation CCS, for certified clinical sociologist, on health sociologists in nonacademic, clinical settings who satisfy their requirements.

THE FUTURE

Employment for sociologists in general is expected to increase in the next decade, and the fastest-growing specialty will most likely be medical sociology. There should also be a significant increase in the demand for social gerontologists in particular, and this prediction may be a large part of the reason why health sociology is expected to grow. Social gerontologists are sociologists who study the special problems faced by aged persons in our rapidly changing society. The American population is not only growing larger, it is growing older.

It is predicted that by the year 2030, one in five Americans will be sixty-five years of age or older, a trend called the "graying of America." More Americans are living longer, and as the "boom" babies, born after World War II and through the 1950s, become senior citizens, there should be a "boom" of elderly Americans requiring health care. With this large, aging population should come new health sociology issues regarding the distribution of illness and patterns of response to health problems and to the delivery of health care. In addition, health care is rapidly changing and becoming more complex. Each change, new discovery, new technique, illness uncovered, illness treated, and illness cured has sociological ramifications and raises sociological questions. It is clearly a very interesting time to be a health sociologist.

For more information about a career as a health sociologist, contact:

American Sociological Association (ASA)
1307 New York Avenue, Suite 700
Washington, DC 20005
asanet.org

Sociological Practice Association
Southwest Texas State University
San Marcos, TX 78666
socpractice.org

HISTOLOGIC TECHNICIAN AND HISTOTECH- NOLOGIST (HTL)

Histologic technicians and histotechnologists prepare human and other animal tissue specimens in microscope slides for examination. Histology is the branch of biology concerned with the microscopic study of the structure of tissues, and histotechnology is the preparation of the slides for microscopic and other types of examination for diagnostic, research, or instructional purposes.

The health-care personnel who are primarily responsible for preparing such specimens are histologic technicians. Histotechnologists usually function as supervisors and instructors and perform the more complex laboratory procedures.

Tissue sections are used to detect and diagnose body dysfunction and malignancies. The methods by which histologic technicians process sections of body tissue include fixation, dehydration, embedding, sectioning, microincineration, mounting, and the use of various contrast stains, all of which are performed so as to make visible discrete changes in the tissue that could indicate disease or another abnormality—or on the other end of the spectrum, that could indicate normality or improvement in a condition.

Many dramatic advances in slide preparation and sophisticated new methods of examining tissue samples allow for important early detection of many types of cancer. Tissue samples are often taken from a patient during surgery, and while the surgical team waits, the samples are immediately prepared by a histologic technician or histotechnologist and promptly examined by a pathologist and/or the attending physician. Depending on what is revealed, the surgery may proceed and abnormal tissue be removed, or it may be determined that additional surgery is not warranted or appropriate. Clearly, the work carried out by histologic technicians and histotechnologists is extremely important and requires intelligence and precision.

SETTINGS, SALARIES, STATISTICS

Most histologic technicians and histotechnologists work in clinics, hospitals, and universities. In the hospital setting, they play an extremely important role as team members in the care of patients. Duties range from performing frozen section stat procedures while the patient is on an operating table to performing special, painstaking staining procedures for infectious disease diagnosis in the lab. Current technology includes immunohistochemistry, flow cytometry, DNA hybridization, and image analysis.

Many histologic technicians and histotechnologists work in the laboratories of chemical, pharmaceutical, petrochemical, personal-care product, and household product manufacturers. Opportunities also exist in the government.

Histologic technicians and histotechnologists usually average forty hours of work per week, with weekend and night shifts sometimes required. There are approximately 30,000 histologic technicians and histotechnologists in the United States, and the majority of them are women.

The median entry-level salary for histologic technicians is about $25,500; for histotechnologists it is slightly more. The average annual salary is reported at $31,500 for histotechnologists, with a salary range of $28,400 to $39,200. Salaries in large cities and on the West Coast tend to be higher.

HOW TO BECOME A HISTOLOGIC TECHNICIAN OR A HISTOTECHNOLOGIST

While histologic technicians were once trained on the job and while some informal training persists, the strong trend today is toward formal histotechnological training. It is hoped that formalized educational programs in this field will upgrade and unify competency standards, and students planning careers in histotechnology should anticipate committing the necessary time to a formal educational program.

More than thirty histologic technician/histotechnologist educational programs are accredited by the National Accrediting Agency for Clinical Laboratory Sciences (NAACLS). The majority of these programs are offered by hospital and medical centers. Several community and junior colleges also have accredited programs.

Associate's degree programs are all approximately twenty-four months long, and all but one require only a high school diploma or its equivalent. Approximately two-thirds of the certificate programs require only a high school diploma, and the rest require associate's degrees or anywhere from one to four years of college preparation.

The curriculum of an accredited program consists of classroom instruction, practical demonstration, and extensive hands-on laboratory experience. The curriculum covers medical ethics, medical terminology, chemistry, laboratory mathematics, anatomy, histology, histochemistry, quality control, instrumentation, microscopy, processing techniques, preparation of museum specimens, and records and administration procedures.

High school students who are interested in becoming histologic technicians or histotechnologists should concentrate on biology, science, chemistry, and mathematics courses.

In addition to an aptitude for and interest in the biological sciences, other personal aptitudes and qualities that are important to success in this career include manual dexterity; good vision, with particularly good color differentiation; attention to detail; a strong sense of responsibility; and maturity. Handling tissue specimens is important medical work requiring care, concentration, and precision.

Histologic technicians and histotechnologists must be temperamentally suited to doing such exacting, often repetitious work and also to handling specimens of diseased tissues. Although modern laboratory safety procedures minimize the risks, exposure to environmental toxicity is a potential hazard.

Certification in this field is available through the Board of Registry of the American Society of Clinical Pathologists (ASCP).

To be eligible for ASCP certification at the histologic technician level, a candidate must successfully complete an NAACLS-accredited histotechnology program or have an associate's degree or at least sixty semester hours, including a combination of twelve in biology and chemistry, of academic credit from an accredited college or university plus at least one year of full-time, supervised clinical laboratory experience in histopathology. (Note that the route requiring a high school diploma or its equivalent plus two years of experience was scheduled to be discontinued as of January of 2005.)

Upon passing the ASCP's examination, a candidate is then entitled to use the initials HT (ASCP), for histologic technician certified by the American Society of Clinical Pathologists, after his or her name.

Histotechnologists seeking ASCP certification must hold a bachelor's degree with a combination of thirty semester hours of biology and chemistry plus one year of full-time, supervised clinical laboratory experience in a histopathology laboratory. Or a candidate may hold a bachelor's degree as described above and complete one of the NAACLS-accredited histologic technician educational programs. Upon passing a competency examination, a candidate may use the designation HTL (ASCP), for histotechnologist who is certified by the American Society of Clinical Pathologists, after his or her name.

Several of the fifty states require histologic technicians and histotechnologists to be licensed.

THE FUTURE

Job opportunities are not as plentiful as were expected by the U.S. Department of Labor and the public in general following 2001, but factors that will contribute to growth in this field include the increased frequency with which doctors are turning to laboratory tests when diagnosing and treating patients; the ever-expanding array of tests available; the growing American population and the aging American population; increased health consciousness; and methods of third-party payment that require certain testing and evaluation. With an economic upturn, jobs in this area will be expected to grow slightly faster than average through 2012.

For more information about a career in histotechnology, contact:

National Society for Histotechnology
4201 Northview Drive, Suite 502
Bowie, MD 20716
nsh.org

Board of Registry
American Society of Clinical Pathologists (ASCP)
2100 West Harrison Street
Chicago, IL 60612-3798
ascp.org

National Accrediting Agency for Clinical Laboratory Sciences (NAACLS)
8410 West Bryn Mawr, Suite 670
Chicago, IL 60631-3415
naacls.org

American Society for Clinical Laboratory Science
6701 Democracy Blvd. Suite 300
Bethesda, MD 20817
ascls.org

CHAPTER 26

HOME CARE AIDE I, II, III

Also Known as Homemaker–Home Health Aide, Personal Care Aide, Home Attendant, Home Helper, Home Nursing Assistant, and In-Home Support Worker

Increasing costs for long-term care of patients in residential facilities; the aging of the American population and its needs for in-home care; and the increasing pressure from third-party agencies, such as insurance companies, for the least costly care is making the field of home health care more visible and much more in demand. As a result, more scrutiny, more training programs, more regulation, higher wages, and more jobs are all in the current forecast for this career.

Home care aides (this term has replaced the lengthy "Homemaker–Home Health Aide" title) are health-care paraprofessionals who visit the homes of the ill, disabled, elderly, socially disadvantaged, and others who are unable to perform basic tasks to provide a wide spectrum of personal and homemaking assistance. The specific functions carried out by the home care aide depend on the nature and extent of the physical, emotional, or social problems affecting the patient and the patient's family.

The personal assistance may include bathing and otherwise aiding the patient in carrying out personal hygiene; helping the patient with walking and any prescribed exercises, especially helping to rotate bedridden patients to prevent bedsores and other complications of inactivity; checking respiration, heartbeat, and blood pressure; administering medications; changing surgical dressings; and helping the patient with orthoses, or braces, and prostheses, or artificial limbs. A home care aide also offers important human contact, comfort, emotional support, and instruction on how to manage and carry out fundamental tasks and, if necessary, how to adapt to the limitations caused by the disability. Homemaking functions carried out by the aide may include changing bed linens and doing the patient's laundry; cleaning the patient's home; planning, shopping for, and preparing meals that often must conform to special dietary restrictions; and caring for, dressing, and feeding any young children in the family.

A home care aide usually works with a particular patient and his or her family over an extended period of time, thereby allowing the aide to observe the progress the patient makes. This progress is reported back on a regular basis to the home care aide's supervisor, usually a registered nurse or social worker, who uses this information to determine if services should be changed.

Home care aides are very important deliverers of direct health care. Because of their efforts, many patients who would otherwise require hospitalization are able to remain in their own homes. Home care aides improve the quality of the lives of many patients struggling at home.

SETTINGS, SALARIES, STATISTICS

Home care aides work for local health and welfare departments, hospitals, community voluntary agencies, and privately owned health-care services. Some opportunities also exist in nursing homes.

Approximately 18,000 agencies across the United States employ home care aides, and this number is growing rapidly. Aides usually work alone in the patient's home, traveling from assignment to assignment. Many aides work part-time, and weekend hours are common.

Home health aides held about 580,000 jobs in 2002, according to the U.S. Bureau of Labor Statistics. Most home health aides worked for privately owned health-care services. Others worked for social assistance agencies, for nursing home and residential facilities, or for employment agencies. A few are independent contractors who find their jobs by advertising or by word of mouth.

Many home health workers are not required by their employers to have high school education or special training. Some employers require a seventy-five-hour training program and a competency evaluation test after four months on the job. Aides who pass this test are then certified and placed on a state list of nursing aides.

Federal guidelines for home health aides apply in cases where the employer receives reimbursement from Medicare or Medicaid. Federal law requires a degree of competency in twelve general areas of care: (1) communication skills, (2) documentation of the patient's status and the care received, (3) reading and recording vital signs, (4) basic infection control procedures, (5) basic body functions, (6) maintenance of a healthy environment, (7) emergency procedures, (8) physical, emotional, and developmental characteristics of patients, (9) personal hygiene and grooming, (10) safe transfer methods, (11) normal range of motion and positioning, and (12) basic nutrition.

The federal government recommends the seventy-five-hour training course to prepare for work and for this test. Courses are available in community colleges and other institutions and must meet the requirements of the Center for Medicare and Medicaid Services.

Salaries tend to be low in this field, and most home care aides earn between $12,000 and $18,000 per year. In 2002, home care aides who worked on an hourly basis earned an average of between $5.90 and $10.67 per hour. Some home care aides work for agencies that provide them with insurance benefits, sick-leave pay, and paid vacations, but most do not receive these benefits at this time.

The title used for workers in this field, such as homemaker, aide, or homemaker–home health aide, will vary geographically. In some parts of the country, the titles homemaker and aide are used to designate two different levels of experience.

HOW TO BECOME A HOME CARE AIDE

Educational requirements in this field are in flux. Previously, preparation typically consisted of a several-week-long training course plus on-the-job training, both of which were provided by the employer agency. The trend today is toward more, and more formal, education.

In addition to the federal requirements for Medicare- and Medicaid-covered care, about half of the states currently require formal training, while many other states recommend it. A significant number of these states use the national standards suggested by the National Home Caring Council (NHCC), which call for sixty hours of training coupled with a fifteen-hour practicum. The NHCC is a division of the Foundation for Hospice and Homecare.

Training programs for home care aides are offered by community colleges, adult basic education programs, state programs for the aging, and private agencies. Typically, a student is taught how to bathe, lift, and turn the patient; plan and prepare nutritious meals; monitor vital signs; administer medications; and manage the patient's household. The home care aide also learns about how to handle the emotional problems common to illness, how to deal with the elderly, and how to offer support at what is often a very stressful time.

In 1994, in the hopes of formalizing and standardizing this profession, the Home Care Aide Association of America (HCAAA) presented a detailed position paper entitled "National Uniformity for Paraprofessional Title, Qualifications, and Supervision," in which a three-level career ladder for home care aides was proposed. These levels have since been recognized by the home health industry and by state and federal government agencies.

- The home care aide I (or HCA I) assists with housekeeping and homemaking duties, such as cleaning, shopping, doing laundry, performing essential errands, and planning and preparing basic meals; maintains a safe environment; observes and monitors the client's condition; and teaches the client those tasks that increase the client's independence. The HCA I does not, however, provide any personal care.
- The home care aide II (or HCA II) assists the client and client's family with home management activities and with nonmedically directed personal care. Specifically, an HCA II performs all of the duties of a HCA I, plus assists with ambulation, bathing, hair care/grooming, dressing, toileting, transfer activities, and special diets. An HCA II does not, however, perform duties under a medically directed plan of care nor would be assigned duties related to assistance with medications or wound care.
- The home care aide III (or HCA III) works under a medically supervised plan of care to assist the client and client's family with both household management and personal care. Specifically, an HCA III carries out all of the functions of an HCA I and an HCA II, plus performs nonsterile wound care, assists with self-

administered medications, assists with prescribed exercises and rehabilitation activities, and helps with assistive devices.

Specific training, supervision, and yearly in-service education requirements for each of these categories are also detailed in the HCAAA's position paper. Because of the great demand for home care services, however, there is often a blurring of roles. With so great a shortage of personnel as the United States is experiencing, job definitions are often obscured.

Personal qualifications for work as a home care aide include maturity, genuine willingness to help people, compassion, patience, common sense, a sense of humor, and enough strength to lift and support patients. Certification, which is voluntary, is offered by the National Association for Home Care (NAHC).

THE FUTURE

Currently all states are experiencing a severe and worsening shortage of home care aides. This demand for home care aides should grow dramatically in the future as a result of the rapidly increasing elderly and chronically ill populations and because of the cost effectiveness of home care.

Of the ten occupations requiring a high school diploma or less that are predicted to grow the fastest by the year 2012, home care aide is listed first; of all occupations, it is ranked second. Job opportunities in this field should increase by more than 100 percent. An additional 500,000 jobs are expected in this field. It is hoped that salaries will increase significantly as well.

Home care is an essential component of health-care reform. Shortened hospital stays mean ever greater importance for the home care aide's services. The Home Care Aide Association of America's HCA I, II, and III classifications and standards reflect the increase in the importance of the home care aide's role. Indeed, the creation of home care aide specialties, such as pediatric, mental health, Alzheimer's disease, developmental disabilities, and HIV/AIDS home care aides, is under discussion.

As hospital and other institutional costs skyrocket, and as hospitals and third-party payers have moved to establish limitations on the lengths of hospital stays, the emphasis on home care is increasing and should continue to grow. It should be noted, however, that recent cuts in Medicare coverage for home care aid has contributed to the shortage as well. Fewer hours of help are covered, making each home visit more strenuous and faster paced and making each day scheduled with more, shorter visits.

For more information about home care aides, contact:

National Association for Home Care (NAHC) and the National Home
  Caring Council (NHCC)
228 7th Street SE
Washington, DC 20003
nahc.org

The Home Care Aide Association of America is an affiliate of the NAHC and can be reached at the NAHC's address.

For more information about training, contact:

National Association of Health Career Schools (NAHCS)
750 First Street NE, Suite 940
Washington, DC 20002
nahcs.org

HORTICULTURAL THERAPIST

The physicians of ancient Egypt often prescribed peaceful walks in beautiful gardens to soothe the physical and emotional pain of their patients. Today, many physicians prescribe working in a garden, greenhouse, crop field, or orchard for certain patients who have mental, physical, and/or social disabilities.

Horticultural therapists work with people who have special physical, emotional, mental, and perhaps spiritual needs. Horticultural therapy programs in veterans' hospitals following World War II gave a major boost to public awareness of this profession because of the numbers of both new programs and patients participating in them. Through guiding patients to learn to grow and care for plants, the therapist helps the patients to grow in competencies and self-confidence.

Horticulture is the practice of growing flowers, fruits, vegetables, and shrubs for ornament and pleasure. Horticultural therapy is the use of gardening activities to evaluate, rehabilitate, train, and otherwise improve the life skills and lives of individuals who are physically and/or mentally impaired.

Horticultural therapy is based on several basic human tendencies and needs. Fundamental to its theory is the universal, almost innate, human delight in perceiving natural beauty. Horticultural therapy brings to its patients natural beauty in the form of flowers, shrubs, and other plant life.

Flowers and organic motifs appear in the art of almost every culture in every age. Plants and flowers are part of our rituals and celebrations. We plant them in our yards and bring them into our homes and even our work-places because they are among the most beautiful things in nature, and that beauty has a positive effect on us. Seeing a garden in bloom can be calming, renewing, and inspiring for any person, but perhaps especially for a patient who has been shut off from the mainstream of life by physical and mental limitations. Perceiving the color, fragrance, and form of a beautiful flower can, in very elemental ways, make a person feel better.

Horticultural therapy is also founded on the concept that work experiences can be therapeutic. Tending a garden is a lesson in patience, responsibility, and faith. Watching day by day as seeds turns into blossoms is fascinating and fun. Harvesting the fruits—and flowers—of one's labors can provide a sense of personal accomplishment. In addition, society not only values the beauty of plants and well-landscaped grounds, it values those individuals with a knack for tending them. On many levels, making things grow can be a personal growth experience.

Horticultural therapists are specially educated and trained members of rehabilitation and therapy teams—which include doctors, psychiatrists, psychologists, occupational therapists, behavioral specialists, vocational skills instructors—who involve the patient in all phases of gardening and, sometimes, in the sale of the produce and plants grown as a means of improving those patients' lives.

Horticultural therapists are experts on the medical and psychological benefits of gardening. Horticultural therapy can enhance self-esteem; alleviate depression; improve motor skills; provide opportunities in problem solving; encourage work adjustment, social interaction, and communication; and teach certain marketable horticultural and business skills—all toward the goal of integrating the individual into the everyday community life stream.

For many patients whose conditions and even treatments have rendered them feeling passive and dependent, having living plants to nurture creates a role reversal. Horticultural therapy places the patient in the care-giving role, and this often engenders confidence and a renewed sense of purpose.

The education required to become a horticultural therapist stresses not only horticulture and agriculture but also psychology and the social and behavioral sciences. Thus the therapist is able to help analyze the patient's problems, assess his or her limitations and cognitive abilities, tailor activities to fit the disabilities and goals set, and gauge his or her progress.

Patients include individuals who are mentally impaired, mentally ill, visually impaired, elderly, socially maladjusted, alcohol and/or drug abusive, or disadvantaged, as well as individuals who are recuperating from surgery, who have sustained spinal cord injuries or a stroke, or who have cerebral palsy or other conditions that cause physical limitations.

The Wheelchair Orchard at Kansas State University's Horticultural Research Farm, now in its twentieth year, is an example of how an understanding of horticulture and disabilities, creative thinking, and sensitivity can happily come together in a horticultural therapy program to provide mental and physical therapy and pleasure to patients who use wheelchairs. In the Wheelchair Orchard, apple and pear trees have been wired and trained to grow onto low overhead trellises, or they are espaliered so that the branches are accessible to the wheelchair-bound gardener. This allows patients to prune, pinch, and otherwise tend these trees—and pick their fruit. Kansas State's orchard has served as a model for other gardens and orchards around the country.

SETTINGS, SALARIES, STATISTICS

Horticultural therapists work in general hospitals; rehabilitation hospitals; psychiatric hospitals; convalescent homes; juvenile centers; nursing homes; schools, work cooperatives, and training centers for individuals who have mental disabilities; public school special education programs; drug and alcohol rehabilitation centers; and correctional facilities. Horticultural therapists work indoors and outdoors, usually with groups but also on a one-to-one basis with patients. In 1879, the Pennsylvania Friends Asylum for the Insane built the first greenhouse in the United States for use with the mentally ill. Today, there are more than 1,000 horticultural therapy programs across the country providing this therapy to an estimated 24,000 individuals.

In 2001, surveys of part-time and full-time horticultural therapists revealed an average annual salary of $31,500. Since part-time therapists' salaries are factored into this average, it can be assumed that full-time, certified horticultural therapists can earn significantly more.

A minimum of a bachelor's degree in horticulture is the professional requirement. At this time, five universities in the United States offer bachelor's degrees in horticultural therapy. Of these, three universities also offer master's degrees and doctorates in horticultural therapy. There are, in addition, four certificate programs, one associate's degree program, and ten schools that offer elective courses in horticultural therapy.

Kansas State University, which has been a pioneering school in this field, offers two distance learning courses in addition to its B.S., M.S., and Ph.D. programs. The curriculum for the distance learning courses typically includes work in agriculture, horticulture, sociology, psychology, the behavioral sciences, and horticultural therapy, as well as an internship.

The American Horticultural Therapy Association (AHTA), formerly the National Council for Therapy and Rehabilitation through Horticulture (NCTRH), has established two professional classifications for horticultural therapists that are based on educational level and employment experience.

- The *horticultural therapist registered* (*HTR*) designation is for horticultural therapists holding a degree in horticultural therapy who also have interned for a minimum of one year (2,000 hours) of paid employment.
- The *master horticultural therapist* (*HTM*) designation is for horticultural therapists who have attained a master's in this field and have worked extensively in horticultural therapy, accumulating a minimum of four years of full-time paid employment.

The horticultural therapy technician (HTT) classification once offered to students who were in the process of obtaining their bachelor's degree and/or practical experience is no longer offered. At this time registration with the AHTA is voluntary, and there are no state licensing laws.

The AHTA advises high school students to obtain well-rounded, solid horticultural backgrounds by taking all of the biology courses available; by spending their summer vacations working in greenhouses, in nurseries, or for landscaping companies; and by volunteering at rehabilitation and other facilities where it is possible to learn about various disabilities.

Of the personal requirements for success in this career, most important are the subtle, special qualities that make an individual a good "relater"—sensitivity, empathy, compassion, patience, the ability to listen, and a genuine willingness to help. While plant care can call for physical strength and dexterity, there are horticultural therapists who themselves have physical limitations.

THE FUTURE

Several recent studies of emerging fields and occupations have identified horticultural therapy as an area that should experience rapid growth in the coming decade. The number of facilities and, therefore, job opportunities should increase as the American population grows older and larger. There are 68 million households in the United States where gardening is regularly carried out. Many people do not have to be told by professionals about the therapeutic effects of gardening—they know about them from experiences in their own backyards. Gardening is pleasurable and inexpensive, and it is expected that as our population ages, more people will naturally continue to garden or turn to gardening as a form of therapy. Gardening is an excellent lifelong activity, and as more programs offering formal horticultural therapy are created or expanded, opportunities for therapists will grow.

For additional information about a career in horticultural therapy and a list of educational programs, contact:

American Horticultural Therapy Association (AHTA)
909 York Street
Denver, CO 80206
ahta.org

The AHTA also publishes the *Journal of Therapeutic Horticulture* and provides many information services.

MEDICAL ASSISTANT

Medical assistants are the people patients may see first when visiting their doctors' offices: they often do receptionist tasks, answer phones, make appointments, do record keeping, take and record patients' vital signs, stock supplies in examination rooms, send out packages to labs, and generally keep things running smoothly.

Medical assistants are multiskilled health-care professionals who perform administrative and/or clinical duties in ambulatory- or immediate-care settings. In large offices, they may report to an office manager; in smaller ones, perhaps to the doctor or a registered nurse. Their work is entirely different from that of physician assistants (see Chapter 48) who examine, diagnose, and/or treat patients under the physician's guidance.

Most medical assistants have both clinical and clerical responsibilities. Clinical functions vary depending on the scope of duties permitted by the laws of each state. Their responsibilities may include helping the physician by obtaining the patient's medical history; taking and recording the patient's height and weight; obtaining and recording vital signs, such as pulse, temperature, respiration, and blood pressure; preparing the patient for examination and/or treatment; drawing blood; assisting in examining and/or treating the patient; performing routine laboratory tests and EKGs; applying dressings; instructing the patient in preparation for x-rays and laboratory examinations; preparing and administering medications as directed by a physician; instructing the patient on medication and home care; preparing the examining room; cleaning and sterilizing instruments; disposing of contaminated supplies; stocking laboratory supplies; and maintaining the examining, consultation, and waiting rooms in a clean and orderly condition.

The clerical, or administrative, responsibilities that a medical assistant may be expected to perform include scheduling and receiving patients; transcribing and maintaining medical records; procedural and diagnostic coding; typing and taking dictation; arranging for hospital admissions and laboratory procedures for patients; and handling telephone calls, correspondence, reports, insurance matters, office accounts, fees, and collections.

The size of the office in which the medical assistant works usually determines the ratio of clinical to clerical work expected. In larger offices with several staff members, medical assistants usually specialize in either patient care or office functions, whereas in a small practice, a medical assistant may have to handle both facets of the work. Although they may carry out clerical responsibilities, by virtue of their education and training, medical assistants are different from medical secretaries, who rarely perform clinical duties.

Medical assistants work in all medical specialties. For example, medical assistants in pediatrics are medical assistants who have had specialized training in pediatrics—the branch of medicine dealing with the development and care of infants and children. Working as members of the pediatric health-care team under the supervision of a pediatrician, pediatric medical assistants perform many of the same clinical and clerical functions carried out by medical assistant–generalists. They prepare examining rooms and patients for examination, take temperatures, measure height and weight, sterilize instruments, and assist the pediatrician as he or she examines and treats the infant or child. A medical assistant in pediatrics may also administer and interpret specific screening and diagnostic tests, recognize acute medical conditions, and administer specific medications—all under the supervision of the pediatrician. Any clerical responsibilities they may assume are also the same as the medical assistant–generalist's and may include secretarial, receptionist, bookkeeping, and medical record-keeping functions.

There are also geriatric medical assistants, podiatric medical assistants, ophthalmic medical assistants (see Chapter 39), orthopedic medical assistants, family medicine medical assistants, and many more.

A medical assistant must adhere to the ethical and legal standards of medical practice, demonstrate professional characteristics, and know how to respond to medical emergencies. Certain specific duties are covered by a variety of laws in some of the states, and the medical assistant must be aware of and follow those that apply in her or his work location.

In addition, medical assistants serve another important purpose. Ideally, they act as a liaison between the patient and the physician and, in the case of a medical assistant in pediatrics, between the family and the physician, as well. A medical assistant can offer important guidance, support, comfort, and warmth to the patient while freeing the physician for more technical functions. The medical assistant's role in understanding, evaluating, and accurately relaying patients' telephone calls for assistance is extremely important. A medical assistant who is efficient and personable can do much to enhance both the delivery of health care to the patient and the atmosphere in which that health care is delivered.

SETTINGS, SALARIES, STATISTICS

More than half of all medical assistants work in the offices of physicians—single practitioners and group practices, primary care physicians as well as specialists—who are in private practice. In fact, more medical assistants are employed by practicing physicians than any other type of allied health personnel. Of the remaining medical assistants, approximately 16 percent work in clinics, 9 percent in managed care or health maintenance organization facilities, 8 percent in hospitals, and 2 percent are employed in independent laboratories, educational institutions, and nursing homes. Although they usually work forty-hour weeks, some evening and weekend office hours may also be required.

Most medical assistants who have specialized in pediatrics are employed by pediatricians who are in solo or group practice. Child-care centers, community and neighborhood health centers, well-baby clinics, and other ambulatory child health-care facilities that are supervised by a physician also employ medical assistants in pediatrics.

Approximately 365,000 medical assistants were employed in the United States in 2002. Most medical assistants are female; however, more and more males are entering the field.

Salaries for medical assistants vary widely. The medical assistant's training, years of experience, and scope of responsibility as well as the volume of the physician's practice and the geographic location can all affect income.

Median annual earnings were $23,940 in 2002, with the lowest-paid 10 percent of medical assistants earning less than $17,640 and the highest-paid 10 percent earning more than $34,130, according to the 2002 research of the U.S. Bureau of Labor Statistics.

Opportunities for direct advancement in the office setting may be limited. In larger offices, promotions to supervisor or office manager may be possible. Most medical assistants who seek greater challenges and salaries undertake additional formal training to enter other allied health professions. Opportunities also exist in teaching and consulting. Many medical assistants work in specialty areas of other types of facilities, such as health information departments, emergency rooms, outpatient treatment centers, and insurance companies.

HOW TO BECOME A MEDICAL ASSISTANT

While some medical assistants are still trained on the job by the physician for whom they work, most medical assistants are graduates of formal education programs offered by postsecondary institutions. Hundreds of public and private vocational schools, community colleges, and junior colleges now offer medical assistant programs providing courses in medical terminology, biology, anatomy and physiology, typing, transcription, accounting and record keeping as well as instruction in laboratory techniques, clinical procedures, and the use of medical equipment.

Medical assistant programs offered by community colleges usually entail two years of class work and supervised clinical experience, leading to an associate's degree. Other programs available are approximately one year in length and award diplomas or certificates. Last year, approximately 23,000 students graduated from formal medical assistant educational programs.

The Commission on Accreditation of Allied Health Education Programs (CAAHEP), an independent accrediting body in which the American Medical Association participates as one of a number of sponsors, currently accredits approximately 400 educational programs for medical assistants. The Accrediting Bureau of Health Education Schools (ABHES) also accredits medical assistant educational programs. An accredited medical assistant curriculum includes courses in anatomy and physiology; medical terminology; medical law and ethics; psychology; written and oral communication; medical assisting administrative procedures, including office procedures, business correspondence, typing, transcription of medical dictation, medical office management, bookkeeping, and insurance; and medical assistant clinical procedures, including examination room techniques, aseptic practices and techniques, the care of supplies and equipment, first aid and cardiopulmonary resuscitation, laboratory orientation, and principles of pharmacology. These programs also require students to extern in qualified physicians' offices, accredited hospitals, and other health-care facilities.

A high school diploma is almost always required for formal education, as well as for on-the-job training in medical assisting. In high school, students should take mathematics, health, biology, typing, and business courses.

Personal qualities that are important to success and satisfaction as a medical assistant include intelligence, common sense, strong oral and written communication skills, friendliness, compassion, conscientiousness, manual dexterity, maturity, respect for the confidential nature of medical information, and a genuine interest in and willingness to help individuals who are ill. Medical assistants in pediatrics should, of course, enjoy children.

Certification in this field is offered by the American Medical Technologists (AMT) and the American Association of Medical Assistants (AAMA). To be eligible for certification by AMT, a medical assistant must complete a medical assisting program accredited by an organization approved by the U.S. Department of Education, complete a medical assisting course in an institution accredited by a regional accrediting commission (the accrediting body for two-year public colleges), or complete an armed forces training course. High school graduates who have a minimum of five years' employment experience in the medical assisting profession may also apply for certification. Upon passing the AMT certification examination, a candidate becomes a registered medical assistant and may use the designation RMA after his or her name.

To be eligible for AAMA certification, a medical assistant must complete an accredited medical assistant educational program. Upon passing the AAMA's written competency examination, a candidate is entitled to use the designation certified medical assistant (CMA) after his or her name.

While voluntary, both AAMA and AMT certification are widely accepted as evidence of a high level of preparation, and both tend to improve job opportunities and starting salaries. Although there is no licensing for medical assistants, some states require a short course or test before medical assistants may draw blood, give injections, take x-rays, and so on.

THE FUTURE

This occupation is projected to be the fastest-growing occupation of all career fields in the United States through 2012.

The job outlook for medical assistants—and especially for medical assistants who have graduated from formal, accredited training programs and who are certified—is excellent. Several factors should contribute to this favorable picture. The increasing population and larger percentage of older Americans as well as increasing health consciousness together create a situation where the demand for health services increases significantly.

For more information about medical assistants, contact:

American Association of Medical Assistants (AAMA)
20 North Wacker Drive, Suite 1575
Chicago, IL 60606-2903
aama-ntl.org

Registered Medical Assistants of American Medical Technologists
   (AMT)
710 Higgins Road
Park Ridge, IL 60068-5765
amt1.com

MEDICAL ILLUSTRATOR

Also Known as Graphic Communicator in Medicine and Medical Artist

Medical illustrators have provided a view into the mysteries of the human body since ancient times. Artists, physicians, alchemists, and philosophers—from the time of the ancient Greeks, Egyptians, and Romans through the Middle Ages and the Renaissance—have left us their drawings to admire and to learn from. In more recent times, the hundreds of astonishing and impeccable drawings—of wrists and fingers, ankles and toes, torsos, ears, heads, and spines—in the classic *Gray's Anatomy* have instructed generations of art students and medical students alike.

A medical illustrator is a highly trained, specialized artist who creates graphic representations of medical or biological subjects for the various bioscience communications media—medical textbooks, professional journals, pamphlets, instructional films and exhibits, general magazines, television, and the Internet.

Medical illustrators are both communicators and educators who use their artistic talents and creative insights to record facts and progress in many health fields. They sometimes work directly with health-care and research teams by using their drafting skills to provide illustrations that assist with research problems or their sculpting skills to model artificial body parts, such as noses, eyes, and ears, to be used when cosmetic or functional improvement is required.

For one assignment, a medical illustrator may be called upon to draw an extremely accurate, representational rendering of an anatomical body part, a microorganism, or even an entire surgical procedure in an operating room. For the next project, the assignment may be to reduce a complex idea to an abstract, easy-to-understand diagram or schematic concept. But a medical illustrator is not just a talented artist—he or she is a talented artist who has a solid knowledge of anatomy and general medicine.

Students preparing at schools of medical illustration learn neuroanatomy and physiology right along with three-dimensional modeling techniques, illustration, and computer graphics. This medical foundation is essential because the artist must understand the demands of an assignment, and the work executed must be authentic and precisely interpreted.

Because of the variety of assignments that a medical illustrator must be able to fulfill, he or she must be accomplished in a variety of artistic techniques and media—drawing, painting, modeling, diagramming, and creating graphic and audiovisual aids. He or she must possess a basic knowledge of typography, layout, and design and know how to prepare artwork for publication. And, of course, most medical illustrators today create their artwork using computers and the various software packages designed for medical illustration.

While the majority of medical illustrators handle an ever-changing variety of assignments, some specialize in a single art medium or concentrate on a particular medical specialty, such as pathology, embryology, ophthalmology. These medical illustrators work only with physicians, research scientists, educators, and authors in that particular specialty.

SETTINGS, SALARIES, STATISTICS

Most medical illustrators are employed by medical schools and large medical centers that have teaching and research programs. Some also work in private, state, and federal hospitals; clinics; dental and veterinary schools; medical publishing companies; pharmaceutical manufacturing companies; and advertising agencies.

Many medical illustrators also take on freelance assignments, and some work exclusively on a freelance basis. Some artists are in solo practice; others are members of large multimedia production units, working with other medical illustrators, graphic designers, chart artists, website designers, art assistants, biological photographers (see Chapter 3), television personnel, and educational specialists.

The number of men and women in this field is relatively small. The Association of Medical Illustrators (AMI), the international professional association for medical illustrators, reports a membership of approximately 900 men and women and estimates that this figure represents 80 percent of the total number of individuals in this field. AMI fosters its members' careers through education, certification, accreditation of college and university curricula, a salon, referrals, and annual and special events.

In the summer of 2004, a major exhibit—a "supershow"—of more than 370 outstanding works of art by AMI members was held in Colorado Springs, Colorado. It presented works by artists from all over North America and included surgical and anatomical illustration, interactive media, animation, three-dimensional art, fine art, and more, in categories ranging from medical publishing, advertising, and broadcast and film media to human genome research and forensic sciences.

The scope of the show emphasized how medical illustration today is much more than just illustration for textbooks and encyclopedias. It makes dynamic use of every modern form of media and is in the forefront of public and medical education—often graphically presenting surprising, even awe-inspiring, concepts that have never before been communicated in visible form.

Salaries at this time are described by the AMI as varying significantly, depending upon the experience and ability of the artist, the type of work, and the area of the country. The average starting salary in an institutional setting for a recent graduate of an accredited program is approximately $40,000 to $45,000 a year, plus benefits. Experienced illustrators earn approximately $45,000 to $75,000 a year. Administrators and faculty members earn more, and salaried illustrators often earn additional income by freelancing. Experienced artists who have established their reputations sometimes work completely independently, freelancing both as artists and as consultants.

Advancement in salaried jobs in this field usually comes in the form of promotion to director/producer of a design, art, or audiovisual service department.

HOW TO BECOME A MEDICAL ILLUSTRATOR

Prospective medical illustrators must first of all be highly talented and second be highly disciplined about the development of their talent. Medical illustrating requires outstanding talent and excellent training in art as well as interest and education in the biological sciences. To become a medical illustrator, specialized training in both disciplines is necessary.

There are very few schools of medical illustration in the United States, and only five of them (the Medical College of Georgia, the University of Illinois, Johns Hopkins University School of Medicine, the University of Michigan, and the University of Texas) are accredited by the Association of Medical Illustrators, which has established standards for the professional training of medical illustrators. Each of these programs accepts only between six and twelve students per year. Membership in the AMI is useful because many employers rely on it as an indication of proficiency.

In 1987, the American Medical Association's Committee on Allied Health Education and Accreditation (CAHEA) recognized the medical illustration occupation, and it accredited medical illustration educational programs until July 1, 1994. The Commission on Accreditation of Allied Health Education Programs (CAAHEP), an independent body that is CAHEA's successor, now accredits programs. At this time, the five programs recognized by the AMI are also accredited by CAAHEP.

All five accredited educational programs for medical illustrators are master's degree programs, and they range in length from two to three years. Requirements for admission to these programs vary to some degree, but basically the following preparation is recommended. In high school, an aspiring medical illustrator should follow the college preparatory program, with a strong emphasis on art. Biology and other science courses should be included. At the college level, a student should concentrate on art, premedical biology, and humanities courses. The art courses should include drawing, life drawing, painting, color theory, design, illustration technique, layout, photography, and typography. The science courses usually required include biology, zoology, comparative vertebrate anatomy, embryology, physiology, chemistry, and histology. Most students admitted to schools of medical illustration have majored in art. Some students, however, choose zoology or anatomy as their undergraduate major or have double or interdisciplinary majors in art/biology. Because these schools accept very few students annually, competition is stiff. A strong academic record is essential, and a portfolio of the candidate's artwork is reviewed.

Although there is some variety from school to school, most educational programs for medical illustrators include courses in human anatomy, including dissection; histology, or the microscopic study of cells and tissues; human physiology; embryology; neuroanatomy, or the nervous system; pathology; illustration techniques for publication, such as wash, carbon dust, pen and ink, watercolor, gouache, acrylics, ink, and airbrush; illustration techniques for nonprint media, such as slide-tape, motion picture, filmstrip, television, the Internet; surgical illustration, including surgical observation; anatomical illustration, including autopsy observation; three-dimensional modeling techniques; chart graph, and table design; exhibit design and construction; prosthesis design and construction; cinematography; animation; medical photography; and computer graphics and imaging.

To succeed in this profession, artistic ability, creativity, the ability to interpret information clearly, and a strong interest in the subject matter are needed.

At this time, certification is optional. There are no state licensing requirements for medical illustrators.

THE FUTURE

Employment opportunities for medical illustrators are favorable. As medical research, new technologies, and new techniques evolve ever faster, the need for artists who can record and communicate these advancements will grow, and medical illustrators holding master's degrees from accredited educational programs will be in the greatest demand.

For more information about medical illustrators and a list of accredited schools of medical illustration, contact:

Association of Medical Illustrators (AMI)
2965 Flowers Road South
Atlanta, GA 30341
medical-illustrators.org

30

MEDICAL SOCIAL WORKER AND PSYCHIATRIC SOCIAL WORKER

The New Freedom Commission on Mental Health, which met during 2002–2003, was established by President George W. Bush and had as its goal the improvement of mental health care for both children and adults in the United States. The members of the commission visited programs, interviewed people, and studied the situation all over the country. It received input from nearly 2,500 people from all fifty states and consulted with professionals in many specialties in the field. The final report was made available on the commission's website, MentalHealthCommission.gov, and has many implications for anyone who is considering a career in this field.

It is widely agreed that health is more than just the absence of disease or illness; it is the complete physical, mental, and social well-being of the individual. Social work is defined as a system of organized activities that is carried out by a person with particular knowledge, competence, and values and that is designed to help individuals, groups, or communities toward a mutual adjustment between themselves and their social environment. A professional social worker helps people cope with complex interpersonal and social problems and obtains for them the resources they need to live with dignity. Professional social workers advocate for the biological, psychological, and social health and well-being of their patients. A *medical social worker* is a social worker who specializes in helping patients and their families cope with personal problems—be they social, emotional, or financial—resulting from severe or long-term illness or disability, recovery, and rehabilitation and who obtains the resources they will need to get through their health situation with a minimum of stress. A *psychiatric social worker* is a social worker who specializes in helping psychiatric patients and others overcome emotionally stressful situations. Once patients overcome their acute problems, the psychiatric social worker helps them reenter the community as well as serves as an important communications link between the patients and their families and between the families and the professionals treating their loved ones.

If a patient's personal problems and fears are severe enough and go unanswered, they can slow his or her progress toward health and well-being. Medical and psychiatric social workers work to understand the patient's concerns and to bring to him or her the hospital personnel and services and the community resources that can alleviate these fears and the conditions that cause them so that the best recovery can be achieved. Medical and psychiatric social workers are vital members of the health-care team along with doctors, nurses, psychiatrists, therapists, and other health-care professionals.

There are more social workers employed in the nation's mental health facilities than any other single profession: 40 percent of the professional staff of all mental health facilities are social workers, 32 percent are psychiatrists, 23 percent are psychologists, and 5 percent are psychiatric nurses. Half of all the mental health treatment in the United States is given by professional social workers. It is often the social worker's sensitivity, knowledge, skills, and insights that make the big difference in a patient's recovery or adjustment.

A complete list of the specific duties carried out by a medical social worker is almost impossible to compile—medical social workers have to respond to the infinite types of problems caused by illness and injury. They assist individuals and their families in coping with a wide range of problems related to physical illness, disability, recovery, and death: for example, directing the parents of a newborn with a congenital disability to the resources in the community that they will need; organizing rehabilitation services and support groups within the community; finding shelter for young children left untended because of their parents' hospitalization; arranging for the regular delivery of special dietetic meals to an elderly patient after he or she is discharged from the hospital and convalescing at home; or easing a patient's transition into a nursing home, should that become necessary.

Medical social workers help patients handle their fears about their medical condition and their worries about how their health may affect future family relationships, work, and finances. They conduct individual and family assessments, educate people about personal health care, refer patients to the appropriate health services, and follow up on these referrals. Medical social workers advocate on behalf of patients and groups of patients, work with groups of people who have similar health problems, help communities secure access to needed health resources and services, direct social service programs in institutional and noninstitutional settings, design programs, teach, and conduct research. The HIV/AIDS epidemic has also presented new challenges to the work of medical social workers.

The specific functions and responsibilities carried out by psychiatric social workers are as numerous and varied as the problems that can be generated or aggravated by mental illness. The psychiatric social worker's fundamental responsibilities include obtaining and preparing a history of each new patient admitted to a mental hospital or other mental health facility; serving as a constant and friendly liaison between the patient and his or her family throughout what is often a long period of treatment; and also serving as a liaison between the family and the psychiatrist and other professionals treating the patient, explaining to them the patient's illness and progress and communicating to the professional staff any family concerns or information that may have bearing on the treatment.

The psychiatric social worker helps smooth the patient's return to a more satisfying, productive life in the community by using a carefully cultivated repertoire of community resources, by producing remedies for the concrete, day-to-day problems that the patient may face as he or she adjusts to the outside world, and by remaining in touch with the patient and providing continuing support and help as he or she works to overcome his or her problems and fears. For psychiatric social workers, too, HIV/AIDS has presented new issues, problems, and interventions. Some psychiatric social workers conduct research, and others teach psychiatric social work.

SETTINGS, SALARIES, STATISTICS

Medical social workers practice in a wide variety of settings: free clinics; union health centers; specialty outpatient clinics; health maintenance organizations; solo and group medical practices; home health agencies; industry; the emergency, intake, discharge, maternity, pediatric, intensive care, psychiatric, burn, surgical, and medical areas of general, specialized, government, and military hospitals (over half of the country's hospitals have social services departments or offer social services); nursing homes; long-term health-care facilities; public health departments; alcohol and drug abuse programs; sex education programs; crisis clinics; rape prevention and child abuse services; national and international voluntary agencies; rural health planning agencies; Native American reservations and Native American health centers in major urban areas; the Department of Health and Human Services; vocational rehabilitation offices; mental health/mental disability boards; health and disaster relief programs; and private practice. They also teach medical social work in schools of social work, medicine, nursing, public health, pharmacy, and dentistry and in allied health para-professional training programs.

This long and diverse list of work settings suggests what is special about the nature of medical social work—medical social workers can be found wherever people are faced with health and medical situations, dilemmas, and problems. Social workers began their involvement with health issues in the United States at the turn of the last century. Their first concerns were with making health services available to the poor and with improving the social conditions that bred tuberculosis and other infectious diseases. Today, medical social workers are found in every aspect of our health-care system.

Psychiatric social workers work in mental hospitals, the psychiatric departments of general hospitals, mental health clinics, hospitals for individuals who are mentally disabled or who have epilepsy, federal and state mental hospitals, rehabilitation organizations, community mental health centers, the courts, and research and educational institutions.

All social workers combined held about 477,000 jobs in 2002, according to the U.S. Bureau of Labor Statistics. This represented about two out of every five jobs in government agencies. Of those, medical and public health social workers made up about 107,000 and mental health and substance abuse social workers made up about 95,000. Job opportunities are expected to grow faster than the average through 2012.

Earnings for medical social workers were at a median annual salary level of $37,380 in 2002, with the lowest-paid 10 percent earning less than $23,840 and the highest-paid 10 percent earning more than $56,320.

Earnings for psychiatric social workers were at a median annual salary of $32,850 as of 2002, with the lowest-paid 10 percent earning less than $21,050 and the highest-paid 10 percent earning more than $52,240.

Salary levels vary in different regions and institutions. Institutions in the West—Arizona, Idaho, Utah, Nevada, Oregon, Washington, California, Hawaii, Alaska, Montana, and Wyoming—tend to offer the highest salaries. Social workers who are employed by the federal government are among the highest-paid members of this profession.

HOW TO BECOME A MEDICAL OR PSYCHIATRIC SOCIAL WORKER

There are three levels of professional social work education: the bachelor's degree (B.S.W.), the master's degree (M.S.W.), and the doctorate (D.S.W. or Ph.D.). Preparation for professional social work requires a minimum of a bachelor's degree, and there are approximately 400 bachelor of social work degree programs that are accredited by the Council on Social Work Education (CSWE). An accredited undergraduate curriculum will include course work in human behavior and the social environment; social welfare policy and services; methods of social work, which is the process of intervening in the flow of events to help solve a problem or develop a resource; research; and field practice.

An M.S.W. is usually required for more advanced medical and psychiatric social work positions. There are approximately 115 universities that offer two-year master's programs. To apply for a graduate degree in social work, a person need not have a bachelor's degree in this field. A number of graduate schools offer health concentrations in their curricula, and a few offer interdisciplinary degrees with public health schools.

A doctorate is usually required for faculty positions in colleges and universities and for most research positions. Administrative positions, such as director of hospital medical social work, usually require a Ph.D. in Social Work. The CSWE currently accredits forty-five doctoral programs.

Personal qualities that are essential for success and career-long satisfaction in the fields of medical and psychiatric social work include a genuine love for people and concern for their needs, warmth, the ability to work as a member of a team, freedom from prejudices, sound judgment, and a special balance of empathy and professionalism, faith and objectivity.

Voluntary certification in this field is available through the Academy of Certified Social Workers (ACSW). To become certified, a candidate must complete a master's degree program in social work, have a minimum of two years of postgraduate work experience, be a member of the National Association of Social Workers (NASW), and pass a written examination. Upon successful completion of the certifying process, a social worker may use the title certified social worker with the initials ACSW. Certification tends to enhance salary and advancement. All fifty states and the District of Columbia require social workers to be registered, licensed, or certified.

THE FUTURE

The U.S. Department of Labor's Bureau of Labor Statistics predicts that between now and 2012, job opportunities for social workers will expand, and social work will be in the top 20 percent of all occupations in terms of growth. Ever-increasing awareness of the importance and application of this work; the expansion of the U.S. population, and specifically of the older population; and the never-ending line of new medical problems and medical solutions, almost all of which present challenges to the patient and to society, should cause growing demand and budgeting for medical and psychiatric social workers.

For more information about what medical and psychiatric social workers do and about education and certification requirements, contact:

National Association of Social Workers (NASW)
Education Office
750 First Street NE, Suite 700
Washington, DC 20002-4241
socialworkers.org

MEDICAL TECHNOLOGIST (MT) AND MEDICAL LABORATORY TECHNICIAN (MLT)

Also Known as Clinical Laboratory Scientist and Clinical Laboratory Technician, Including Clinical Assistant

Most of the tests that are done in hospital and doctor office visits are performed by medical technologists or medical laboratory technicians. When the nurse in a doctor's office says that a test will be sent to the lab, chances are that it is going to one of these specialists.

Medical technologists (MTs) and medical laboratory technicians (MLTs), increasingly known as clinical laboratory scientists (CLSs) and clinical laboratory technicians (CLTs), respectively, perform diagnostic laboratory tests that play a crucial role in the detection of diseases and the treatment of patients. Using microscopes, a variety of chemicals, complex precision instruments, and computers, they carry out serology, parasitology, toxicology, cytology, histology, bacteriology, urinalysis, environmental chemistry, hematology and blood typing, general chemistry, immunochemistry, nuclear medicine, and other tests that tell physicians and patients much about the nature and progress of health conditions.

In a recent year, Americans spent about $32 billion on the more than 1,000 different medical laboratory tests that are available today. A major hospital may process more than 2 million different laboratory tests in one year, and much of this laboratory work is computerized. From one two-milliliter blood sample (about forty drops), more than twenty different tests can be run simultaneously, with the results being handled by laboratory information systems that can interface with patient care centers. Some laboratory tests are so sophisticated and specialized that they are performed by only one or a few laboratories nationwide.

A hospital laboratory never completely shuts down. The need for vital laboratory information exists around the clock, and timely handling of important laboratory information leads to better patient care.

Medical technologists must have a baccalaureate degree. They supervise laboratories and make critical judgments about laboratory results as well as carry out complex testing procedures. Because of their comprehensive science background, MTs know how to solve problems and troubleshoot analytical systems. They understand the scientific theory behind a test, and they also are able to evaluate the effects that various pathological conditions may have on test results. They understand quality issues and monitor laboratory output for precision and accuracy as well as design and implement new test procedures.

Some MTs, known as generalists, are employed in facilities where they work in all the laboratory disciplines. Others specialize in clinical areas and become experts in that area. Medical technologists are also employed in research, public health, and reference laboratories as well as perform private consulting for physician office laboratories.

Medical laboratory technicians usually have a two-year associate's degree. Working under the supervision of the medical technologist, an MLT performs laboratory tests that are less complex and require less theoretical and technical knowledge. Medical laboratory technicians are expected to microscopically examine specimens, perform blood counts, operate automated testing equipment, and inoculate culture media to identify bacteria. With experience, they may take on more responsibility and use more independent judgment.

Medical laboratory technicians who hold certificates from one-year educational programs are referred to as clinical assistants (CAs). CAs assist MLTs. They are trained to perform the most routine, least complicated laboratory procedures under direct supervision. These procedures involve the use of laboratory instruments in processes where discriminations are clear, errors few and easily corrected, and results can be confirmed with a reference test or source within the working area.

SETTINGS, SALARIES, STATISTICS

More than half of all medical laboratory personnel work in a hospital laboratory. Other opportunities exist in independent laboratories; physicians' offices; clinics; health maintenance organizations; pharmaceutical companies; public and private research institutions dedicated to the study of specific diseases; the armed forces; and city, state, and federal health agencies; as well as on the teaching staffs of programs that prepare medical laboratory personnel. A growing demand exists for private consultants to interface with physician office laboratories.

The workweek for medical technology personnel is usually forty hours long. Part-time opportunities exist at many work sites, and flexible hours are possible as hospital laboratories are staffed for three shifts per day. As many as 20 percent of all medical laboratory personnel work part-time. Because most hospital laboratories never close, hospital laboratory personnel can also expect to work evening, weekend, and holiday hours, and rotating shifts are common. In times of emergencies, seasonal infections, and other occasional heavy needs for laboratory work, the workload can be extremely heavy.

Median annual earnings for medical laboratory technologists in 2002 were $42,910, with those in the lowest 10 percent earning less than $30,530 and those in the highest 10 percent earning more than $58,000.

For medical laboratory technicians, the median annual salary in 2002 was $29,040. Those in the lowest 10 percent earned less than $19,070, and those in the top 10 percent earned more than $43,960.

Salaries in hospitals were the highest for both groups, and salaries in medical and diagnostic laboratories and physicians' offices were somewhat lower.

Salaries in this field depend on educational level, certification, region, and institution. Generally, medical laboratory personnel who work in large cities earn the highest salaries.

Medical laboratory technology is a field where "career laddering" is possible but not common. The experience and training necessary to function at one level are not easily applied to the attainment of the higher levels. Without losing any credit or time, medical laboratory technicians can add course work and experience to their certificates or associate's degrees and qualify for medical technologist status; similarly, medical laboratory technicians with certificates may apply their training toward the educational and experiential requirements for a medical laboratory technician associate's degree. In reality, however, this advancement rarely occurs.

Technologists may advance to supervisory positions, and, with additional time and experience, a medical technologist may become the administrative medical technologist in a large hospital. Graduate education tends to enhance salaries and advancement.

HOW TO BECOME A MEDICAL TECHNOLOGIST OR MEDICAL LABORATORY TECHNICIAN

The educational requirement for an entry-level position as a medical technologist is a baccalaureate degree, including or in addition to the completion of a hospital internship. As an undergraduate, a student medical technologist will generally take course work in biology, chemistry, and mathematics, which will provide a solid scientific foundation for the clinical internship in which he or she will participate.

Medical technologist educational programs are offered by many colleges, universities, and hospitals around the United States. The curriculum offers courses in theory and extensive laboratory experience in hematology, microbiology, immunology, transfusion medicine, and clinical chemistry. Some programs are integrated and the student receives instruction in medical laboratory technology course work as a component of the baccalaureate degree. Other programs are referred to as "three plus one programs": students spend three academic years on a college or university campus studying the background foundational sciences and then relocate to a hospital setting for their final year of education.

Of the medical technologist educational programs offered nationwide, approximately 275 are accredited by the National Accrediting Agency for Clinical Laboratory Sciences (NAACLS).

Many institutions offer graduate work in medical laboratory technology. This graduate study prepares medical technologists for teaching, administrative, and research positions and enables professionals to gain specialist certification in particular areas of the laboratory.

Getting the education necessary to become a medical laboratory technician can take one of two formal educational options. After high school, students can enroll in a two-year, community or junior college associate's degree program that will prepare them to carry out the more complicated technical functions of laboratory work, or they may enroll in a one-year certificate program for medical laboratory technicians offered by a hospital, college, community college, or vocational/technical school. In addition, many practicing medical laboratory technicians learn their skills in the military, and some have been trained on the job. Several agencies accredit medical laboratory technician educational programs.

The NAACLS accredits associate's degree programs and certificate programs. The NAACLS also grants approval status to clinical assistant programs. The Accrediting Bureau of Health Education Schools (ABHES) and the Accrediting Commission of Independent Colleges and Schools (ACICS) also accredit medical laboratory technician educational programs.

Students in two-year medical laboratory training programs learn more theory than certificate students. The emphasis in the two-year program is on general knowledge, basic skills, and mastering laboratory testing procedures, and the curriculum teaches procedures in hematology, serology, chemistry, microbiology, and immunohematology. Medical laboratory technician students in the certificate programs take introductory course work in medical ethics and conduct, medical terminology, laboratory solutions and media, blood collecting techniques, microbiology, hematology, serology, and immunohematology.

Abilities and personal qualities that can contribute to effective and enjoyable performance in this field include an aptitude for science, attention to detail, manual dexterity, good or good corrected vision, the ability to distinguish between fine color gradations, and the ability to work well under pressure.

Many states and cities require medical laboratory personnel to be licensed. Information on licensure is available from state departments of health. Certification in medical laboratory work is offered by several national certifying agencies. The Board of Registry of the American Society of Clinical Pathologists (ASCP) is the oldest and largest of these certifying agencies.

The Board of Registry has specific combinations of education and experience that entitle a candidate to sit for its examinations. Medical technologists who satisfy these requirements earn the designation MT (ASCP), which stands for medical technologist certified by the American Society of Clinical Pathologists. A medical laboratory technician who satisfies the requirements may use the designation MLT (ASCP), for medical laboratory technician certified by the American Society of Clinical Pathologists, after his or her name.

The National Certification Agency for Medical Laboratory Personnel (NCA) also certifies medical technologists and medical laboratory technicians. A medical technologist who satisfies the NCA's educational, experience, and examination requirements is designated a CLS (NCA), for clinical laboratory scientist, and a medical laboratory technician fulfilling the requirements is designated a CLT (NCA), for clinical laboratory technician.

The American Medical Technologists (AMT) also certifies medical laboratory personnel, offering the designations MT (AMT) and MLT (AMT) to medical technologists and medical laboratory technicians, respectively, who meet its educational and experience requirements. In 1999, the AMT began granting a new certification, the CLC (AMT), which stands for certified laboratory consultant. A laboratory consultant helps to set up labs that comply with Occupational Safety and Health Administration (OSHA) and other regulations and that meet the needs of the testing to be carried out. Six years of experience in the laboratory are required for certification. So far, forty CLCs (AMT) have been granted.

Finally, certification is available from the International Society for Clinical Laboratory Technology (ISCLT). A medical laboratory technician who satisfies the ISCLT's preparation requirements and who passes its competency examination is designated an RLT, for registered laboratory technician. A medical technologist who satisfies the various requirements is designated an RMT, or registered medical technologist. ISCLT certification satisfies the licensing requirements in several states.

Certification is an important enhancement to employment, salaries, and advancement in this field, and in many cases it is a requirement for employment. Many medical laboratory workers are certified by more than one agency. The agencies' certification requirements are numerous and varied, and it is strongly recommended that students contact these organizations directly. In some parts of the country, certification by a particular agency is preferred by employers.

THE FUTURE

The job outlook for this profession is expected to continue to be very good, and the number of job openings is expected to exceed the number of trained personnel available. Several factors affect the employment outlook for medical laboratory personnel. The American population is growing larger, and a larger percentage of it is older (a trend that is expected to continue at least for several decades); therefore, the number of people potentially requiring laboratory tests should increase. Simultaneously, that population is growing more and more health conscious and is willing to undergo medical tests.

In addition, the number of tests available is growing, and their use by physicians to pinpoint diagnoses is also growing. These factors should contribute to an increased demand for laboratory tests and, therefore, an increased demand for laboratory personnel. At the same time, however, the student population is smaller today.

A potentially complicating factor, however, is the greater efficiency that accompanies the greater labor- and cost-effectiveness of computerized testing methods. Procedures that once were done one at a time, by hand, are now carried out with the push of a button by computers that are able to turn out large batches of results quickly and inexpensively.

Adding these influences together, however, it is expected that employment opportunities should grow faster than the average for all occupations through 2012, with new positions opening up. Many areas of the country are reporting acute shortages of laboratory personnel. More than 50 percent of the states and territories surveyed by the American Society for Medical Technology report a shortage of technologists. More than 45 percent report shortages of technicians. Some facilities have been forced to hire temporary technologists at very high fees from temporary and contracting agencies. Other facilities are offering substantial bonuses to employees who will commit to at least one year of employment in a rural hospital, where the labor shortage is greatest.

For more information about medical laboratory personnel, contact:

American Society of Clinical Pathologists (ASCP)
2110 West Harrison Street
Chicago, IL 60612
ascp.org

American Medical Technologists (AMT)
710 Higgins Road
Park Ridge, IL 60068
amt1.org

National Credentialing Agency for Medical Laboratory Personnel (NCA)

P.O. Box 15945-289

Lenexa, KS 66285

nca-info.org

International Society for Clinical Laboratory Technology (ISCLT)

917 Locust Street, Suite 1100

St. Louis, MO 63101-1419

National Accrediting Agency for Clinical Laboratory Sciences (NAACLS)

8410 West Bryn Mawr, Suite 670

Chicago, IL 60631-3415

naacls.org

MUSIC THERAPIST

Also Known as Adjunctive Therapist, Creative Arts Therapist, Music Specialist, Rehabilitation Therapist, Therapeutic Activities Worker, and Expressive Arts Therapist

"**M**usic has charms to soothe a savage breast. . ." the poet said, and we instinctively know that this is true. The recognition that music has healing value is at least as old as recorded history. Today, for many kinds of patients in hospitals, rehabilitation centers, nursing homes, drug abuse treatment centers, schools, and mental health facilities, music is part of the prescribed treatment plan.

Modern music therapy is the systematic application of music in a therapeutic environment to bring about desirable changes in a patient's behavior. It is a useful therapeutic tool in the rehabilitation of patients with a variety of behavioral, learning, and physical disorders, and it has been demonstrated to be effective in improving self-control and self-esteem, relieving depression, enhancing attention span, and, in other ways, giving patients new insight into themselves and a better understanding of the world around them. Research also suggests that listening to music can affect pulse, blood pressure, and muscle response. Indeed, neuroscientists think that music might be able to build and strengthen neural connections in the cerebral cortex.

Music therapists are the trained health-care professionals who plan and carry out the specific musical activities used in the rehabilitation of persons with disabilities. They work with socially and emotionally maladjusted adults and adolescents; people with developmental disabilities of all ages; geriatric patients; children with learning problems; individuals with hearing loss or visual and physical impairments; the homeless; patients with

HIV/AIDS; substance abuse patients; individuals with cerebral palsy, stroke, Parkinson's disease, and Alzheimer's disease; and persons with multiple disabilities. They use a combination of music and psychology to achieve certain treatment goals involving the restoration, maintenance, and improvement of the patient's mental and physical health.

The programs devised by music therapists are designed to gain and maintain the patient's interest. Group and individual singing, musical instruments, and often dance and body movements are part of the therapy.

The music therapist is a member of the health-care team, often working with other therapists, psychiatrists, psychologists, and social workers to analyze the patient's problems and establish treatment goals. How music therapy may help a particular patient is discussed, then specific group and individual activities designed to meet the patient's needs are planned and implemented by the music therapist. Patients are periodically evaluated to gauge the effectiveness of the music therapy.

SETTINGS, SALARIES, STATISTICS

More than 5,200 music therapists practice in the United States, working in general and psychiatric hospitals, clinics, mental retardation centers, adult day-care facilities, government and community health agencies, nursing homes, hospices, halfway houses, correctional facilities, special education programs in public and private schools, and the research departments of universities where work on projects in biofeedback, relaxation, and other areas where music therapy may play a role is conducted. Some music therapists have their own practices and work with children and adults who are referred by psychiatrists and other health professionals. Most music therapists have regular workweeks but may occasionally be called on to work evening or weekend hours. While the great majority of music therapists is made up of women, the number of men entering this field is growing steadily.

According to the American Music Therapy Association, starting salaries in 2004 for music therapists were running at about $23,000 to $28,000, depending on the location and the type of facility. Some jobs are done on contract, rather than as employees, and in those cases the music therapist will probably not receive benefits.

Experienced music therapists earn $32,000 or more per year on average. Prior education, experience, and location will affect these figures. Some music therapy professors report earnings as high as $70,000 per annum. Music therapists who work in hospices or who specialize in gerontology tend to earn the least. Salaries are generally highest in the New England and western states and lowest in the south central states.

Advancement in the music therapy field involves positions such as department supervisor, to which a music therapist may be promoted, but such promotions usually entail a reduction in therapy activities and increased administrative duties.

HOW TO BECOME A MUSIC THERAPIST

The people who are working as music therapists today bring to their careers a wide range of prior training and experience. Some have advanced degrees in music therapy from institutions offering special programs in this field; others have study and experience combinations that have led to employment in the music therapy field.

As this form of therapy grows, however, more rigid educational standards are being established and adopted by more employers. Therefore, satisfying these standards is recommended to students starting in the field. The curriculum typically leading to a bachelor's degree in music therapy includes music and music therapy courses (60 percent of the program work), behavioral/health/natural science courses (20 percent), and general studies (20 percent).

Approximately seventy colleges and universities offer bachelor's degree programs in music therapy. Of these, about a dozen also offer master's and doctoral programs.

The approved curriculum for entry-level study in music therapy includes course work in music therapy; psychology; music; biological, social, and behavioral sciences; disabilities; and general studies. Study includes practical application of music therapy procedures and techniques learned in the classroom through required fieldwork in facilities in the community and a supervised clinical internship upon completion of the course work. As students, music therapists learn to assess the needs of clients, develop and implement treatment plans, and evaluate and document clinical changes.

Those graduates who complete an approved clinical internship and who pass an exam given by the Certification Board of Music Therapists (CBMT) earn the credential MT-BC, for music therapist–board certified, thereby demonstrating entry-level skills in the profession. The CBMT is an independent, nonprofit corporation fully accredited by the National Commission for Certifying Agencies. The CBMT programs meet or exceed the same standards licensing boards adhere to in test development and administration. The MT-BC credential is maintained through certification reexamination every five years or through successful completion and documentation of 100 Music Therapy Continuing Education Units (CEUs).

In addition to the MT-BC credential, other recognized professional designations are registered music therapists (RMTs), certified music therapists (CMTs), and advanced certified music therapists (ACMTs) listed with the National Music Therapy Registry (NMTR). The NMTR is a separate entity from the CBMT that will maintain a list until the year 2020 of other qualified music therapists using the professional designations of RMT, CMT, and ACMT. Any individual who does not have proper training and credentials is not qualified to provide music therapy services.

Personal qualities important to a successful and satisfying career in music therapy include good physical health, stamina, the emotional stability both to handle patients and to be a good role model for them, tact, patience, compassion, a healthy sense of humor, the ability to withstand frustration, and creativity. It is also important to work well as part of a team.

At this time, licensure is not required, except in the case of music therapists who work in public schools and who may therefore be licensed as special education instructors in the states in which they work.

THE FUTURE

The employment picture for this career looks very good. Music therapy is gaining in acceptance and popularity as the medical profession and the public recognizes the benefits of alternative forms of medical care. Indeed, music therapy's significant benefits to the growing elderly population have been the topic of governmental hearings, and in 1992, when amendments to the Older Americans Act became law, music therapy, as well as art therapy (see Chapter 2) and dance/movement therapy (see Chapter 11) were included and defined. This recognition has made certain federal grant money available for study and treatment.

Research into music's part in biofeedback and relaxation as well as exciting new work on music's role in enhancing special education continue to increase interest in this therapy and create a demand for therapists. As with other auxiliary health care, however, the future of music therapy depends on the economy, coming health-care trends, governmental support, and financing of health-care and managed-care policy.

Work as a music therapist can be challenging, creative, and personally satisfying. Music therapy is an important form of rehabilitation for many patients today. If the economy and health-care delivery systems are favorable, jobs in this important field should open up.

For more information about music therapists, contact:

American Music Therapy Association
8455 Colesville Road, Suite 1000
Silver Spring, MD 20910-3392
musictherapy.org

CHAPTER 33

NUCLEAR MEDICINE TECHNOLOGIST (NMT)

Also Known as Radioisotope Technologist

Nuclear medicine is the science and clinical discipline of administering radioactive compounds—radionuclides and radiopharmaceuticals—to patients or to specimens of the patient's body in order to diagnose, treat, and investigate various health problems. When these compounds are used directly on the patient, they are administered intravenously, intramuscularly, subcutaneously, or orally.

Nuclear medicine technologists (NMTs) are specialists who use very low doses of these radioactive substances to trace shapes and movements inside a patient's body, making an image on film or on a computer that helps nuclear medicine physicians in diagnosing problems without invasive surgical procedures.

In diagnostic procedures, tiny amounts of these isotopes are introduced into the patient's body to act as tracers. In the course of their journey through the body, the isotopes are altered or they attach to certain tissues. The technologist positions a special camera over the region of interest, such as the brain, liver, lungs, thyroid gland, bones, or even whole systems, and when the radioactivity has concentrated in that region, it is detected and translated into spots of light that expose the camera's film.

The developed film is called a scan or a scintigram. The image created by the radioactive tracer allows the physician to detect a variety of structural and functional abnormalities. By observing how and where the radioactive compounds go, a nuclear medicine physician is able to gain unique and valuable information about changes in the body's biological processes as well as changes in anatomy.

When administered for therapeutic purposes, the radioactive compounds are used to selectively destroy diseased tissue.

A good example of how nuclear medicine is used to diagnose and evaluate health problems is the nuclear cardiology procedure known as the thallium scan, which is a test performed to detect blockage in the coronary arteries that supply the heart. In this procedure, the patient is connected to an electrocardiograph that constantly monitors his or her heart activity. He or she then begins exercising on a treadmill.

While the patient exercises, the radioisotope thallium 201, a low-dose radioactive tracer, is injected into a vein in the patient's arm. It enters the patient's bloodstream and circulates throughout the body. A gamma scintillation camera is positioned over the patient's chest, and it picks up the isotope as it progresses to the coronary arteries leading to the heart muscle. A computer translates the signals given off by the thallium and from them produces a computerized printout displaying the distribution of the thallium in the heart muscle.

Where the blood flows unimpeded, the tracer also flows, giving off its radiation and creating spots of light on the scan. Where circulation is poor or a blockage exists, the flow of blood and the tracer are impeded, and the computer picture will show a "cold spot." This test can reveal much about the patient's heart and is very accurate, while being almost noninvasive—only an injection is required. The radiation dose used is only slightly greater than that in a conventional chest x-ray.

A common example of nuclear medicine used in the treatment of diseases is the radioactive iodine capsule or liquid given to patients suffering from hyperthyroidism, which is overactivity of the thyroid gland. In this procedure, the patient swallows a carefully controlled amount of radioactive iodine. When it reaches the thyroid gland, the radioactive iodine destroys the over-functioning tissue, thereby relieving the potentially serious symptoms. The advantage of using radioactive iodine is that it destroys this tissue nonsurgically, eliminating the hospital stay, greater expense, and potential trauma and risk that surgery entails.

Nuclear medicine technologists are the health-care professionals who, working under the supervision of the nuclear medicine physician and other professionals in this field, position the patient; calculate, prepare, and administer the correct dosages of the radioactive drugs; run the gamma ray detecting equipment; examine the quality of the image made, either on film or on a computer screen; and then process the test, increasingly with the help of a computer.

For most NMTs, diagnostic scanning is their primary function. They also perform certain in vitro diagnostic procedures (*in vitro* is Latin for "in glass"—that is, occurring not in the patient's body but in a laboratory situation). In these laboratory procedures, known as radio assay, radioactive materials are added to body specimens, such as urine and blood, to measure tiny amounts of substances such as hormones, vitamins, or vital drugs.

NMTs must, of course, be proficient in laboratory procedures. Nuclear medicine technologists apply their knowledge of radiation physics and radiation safety procedures so that radiation exposure to the patient, to the public, and to the radiation workers is kept within minimum levels. Nuclear medicine workers are also responsible for purchasing, handling, and properly disposing of the radioactive drugs; maintaining quality control; and maintaining patient records.

Nuclear medicine technologists must understand and relate to the patient's concerns and fears about his or her illness and pending diagnostic procedures or therapies. They must be able to recognize emergency situations and know how to initiate lifesaving first aid.

SETTINGS, SALARIES, STATISTICS

About 65 percent of all NMTs work in hospitals. NMTs also work in public health institutions, doctors' offices, and research institutions. Some NMTs teach nuclear medicine technology in colleges and universities.

In 2002, there were approximately 17,000 nuclear medicine technologists in the United States, and about two-thirds of them worked in hospitals.

Salaries vary according to the technologist's experience and responsibilities, the type of institution, and the geographic area. In 2002, median annual salaries for nuclear medicine technologists were $48,750, with the lowest-paid 10 percent earning less than $35,870 and the highest-paid 10 percent earning more than $68,710. Salaries tended to be higher on the West Coast.

Advancement in the field of nuclear medicine technology may come in the form of promotion to supervisory and administrative positions. A bachelor's degree is important for such promotions and essential for teaching positions.

HOW TO BECOME A NUCLEAR MEDICINE TECHNOLOGIST

There are several ways to attain the education and clinical experience necessary to become a nuclear medicine technologist. Formal education programs of different lengths, usually twelve months to four years, accommodate the prior training and needs of candidates coming to this field from various backgrounds: certified radiographers, certified radiation therapy technologists, RNs, medical technologists, and holders of associate's and bachelor's degrees in physics and the biological sciences. The length of the program and the credential awarded—certificate, associate's degree, or bachelor's degree—will depend on prior preparation, the educational needs of the student, and the specific institution. One-year certificate and two-year associate's degree programs are most common. On-the-job experiences also can provide the training necessary for employment as an NMT, but such training is becoming rarer and is considered by many employers to be insufficient.

Programs in this field are accredited by the Joint Review Committee on Nuclear Medicine Technology (JRCNMT). In 2002, there were approximately ninety-two accredited programs in the United States and Puerto Rico. Slightly more than half are offered by colleges and universities, and one-third are offered by hospitals and medical centers. Accredited programs also are offered by community colleges and the military.

The curriculum in a formal program includes courses in patient care, nuclear physics, instrumentation, statistics, health physics, biochemistry, immunology, radionuclide chemistry, radiopharmacy, administration, radiation biology, clinical nuclear medicine, in vivo—in the patient's body—and in vitro studies, radionuclide therapy, and computer application and operation.

In many settings—hospitals, primarily—to work as a nuclear medicine technologist, a candidate must be certified and/or registered. Two organizations certify NMTs: the American Registry of Radiologic Technologists

(ARRT) and the Nuclear Medicine Technology Certification Board (NMTCB). Many NMTs are certified by one or by both, depending on the employment requirements in their region and their long-range career goals. The ARRT offers its certification examination three times a year in approximately 100 locations nationwide and in Puerto Rico. This three-hour-long test of competency is used not only by employers as a standard of preparation but also by those states that require licensing.

To be eligible for this examination, a candidate must have graduated from an accredited nuclear medicine educational program. In certain specific cases, candidates who have not attended one of these programs may file an appeal to sit for the examination. Upon passing the ARRT examination, a nuclear medicine technologist may use the title registered nuclear medical technologist and the letters RT (N) (ARRT) after his or her name. The letters stand for radiologic technologist in nuclear medicine certified by the American Registry of Radiologic Technologists. ARRT certification is recognized by Great Britain, Canada, Australia, and South Africa.

The NMTCB also requires its candidates to graduate from accredited schools of nuclear medicine technology. Certification options for nuclear medicine technologists who have been trained on the job exclusively have been phased out. To sit for the NMTCB examination, a candidate must either be a graduate of an accredited educational program in nuclear medicine technology or have taken the exam before within the past five years.

Upon successful completion of the NMTCB's qualifying examination, the candidate may use the title certified nuclear medical technologist and its abbreviation CNMT after his or her name. The NMTCB has reciprocity with the Canadian Association of Medical Radiation Technologists, which means that certification by the NMTCB is recognized in Canada and vice versa.

At this time, more than half of the states and Puerto Rico require nuclear medicine technologists to be licensed. However, recent federal legislation encouraging state licensing should result in a trend toward more state regulation in the near future. Nuclear medicine technologists must meet the minimum federal standards for the administration of radioactive drugs and the operation of radiation detection equipment.

Individuals who are interested in nuclear medicine technology should have good verbal and numerical skills; manual dexterity; appreciation for the importance of accuracy; respect for the potentially dangerous materials being handled; the ability to work well and communicate well both with other health-care professionals and with a wide variety of patients, many of whom are very anxious, very ill, or dying; compassion; patience; and the physical strength to lift and position patients.

THE FUTURE

Job opportunities are expected to grow faster than the average in all occupations through 2012. However, the job outlook for nuclear medicine technologists will depend largely upon what future technological advances dominate the field.

Competing with nuclear medicine imaging methods are many newer, less invasive methods such as magnetic resonance imaging (MRI) and computerized tomography (CT) scanning. In turn, these innovations are likely to be replaced with the next generation of sophisticated, noninvasive diagnostic techniques. Simultaneously, new applications for nuclear medicine in tumor treatment and in coronary output evaluation that are more effective and/or safer than earlier procedures should increase the need for NMTs. Most NMTs work in hospitals, so hospital efforts at cost containment must also be factored into the job outlook.

For more information about nuclear medicine technologists and the educational and other requirements for a career in this field, contact:

American Society of Radiologic Technologists (ASRT)
15000 Central Avenue SE
Albuquerque, NM 87123-3917
asrt.org

The Society of Nuclear Medicine (SNM) Technologists Section
1850 Samuel Morse Drive
Reston, VA 20190-5316
snm.org

American Registry of Radiologic Technologists (ARRT)
1255 Northland Drive
Mendotta Heights, MN 55120-1155
arrt.org

Nuclear Medicine Technology Certification Board (NMTCB)
2970 Clairmont Road NE, Suite 935
Atlanta, GA 30329-1634
nmtcb.org

For information about accredited educational programs in nuclear medicine technology, contact:

Joint Review Committee on Education Programs in Nuclear Medicine
    Technology (JRCNMT)
One 2nd Avenue East, Suite C
Polson, MT 59860-2320
www.jrcnmt.org

CHAPTER

34

NURSE

Including Licensed Practical Nurse
(LPN), Registered Nurse (RN),
Advanced Practice Nurse, and
Clinical Specialties

With more than 3 million jobs, nurses make up the largest occupational group in the United States. Registered nurses (RNs) alone held more than 2.3 million jobs in 2002 and licensed practical nurses (LPNS) held 702,000 more.

For a century and a half, nurses have been considered to be essential suppliers of health care in America. Working in a broad range of institutional and community settings, nurses care for and comfort the ill, the injured, and the disabled. In addition, they teach good health, safety, sanitation, and nutrition practices. Nursing has traditionally been very people-oriented work that provides significant personal challenges and personal satisfactions.

There are four educational routes in nursing: (1) practical, or vocational, nursing programs; (2) associate's degree programs; (3) diploma programs; and (4) baccalaureate programs. All four options prepare the student to provide nursing services, but they provide preparation for four distinct levels of the nursing profession and differ in the depth and breadth of intellectual, interpersonal, and technical skills taught. One educational route trains the student to become a licensed practical nurse; the other three prepare the student to become a registered nurse.

The first educational option entails one year of formal education plus supervised clinical instruction, which prepare students to become licensed practical nurses, or *licensed vocational nurses* (*LVNs*) as they are called in Texas and California. LPNs provide bedside care to ill, injured, convalescent, and physically disabled patients in hospitals, clinics, nursing homes, and similar institutions.

Working under the supervision of registered nurses, LPNs provide nursing care that requires technical knowledge and skill, but not the in-depth professional education and training of a registered nurse. Their functions may include taking and recording the patient's temperature, blood pressure, pulse rate, and respiration rate; dressing wounds; giving alcohol rubs, massages, and injections; applying compresses, ice bags, and hot water bottles; administering certain medications; helping the patient with bathing and other personal hygiene routines; preparing the patient for medical examination; assisting the physician and registered nurse in examining the patient and carrying out nursing procedures; assisting in the delivery, care, and feeding of newborns; and observing the patient and reporting any significant symptoms, reactions, and changes in the patient's condition to the physician or nurse in charge.

Licensed practical nurses who work in clinics and doctors' offices may prepare the patients for examination, apply dressings, instruct patients on home health care, and handle such administrative responsibilities as record taking and managing the appointment calendar.

An associate's degree, diploma, or baccalaureate program prepares the student to become a registered nurse. The nursing profession encompasses many health-care functions applied in a wide variety of settings. Where an RN works, and which area of nursing or specialty he or she chooses will define the specific functions that will be expected, personal qualities needed, and any other supplemental training required.

Hospital nurses plan, carry out, and evaluate a patient's nursing needs in conjunction with the medical care plan prescribed by the physician who is the primary care provider. This care may include observing, assessing, recording, and reporting the patient's progress; administering medications; giving injections; and implementing treatments.

RNs in hospitals also supervise the activities of LPNs, nursing aides, and orderlies. Nurses document patients' status on the patient chart and spend time teaching patients how to care for themselves after they are discharged from the hospital.

Hospital nurses may become experts in a particular clinical specialty, which means that they concentrate their efforts in one particular area of nursing. Specialization entails additional training and education.

Community health nurses, or public health nurses, care for patients in community settings such as clinics and schools and in patients' homes. They provide nursing care in conjunction with the patient's plan of care; teach patients and their families, as well as community groups, about management of health conditions, good nutrition, and preventive health care; and act as a liaison between the community and the hospital. They may also arrange for and implement immunization programs and conduct treatment programs for special groups in the community, such as alcohol abusers and other groups of individuals who share a common health problem.

Private duty nurses are self-employed nurses hired directly by the patient or the patient's family to provide constant personal nursing care in a hospital setting or in the home.

Office nurses assist physicians, dental surgeons, dentists, nurse practitioners, and nurse-midwives who are in private practice or who work in clinics. In addition to nursing duties, office nurses may be expected to perform routine laboratory tests and office functions.

School nurses are hired by individual schools and by boards of education to provide various health and nursing services in individual schools or for entire school systems. They serve as consultants to the school's administration, parents, and students regarding health matters; handle school medical emergencies; implement state health code statutes regarding immunization and communicable diseases; assist in administering physical examinations to students and reporting the findings to parents; and alert parents to any evidence of emotional problems in their children.

Occupational health nurses and *industrial nurses* are independent practitioners who work in government facilities, factories, corporations, and other work sites. They provide nursing care to employees by treating minor injuries and illnesses occurring in the workplace, assisting in physical examinations, and carrying out educational programs designed to improve the health of workers.

Nurse educators work in schools of nursing and nursing programs providing classroom instruction for nursing students and continuing education for men and women who are already nurses. They also work in health-care facilities providing self-care information to patients.

Operating room nurses use nursing concepts and judgment, together with special scientific knowledge and technical skills, to provide a continuous cycle of patient care before, during, and after surgical procedures.

Preoperatively, they assess the patient. Intraoperatively, they are responsible for maintaining an environment conducive to quality patient care by promoting effective working relationships, the smooth functioning of the department, quality control of materials and techniques, and safe and properly equipped operating rooms. Working at the patient's side, the operating room nurse must anticipate the needs of the surgical team. Postoperatively, they visit the patient to evaluate postoperative care. Some operating room nurses specialize in a particular type of surgery, such as neurosurgery, orthopedic surgery, thoracic surgery, or cardiac surgery.

There are approximately 60,000 operating room nurses in the United States. To become an operating room nurse, an RN must supplement her or his basic nursing education by enrolling in a formal operating room course or by participating in a hospital-sponsored in-service program that focuses on the development of the various skills necessary to function as an operating room nurse.

Critical-care nurses are registered nurses who are specially educated in the care of critically ill patients, which prepares them to recognize physiological changes in the patient's condition, administer complex nursing support to the patient, and operate highly sophisticated monitoring equipment. Their education provides them with both in-depth knowledge of the physiology of the body systems and the social skills needed to deal with stress in the patient's family.

Rehabilitation nurses work with children and adults who suffer from permanent or temporary physical, mental, or emotional impairments caused by accident, illness, congenital anomaly, birth injury, surgery, or old age and who need assistance to attain an optimal level of functioning in their lives. They work with patients who are physically disabled from strokes, spinal cord injuries, brain injuries, amputation, cancer, heart or lung disease, neurological disease, and other maladies, providing treatments, exercises, and emotional support that will help them to regain lost abilities and to adapt where loss is permanent. There are approximately 10,000 rehabilitation nurses nationwide. To become a rehabilitation nurse, a registered nurse typically completes a post-RN course in rehabilitation nursing, or he or she may obtain a master's degree in rehabilitation nursing.

Advanced practice nurse (*APN*) is an umbrella term given to a registered nurse who has met advanced educational and clinical practice requirements beyond the two to four years of basic nursing education required of all RNs. Under this umbrella fall four principal types of APNs: (1) nurse practitioner, (2) certified registered nurse anesthetist, (3) clinical nurse special-ist, and (4) certified nurse-midwife. There are more than 140,000 advanced practice nurses, and this number is rapidly growing.

Nurse practitioners (*NPs*) are qualified to handle a wide range of basic health problems. Most have a specialty, such as adult, family, pediatric, or geriatric health care. NPs conduct physical examinations, take medical his-tories, diagnose and treat common acute minor illnesses and injuries, order and interpret laboratory tests and x-rays, and counsel and educate patients. In forty-eight states, they may prescribe medications. Most of the approx-imately 150 nurse practitioner education programs in the United States today confer a master's degree. NPs work in clinics, nursing homes, hospi-tals, or in their own offices.

Certified registered nurse anesthetists (*CRNAs*), working either with an M.D. anesthesiologist or independently, administer more than 65 percent of all anesthetics given to patients each year. In about 85 percent of rural hospitals, they are the sole providers of anesthetics. Two to three years of additional training beyond the four-year bachelor of science in nursing degree, plus national certification and recertification, are required. CRNAs work in almost every setting in which anesthesia is administered, such as operating rooms, dentists' offices, and ambulatory surgical settings. Nurse anesthetists were the first nurses to specialize beyond general duty nursing. This specialty has been recognized for almost a century.

Clinical nurse specialists (*CNSs*) are registered nurses with advanced nursing degrees (a master's or a doctorate) who are experts in a specialized area, such as cardiac or cancer care, mental health, or neonatal health. Besides delivering direct patient care, CNSs work in a variety of consulta-tive, research, education, and administrative roles. They provide primary care; develop nursing care techniques and quality control methods; teach nurses and other health-care professionals; and act as clinical consultants. CNSs work in clinical settings, community- or office-based settings, and hospitals.

Certified nurse-midwives (*CNMs*) provide prenatal and gynecological care; deliver babies in the home, in hospitals, and in birthing centers; and follow mothers postpartum (see Chapter 35).

Many nursing specialties exist. Included below is a list of specialty nurs-ing organizations in the United States that will provide an overview of the wide variety of these specializations. Each association provides additional

information to students considering careers, its members, and the general
public.

American Academy of Ambulatory Care Nurses (AAACN)
P.O. Box 56
Pitman, NJ 08071-0056
inurse.com/-aaacn

American Academy of Nurse Practitioners (AANP)
P.O. Box 12846
Austin, TX 78711
aanp.org

American Association of Critical-Care Nurses (AACN)
101 Columbia
Aliso Viejo, CA 92656-4109
aacn.org

American Association of Neuroscience Nurses (AANN)
4700 West Lake Avenue
Glenview, IL 60025
aann.org

American Association of Nurse Anesthetists (AANA)
222 South Prospect Avenue
Park Ridge, IL 60068-4001
aana.com

American Association of Occupational Health Nurses (AAOHN)
2932 Brandywine Road, Suite 100
Atlanta, GA 30324
aaohn.org

American Association of Spinal Cord Injury Nurses (AASCIN)
75-20 Astoria Boulevard
Jackson Heights, NY 11370-1177
aascin.org

American College of Nurse-Midwives (ACNM)
8403 Colesville Road, Suite 1550
Silver Spring, MD 20910
midwife.org

American Nephrology Nurses' Association (ANNA)
P.O. Box 56
Pitman, NJ 08071
annanurse.org

American Organization of Nurse Executives (AONE)
One North Franklin Street, 32nd Floor
Chicago, IL 60606
aone.org

American Society of Opthalmic Registered Nurses (ASORN)
P.O. Box 193030
San Francisco, CA 94119

American Society of Plastic Surgical Nurses (ASPSN)
P.O. Box 56
Pitman, NJ 08071
aspsn.org

American Society of PeriAnesthesia Nurses (ASPAN)
10 Melrose Avenue, Suite 10
Cherry Hill, NJ 08003
aspan.org

Association of Nurses in AIDS Care
3538 Ridgewood Road
Akron, OH 44333
anacnet.org/aids

Association of Operating Room Nurses (AORN)
2170 South Parker Road, Suite 300
Denver, CO 80231-5711
aorn.org

Association of Pediatric Oncology Nurses (APON)
4700 West Lake Avenue
Glenview, IL 60025-1485
apon.org

Association of Rehabilitation Nurses (ARN)
4700 West Lake Avenue
Glenview, IL 60025-1485
rehabnurse.org

Association of Women's Health, Obstetric, and Neonatal Nurses
    (AWHONN)
2000 L Street NW, Suite 740
Washington, DC 20036
awhonn.org

Dermatology Nurses Association (DNA)
East Holly Avenue P.O. Box 56
Pitman, NJ 08071
dna.inurse.com

Emergency Nurses Association (ENA)
915 Lee Street
Des Plaines, IL 60018
ena.org

National Association of Orthopedic Nurses (NAON)
401 North Michigan Avenue, Suite 2200
Chicago, IL 60611
inurse.com

National Association of Pediatric Nurse Associates and Practitioners
    (NAPNAP)
20 Brace Road, Suite 200
Cherry Hill, NJ 08034
napnap.org

Air & Surface Transport Nurses Association
  (Also known as the National Flight Nurses Association)
9101 East Kenyon Avenue, Suite 3000
Denver, CO 80237
astna.org

National Federation for Specialty Nursing Organizations (NFSNO)
P.O. Box 56
Pitman, NJ 08071
nfso@mail.ajj.com

National Nurses Society on Addictions (NNSA)
4101 Lake Boone Trail, Suite 201
Raleigh, NC 27607
nursingworld.org

Oncology Nursing Society (ONS)
125 Enterprise Drive, RIDC Park West
Pittsburgh, PA 15275-1214
ons.org

Society of Otorhinolaryngology and Head/Neck Nurses (SOHN)
116 Canal Street, Suite A
New Smyrna Beach, FL 32168
sohnnurse.com

SETTINGS, SALARIES, STATISTICS

Nurses work in a wide variety of health care environments including private homes, corporate and non-profit organizations, and military and governmental installations.

Licensed Practical Nurses/Vocational Nurses

More than half of all LPNs work in general hospitals. Other opportunities exist in nursing homes, which are the second biggest employer; health maintenance organizations; rehabilitation centers; clinics; sanitariums; day-care centers; industry; psychiatric hospitals and other long-term facilities; doctors' and dentists' offices; correctional institutions; and patients' homes, where responsibilities may also include meal preparation and teaching the patient's family how to perform simple nursing tasks.

Of the 702,000 LPNs holding jobs in 2002, most were women, but the number of men in the field is gradually growing.

LPNs received median annual salaries of $31,440 in 2002. The lowest-paid 10 percent earned less than $22,860, and the highest-paid 10 percent earned more than $44,040. LPNs employed by nursing homes and the Department of Veterans Affairs tend to earn slightly less. These amounts also vary geographically.

Registered Nurses

RNs work mostly for hospitals, community service agencies, and doctors' offices. About 60 percent of all registered nurses work in hospitals where, on average, they make up more than 20 percent of the entire staff. Another 30 percent of all RNs work in community health agencies, such as public health departments, visiting nurse associations, and home health-care agencies. They also work in nursing homes, physicians' offices, and nursing schools.

Additional opportunities for RNs exist in business and industry, public schools, and research. Approximately 33,000 nurses work as private-duty nurses who take care of a single patient, often in the patient's home.

A nurse's hours and workweeks vary; the number of hours spent on the job each week will depend on the area of nursing in which he or she works. If emergencies are common to a particular specialty, as in the case of nurse anesthetists, for example, then erratic schedules can be expected. In other specialties, such as school nurse or industrial nurse, more predictable, forty-hour—or less—workweeks can usually be expected.

Rotating night, weekend, and holiday shifts are often necessary in hospitals and residential care facilities. If other nurses are ill or away unexpectedly, a nurse's shift can suddenly require overtime.

About one in five RNs work part-time, and others do private-duty nursing in addition to their regular workweek hours. Very long work shifts for medical personnel have recently received legislative attention in many of the states, some of which have begun processes to limit the number of hours that a person can be required to work without adequate time off for rest.

There are approximately 2.6 million registered nurses in the United States, 2.3 million of whom are currently practicing. Of these, approximately 64,000 are nurse practitioners, about 30,500 are certified registered nurse anesthetists, 54,000 are clinical nurse specialists, and 6,540 are certified nurse-midwives. Approximately 96 percent of all RNs are female, but the number of men entering this field is increasing, and, whereas male nurses once worked almost exclusively in the emergency room, today they function in all areas of the hospital, and many do private-duty assignments as well.

The average annual salary for RNs nationwide is approximately $48,090. The lowest-paid 10 percent earned less than $33,970, and the highest-paid 10 percent earned more than $69,670. Much depends on the amount of nursing education an RN has, especially for those with graduate study; the type of position held; the specialty; and the geographic location.

Advanced practice nurses tend to earn more, and some nurse executives who are in charge of patient care management, human resources management, and/or fiscal and human resources management for large hospitals or multihospital systems earn more than $100,000 annually. Salaries in most specialties are highest in the major urban areas and in the West.

HOW TO BECOME A LICENSED PRACTICAL NURSE OR A REGISTERED NURSE

In all fifty states and the District of Columbia, both registered nurses and practical nurses must be licensed.

Licensed Practical Nurse Program

To become licensed, a student must complete a twelve- to eighteen-month state-approved practical nursing course and pass a written examination. At this time, there are about 1,000 state-approved practical nurse training programs nationwide. Most of the programs are offered by trade and vocational/technical schools. Hospitals, community and junior colleges, and health agencies also offer practical nurse training.

The curriculum for a practical nurse program typically includes courses in anatomy and physiology; medical-surgical nursing; psychiatric nursing, or the care of mentally ill patients; pediatrics, or the care of children; obstetrics, or the care of mothers and newborns; the administration of medications; first aid; nutrition and diet therapy; family living; growth and development; community health; nursing concepts and principles; and elementary nursing techniques.

Supervised clinical experience, usually conducted in a hospital, is also part of the training. A high school diploma is usually necessary for admission to a practical nurse training program.

Upon successful completion of a practical nurse educational program, students are awarded a diploma or certificate. They may then sit for the state board licensing exam in the state(s) in which they seek employment.

Registered Nurse Program

To obtain a license, a student nurse must graduate from a state-approved school of nursing and pass a state board examination.

There are three educational routes to becoming a registered nurse.

- The first option entails two academic years of education and training in an accredited program offered by a community, junior, or technical college. Upon satisfactory completion of a two-year nursing program, the student is awarded an associate of applied science or associate of science degree.
- The second option entails three academic years of accredited preparation. These programs are offered by hospitals, and a diploma is awarded.
- The third option entails four years of study and training. Accredited programs are offered by four-year colleges and universities, and upon graduation a bachelor of arts or bachelor of science in nursing is awarded.

All three educational options prepare candidates to sit for the state nursing board exams.

A minimum of a high school diploma and a minimum of a C average in high school are necessary for admission to two-, three-, and four-year nursing programs. The type of nursing program selected—two-, three-, or four-year—will affect the student's employment potential. The more education, the greater the possibilities and, hence, the higher the obtainable salaries. The type of education will also affect the level of responsibilities assigned; often, the greater the responsibility, the greater the intellectual and emotional challenges involved.

Public health and school nurse jobs, supervisory and administrative positions, graduate programs in nursing, and many clinical specialties and nurse practitioner training programs all require a minimum of a bachelor's degree in nursing. The type of program a student selects should depend on her or his career and personal goals, interests, and abilities. A bachelor's degree program is recommended, however, because of the trend toward upgrading criteria in this field. Transfer from one type of nursing program to another is sometimes possible.

All two-, three-, and four-year nursing programs consist of classroom instruction plus supervised nursing practice. The curriculum—which varies in depth and breadth according to the length of the program—includes courses in anatomy and physiology, psychology, English, nursing concepts and techniques, microbiology, sociology, and philosophy. In the bachelor's degree nursing program, these subjects are taught in greater depth, and courses in chemistry, biology, precalculus mathematics, cultural anthropology, organic chemistry, parent-child nursing, epidemiology, nursing research, health care in the social system, community nursing, and nursing trends are added.

In 2003, there were 700 associate's degree, 120 diploma, and 678 bachelor's degree nursing programs in this country. The number of diploma programs has been steadily declining, while more programs at the bachelor's level have been instituted. Some accelerated programs for people who already have a bachelor's degree in a related field are also available; these take about twelve to eighteen months to complete. Accelerated programs at the master's level take about three years to complete.

All states licensing programs require regularly updating nursing licenses, and continuing education credits are required to maintain the currency of the nurses' education.

Increasingly, a bachelor's degree is a requirement for many entry-level jobs. A nurse may advance on a career path through supervisor, assistant head nurse, head nurse, assistant director, director, and vice president in hospital settings, and an advanced degree is almost universally necessary for promotion through these levels. Similar or somewhat different titles may apply in other settings.

A recent study showed that there were 243 master's degree programs and 55 doctoral degree programs, which provide the advanced nursing education necessary to carry out administrative, teaching, and research activities.

Characteristics

Personal qualities that are essential to success and satisfaction in the important profession of nursing include compassion, patience, good physical and emotional health, the ability to work well as part of a team, the willingness to assume responsibility, the ability to react quickly and correctly in emergency situations, a genuine love of people, the desire to help all kinds of patients in need of all kinds of medical care, and optimism.

Despite the many factors that are pressing on this profession, nursing has been and continues to be a source of great personal satisfaction for millions of individuals. When a patient leaves a hospital, it is often the help, encouragement, comfort, and kind words of a nurse that he or she takes home as a lasting image.

THE FUTURE

The recent history of employment for nurses in the United States has been an acute shortage, followed by a surplus, followed by another acute shortage, followed by yet another surplus. Why is the job picture for nurses so volatile?

In the late 1970s, there was a severe shortage of nurses. Job offers were plentiful, and for several years nurses' salaries rose by up to 14 percent a year.

Then in the early 1980s, in what would be a harbinger of things to come, Diagnostic Related Groups were established and instituted. Diagnostic Related Groups (DRGs) are standards that place limits on the number of days a patient may occupy a hospital bed. The DRG philosophy is fiscal and medical, applying statistically likely outcomes to personal medical situations. Because a quarter of all nurses worked in hospitals at that time, one of the many side effects of DRGs was a surplus of nurses; hospitals, facing the prospect of empty beds, cut or did not refill nursing jobs. Across the country, the annual rate of increase in nurses' salaries fell to 3 percent. Nursing school enrollment fell off by 30 percent, setting the stage for a future shortage.

The shortage of nurses became so acute that, in January 1988, the Department of Health and Human Services of the federal government established a Federal Commission on Nursing to determine what factors were discouraging students from pursuing careers in nursing. Conditions in the workplace, salaries, competition from other professions, and educational requirements were studied. The federal government projected that by 2000 there would be a shortfall of at least a million nurses. This shortage resulted in great competition for nurses and impressive gains in nurses' salaries, with some hospitals in major cities sweetening their job offers with such enticements as a year's paid rent.

In the early 1990s, the employment picture was again different, this time because of the economic recession. As nurses retired, they were not being replaced. Many nurses were being laid off. Salaries were flat. The mid- to late 1990s saw an upsurge again, and then after 2000 another recession occurred.

As of 2004, the need for nursing services is as great as ever. With an ever-increasing general population; a rapidly growing elderly population; expanding medical technologies and techniques; more people than ever being treated for and surviving traumas, such as burns or spinal cord injuries, diseases, and congenital conditions that until recently were thought insurmountable; the number of Americans with HIV/AIDS; and the needs of returning veterans from Afghanistan and Iraq, nurses' services are in strong demand.

In most locations, aggressive cost containment continues to be a powerful factor in the patient needs/patient care equation. This cost containment is in reaction to soaring medical costs during the 1980s and beyond. Today, the major agent of cost concerns is the Prospective Payment System (PPS), which holds courses of medical treatment to economic tests. Many health-care organizations around the country, faced with economic pressure from third-party payers, have pared their nursing staffs and increasingly rely on less qualified, unlicensed assistive personnel (UAPs), a move that can pose serious risks to patient care and safety. One study found that a short-staffed hospital unit actually drove up costs because the hospital had to absorb the cost of extra patient days incurred by complications.

It should be noted that since 1985, labor costs as a percentage of total hospital expenses have declined. In addition, the nursing profession itself is aging, with many nurses leaving the employment setting. Finally, student enrollment in nursing programs has decreased. A shortage looms once again.

What, then, is the future for LPNs and RNs? The American Nurses Association (ANA) predicts that after a period of adjustment to the effects of cost containment, the outlook for RNs should be bright. The hospital sector of the profession will continue to shrink, and more LPNs and RNs will find themselves carrying out their important duties in less-expensive outpatient ambulatory settings in the community, which will increase in number and scope. The sickest patients will remain in hospitals, and to care for them, hospitals will need more nurse practitioners and other nurse specialists.

Faster-than-average job growth for registered nurses is projected by the U.S. Department of Labor through 2012. LPNs, too, can expect a similar rate of growth in their profession.

New jobs in outpatient care facilities, especially those providing one-day surgical and treatment services, are expected. Fewer jobs in hospitals may be a factor, as financial pressure mounts to decrease inpatient hospital stays. Opportunities should be particularly plentiful in nursing homes and residential care facilities.

Many more men are being attracted to the challenges of the clinical specialties and to the job security and relatively high pay offered by nursing. For years, men have made up 3 to 5 percent of registered nurses, but in some recent years they have made up approximately 10 percent of all student nurses.

For more information about a career in nursing, contact:

American Nurses Association (ANA)
600 Maryland Avenue SW, Suite 100W
Washington, DC 20024-2571
nursingworld.org

National League for Nursing (NLN)
61 Broadway
New York, NY 10006
nln.org

National Federation of Licensed Practical Nurses (NFLPN)
605 Poole Drive
Garner, NC 27529
nflpn.org

National Student Nurses Association (NSNA)
45 Main Street, Suite 206
Brooklyn, NY 11201
nsna.org

Information is also available from the boards of nursing of individual states, as well as from the nurses' associations of the various states. For information for the state boards, contact:

National Council of State Boards of Nursing (NCSBN)
111 East Wacker Drive, Suite 2900
Chicago, IL 60601
ncsbn.org/regulation/boardsofnursing_boards_of_nursing_board.asp

NURSE-MIDWIFE (NM, CNM)

Although midwifery is as old as maternity, specially educated and trained nurse-midwives are relatively new members of the modern professional health-care team. Nurse-midwives (NMs) provide care for women during pregnancy and childbirth and provide some newborn and general gynecological services as well. Their duties differ from nurse practitioners (NPs) in that NPs care for women's health in general, while the NM duties emphasize the care that surrounds pregnancy and childbirth.

After World War I, the national trend was away from midwife-attended home births and toward in-hospital deliveries attended by an obstetrician. In recent years, although there has been only a slight increase in the number of home deliveries (ninety-nine out of every hundred American babies are born in a hospital), there has been substantial renewed interest in the use of nurse-midwives in normal deliveries.

The word *midwife* comes from Old English and means "with woman." Today's NMs are health-care professionals who, in addition to being a registered nurse (RN), have successfully completed an accredited program of study and clinical experience in obstetrics—the branch of medicine concerned with the care and treatment of women during pregnancy, childbirth, and the period immediately following—which qualify them to provide professional health care to women and their babies throughout pregnancy, labor, delivery, and after birth. NMs care for women who, after careful screening, appear likely to have uncomplicated deliveries. Patients with certain health problems and those with a history of complicated births are handled solely by a physician or in collaboration with a physician. Nurse-midwives maintain a consultative affiliation with physicians and other health-care professionals so that this additional medical assistance is readily available when needed.

The number of in-hospital births attended by certified nurse-midwives (CNMs)—nurse-midwives who have satisfied the educational and examination requirements of the American College of Nurse-Midwives (ACNM)—has grown from 20,000 in 1975 to approximately 250,000 at this time; that is, almost 5 percent of all U.S. births. It is estimated that by 2010 this number will be approximately one in ten births in the United States. Worldwide, about two-thirds of all births are nurse-midwife assisted. This dramatic increase is expected to continue.

The reasons for this revival range from the practical to the philosophical. Many prospective mothers believe nurse-midwives provide more personal care during pregnancy, labor, and delivery than do busy obstetricians. Also, the NMs' philosophy of prepared, and preferably drug-free, natural childbirth is appealing to many women. Nurse-midwife–attended deliveries often take place at home, in hospital birthing rooms, or in birthing centers, and these noninstitutional, homey settings are, for many women, an appealing alternative to a hospital delivery room. In addition, NMs promote family-centered childbirth—that is, the presence and participation in the birth not only of spouses but of other relatives, children, and friends is encouraged, and in most cases such a birthing experience is available only with a nurse-midwife attending. Cost is also a factor: nurse-midwife–attended births cost less than physician-attended births.

A sign of the building interest in and acceptance of nurse-midwife care is the continuing trend toward state legislation requiring insurance coverage to be extended to include maternity care provided by certified nurse-midwives working under the guidance of a doctor and in conjunction with a hospital or clinic. As of 1987, both Medicare and Medicaid coverage apply.

The prenatal, or before birth, care a nurse-midwife typically provides includes performing physical examinations of the pregnant woman, including breast, abdominal, and pelvic examinations, and regularly monitoring the progress of the pregnancy. The NM also educates the prospective mother regarding nutrition; exercise during pregnancy, labor, and postpartum, or after the baby's birth; parent-infant bonding; child care; breastfeeding; bottle feeding; preparing for the newborn; and family adjustment to the new addition. The nurse-midwife teaches and counsels the mother-to-be about preparation for labor and delivery. The woman and her spouse or support person are encouraged to read about childbirth and attend childbirth classes, and, prior to delivery, the nurse-midwife will discuss with them a plan of care during birthing that will accommodate their needs and desires.

Throughout labor and delivery, the nurse-midwife stays with the woman, providing emotional support and comfort measures and supervising and evaluating the progress of the labor. Should pain-relieving medications be required, the nurse-midwife may prescribe and administer them. The NM performs the delivery of the baby and is responsible for all related procedures. Nurse-midwives do not, however, perform cesarean-section deliveries. Should such a surgical situation suddenly develop, an obstetrician is called in immediately.

Immediately after delivery, the NM examines and evaluates the condition of the newborn and provides care, including resuscitation, if needed. The nurse-midwife then provides follow-up care for mother and baby and assists the new mother with self-care, nursing or bottle feeding, and infant care.

In addition, nurse-midwives perform routine gynecological checkups for nonpregnant patients and prescribe and provide various methods of contraception.

SETTINGS, SALARIES, STATISTICS

While the important contribution nurse-midwives have made in bringing professional health care to mothers and babies in rural America cannot be overstated, in fact, an even greater percentage of inner-city women (35.8 percent) and suburban women (28.9 percent) are served by nurse-midwives.

Nurse-midwives work in private practices; in university teaching hospitals; in city hospitals—in their regular maternity sections and, in some cases, in specially outfitted birthing rooms; in rural outreach centers; in group health maintenance organizations; in the military; at family planning centers; on Native American reservations, in public health facilities, in alternative birth centers; and, if certain criteria are met, in patients' homes. Currently, there are more than 6,700 certified nurse-midwives registered with the American College of Nurse-Midwives, and approximately 5,700 of them are in clinical practice in the United States. This profession is dominated by women, but the ACNM records that approximately 2 percent of its members are male.

It should be noted that in addition to the certified nurse-midwives, there is an unknown number of noncertified midwives who attend home deliveries—mostly in rural settings—many of whom have no formal training. To practice professionally, however, specific educational requirements must be met, and certification by the ACNM is generally required to obtain a state license to practice.

As of July, 2004, the median annual salary for certified nurse-midwives in clinical practice was approximately $75,891. Certified nurse-midwives who serve lower socioeconomic and poor rural populations do not earn as much, unless they work for a federally supported program. Salaries for CNMs depend on the practice setting and the geographic location. States where CNMs typically earn the highest salaries include Alaska, California, New York, Pennsylvania, and Florida. The top 25 percent of practitioners earn a median income of $81,497 annually.

Because babies are born year-round and at all hours, late-night, all-night, weekend, and holiday deliveries are routine. Nurse-midwives tend to work erratic, long hours. Most have regular office hours and patient rounds, then are on call.

HOW TO BECOME A NURSE-MIDWIFE

Certified nurse-midwives are educated in both nursing and midwifery, must be registered nurses, and must have a bachelor's degree.

Several education courses may be followed—certificate, master's degree, or combined RN/master's degree—all of which can lead to certification as a nurse-midwife.

A certificate program usually entails nine to twelve months of intensive study and clinical experience. To qualify for a certificate program, one must currently be licensed as a registered nurse in the United States or in one of the U.S. territories.

The master's degree nurse-midwife programs are usually sixteen to twenty-four months long and lead to a certificate in nurse-midwifery plus a master's degree. To enter these programs, one must be a currently licensed registered nurse and have a bachelor of science in nursing.

The third route, that is, the combined RN/master's degree program for nonnurses, requires a bachelor's degree. Combined programs typically require three years of education and training. The first intense twelve months are dedicated to nursing education, after which a candidate may sit for the RN examination. After passing this examination, the candidate then chooses a specialty, and, if that specialty is nurse-midwifery, he or she enters a nurse-midwife master's degree program.

Among the courses in a typical nurse-midwife educational program are antepartum, or before birth, care; intrapartum, or during birth, care; postpartum care, contraceptive gynecology, and childbirth education.

Most schools consider it advisable for applicants to have some clinical experience in obstetrical nursing prior to enrollment in a nurse-midwife educational program. At this time, forty-five nurse-midwife programs are approved by the ACNM. These programs admit small numbers of students annually, and competition for admission is strong.

Nurse-midwife educational programs attract students of all ages. While many students are in their twenties and thirties, people in their forties and fifties are regularly embarking on nurse-midwife educations, which suggests that nurse-midwifery is an appealing second career for many.

Personal prerequisites important for success and satisfaction as a nurse-midwife include good health, sensitivity, humaneness, assertiveness, decisiveness, integrity, and, perhaps, a special sense of joy. Nurse-midwives do very special work.

All graduates of nurse-midwife educational programs approved by the American College of Nurse-Midwives are eligible to take the national certification examination given by the ACNM. Upon passing this examination, an individual is entitled to use the initials CNM, for certified nurse-midwife, after his or her name. All states recognize the legality of certified nurse-midwife practice, and most accept certification by the ACNM as the standard for licensing nurse-midwives.

THE FUTURE

The outlook for nurse-midwives is excellent. The American College of Nurse-Midwives predicts the need for at least 6,000 more nurse-midwives by the year 2010.

Interest in nurse-midwifery education is burgeoning. More and more prospective mothers see their pregnancies and deliveries not as infirmities requiring doctors, hospitals, and days of confinement but as natural events for which less medical intervention and more emotional and educational support is preferable. They are seeking birthing experiences that include family, care that is more personal, and birthing settings that are less institutional. Increasingly, pregnant women are choosing the nurse-midwife alternative because they see nurse-midwives as being providers not only of the type of physical care they want but also of the physical setting and overall philosophy they desire. Lower costs and the trend toward insurance reimbursement further enhance the nurse-midwife alternative and the outlook for it.

Today, up to 70 percent of the care provided by certified nurse-midwives is to women from traditionally underserved communities. Well over half of the women and infants seen by CNMs have their care paid for by government sources through Medicaid, Medicare, or the Indian Health Service—more than twice the percentage seen by obstetricians. Because of the high quality of the care they provide and the lower cost of their services—and because both of these features have long and well-documented histories—nurse-midwives will probably find that their profession plays prominently in health care under any future reform.

For more information on nurse-midwives, including a list of accredited educational programs, contact:

The American College of Nurse-Midwives (ACNM)
818 Connecticut Avenue NW, Suite 900
Washington, DC 20006
midwife.org

NURSING AIDE AND PSYCHIATRIC AIDE

Also Known as Nurse's Aide,
Nursing Assistant (CNA), Hospital Attendant, Auxiliary
Nursing Worker, Geriatric Aide, Psychiatric Nursing Assistant,
and Ward Attendant

Paradoxically, although nursing aides and psychiatric aides often are at the bottom of the health-care personnel hierarchy—working under the doctors, registered nurses (RNs), and licensed practical nurses (LPNs); earning the least; and performing almost all of the routine patient care— they are very often the health-care givers who matter the most to patients.

Working under the supervision of RNs and LPNs, nursing aides and psychiatric aides feed, bathe, dress, help out of bed, and walk patients who need assistance; serve meals; take temperature and pulse readings; make beds; give massages; deliver messages; empty bedpans; provide important skin care to patients confined to bed for extended periods; escort patients to and from operating, examining, and treatment rooms; and respond when patients buzz for help. In short, aides deliver much of the human-touch care that comforts and calms a patient.

Nursing aides perform these duties for patients who are physically ill or disabled. Their responsibilities are much the same as those of home care aides. Psychiatric aides perform these duties for patients who are mentally impaired or emotionally disturbed. Because of their patient population, psychiatric aides must sometimes restrain violent patients.

Most nursing aides and psychiatric aides work in settings that provide long-term care. Almost half of all nursing aides work in nursing homes, where they may have contact with a patient for months or years. In nursing homes, aides are the principal caregivers, and often a warm bond develops between patient and aide. The very nature of inpatient psychiatric treatment entails extended hospitalization, so psychiatric aides also often establish ongoing relationships with the patients they help every day. In both cases, because aides have so much close contact with a patient over what is often a prolonged period of time, they are in an important position to affect the patient's attitude, communicate to and for the patient to the rest of the health-care staff, and monitor the patient's progress.

SETTINGS, SALARIES, STATISTICS

Almost 50 percent of all nursing aides are employed by nursing homes and are sometimes called geriatric aides. Another 25 percent of all nursing aides work in general hospitals. Opportunities also exist in special hospitals and other long-term care facilities such as assisted-living facilities.

More than 90 percent of all psychiatric aides work in hospitals, such as state and county facilities, on the psychiatric floors of general hospitals, in private psychiatric hospitals, in community mental health centers, in residential facilities for the mentally retarded, and in alcohol and drug rehabilitation facilities. Three percent work in nursing homes.

There were approximately 2,000,000 nursing, psychiatric, and home health aides employed in the United States in 2002. Of these, approximately 59,000 were psychiatric aides, down from 105,000 in 1999.

Salaries are not high. According to the 2004 Occupational Outlook Handbook, nursing aides' median hourly wages were $9.59 per hour in 2002, or nearly $20,000 per year. Psychiatric aides earned more at $11.04 per hour. Home health aides earned less, at a median of $8.70 per hour. The mounting shortage of aides is expected to improve salaries.

A forty-hour workweek is typical. Evening, night, weekend, and holiday hours are rotated in.

HOW TO BECOME A NURSING AIDE OR PSYCHIATRIC AIDE

Educational and training requirements for employment are minimal. Some employers—especially nursing homes—require neither a high school diploma nor prior experience. Proficiency in English is not always necessary. Because the prerequisites are few, being an aide is a very accessible occupation for many individuals who want to be part of a health-care community. Most hospitals, however, require aides to have at least one year of experience. Often this experience is as a home care aide (see Chapter 26).

Until recently, most aides' education and training were provided on the job by employers. This preparation typically lasted six weeks to three months. In recent years, however, efforts to upgrade and standardize nursing aide and psychiatric aide education have resulted in half of the states passing laws or regulations requiring aides to successfully complete approved training courses either before starting to work or within a specific period of time after being hired. Nursing aide training programs are offered by community colleges, vocational/technical schools, nursing homes, and hospitals. Anatomy, physiology, infection control, nutrition, and communication skills are taught. There is, however, significant latitude in the length and depth of these courses from state to state. Aides who successfully complete state-mandated programs are awarded certificates.

Once on the job, a new aide is given an orientation that may last from one week to several months.

Important personal prerequisites for this work include dependability, patience, tact, emotional stability, and physical strength.

Some aides go on to seek the additional education necessary for higher professional responsibility as LPNs or RNs.

THE FUTURE

Job turnover in this profession is unusually high, and there are increasing needs for nursing aides of all kinds in hospitals, nursing and rehabilitation centers, and long-term care residential institutions.

The employment forecast is excellent. Up to 500,000 new jobs for nursing aides should open up between now and 2012, according to the U.S. Department of Labor, which ranks nursing aides as the tenth-fastest-growing occupation requiring a high school diploma or less in the coming decade. Salaries should increase as well. Many of the reasons for this growth are the same as the ones that are spurring demand for more home care aides and many other types of direct caregivers: our population is growing, it is growing older, and long-term care facilities and programs for the chronically ill are expanding. Specifically, employment opportunities for nursing aides should increase in nursing homes and other long-term care facilities while decreasing in general hospitals, which, increasingly, are focusing only on the seriously ill who require high-technology medical care.

The employment picture for psychiatric aides is not quite as bright. Cost constraints and a continuation of the forty-year trend toward the deinstitutionalization of all but the most seriously ill patients will result in lower-than-average growth in public mental hospital settings. In private psychiatric facilities, however, the rapidly growing elderly population and ever-expanding treatment options should create employment opportunities in the coming decade.

For more information about nursing aides and psychiatric aides, contact:

American Hospital Association, Division of Nursing (AHA)
840 North Lake Shore Drive
Chicago, IL 60611
aha.org

American Health Care Association (AHCA)
1201 L Street NW
Washington, DC 20005
ahca.org

OCCUPATIONAL THERAPIST (OT) AND OCCUPATIONAL THERAPY ASSISTANT

Occupational therapy is the art and science of employing various educational, vocational, and rehabilitational activities for the purpose of improving the mental abilities, physical abilities, and general health of individuals suffering from developmental deficits, physical injuries or illnesses, psychological or social disabilities, the aging process, poverty and culture differences, or other conditions that threaten or impair their ability to cope with the tasks of living.

Occupational therapists and occupational therapy assistants analyze patients' potentials and limitations and then select and implement specific activities that teach their minds and their bodies how to maximize their potentials and to minimize their limitations so that they may function more effectively and happily. The goal of occupational therapy is improvement. Whether this improvement is the acquisition of skills never before attained, the restoration of abilities lost to injury or illness, adaptation to permanent limitations, or the alleviation of pain, the objective is to help the patient attain his or her highest functional level.

OCCUPATIONAL THERAPISTS

Occupational therapists (OTs) are educated in the origin, progression, management, and prognosis of congenital and developmental impairments and deficits; diseases; and physical, emotional, and environmental stresses and traumas. They know how to recognize and identify manifestations and symptoms of wellness and illness in their patients or clients. They work with physicians, physical therapists, vocational counselors, and other professionals in evaluating patients and in developing short- and long-term goals for them. In planning an occupational therapy program, therapists consider the patient's physical capacity, developmental level, intelligence, and interests.

Because they are tailored to treat the patient's specific disability problems, occupational therapy's purposeful activities are as numerous and diverse as there are physical, mental, and social limitations. OTs may conduct programs designed to improve sitting and standing tolerances for patients with chronic pain; teach muscle reeducation to persons who have experienced strokes and others with neurological disabilities; monitor the heart rates and energy requirements of heart patients as they practice self-care or homemaking activities; make home evaluations to recommend modifications that will maximize the patient's function and safety at home; design and construct splints and other orthoses for injury and surgery patients; adapt daily activities for persons who need to develop skills using only one hand; evaluate the developmental levels of high-risk infants and plan treatment programs to ensure their healthy growth; initiate group and individual treatment activities designed to help clients in mental health centers to learn personal and social behavior skills, to become more independent in daily life, and to become more effective in interacting with others; teach compensatory skills to patients with perceptual deficits; help injured workers return to the job or adapt their work environment to compensate for their disabling conditions; and conduct community living skills programs that prepare recovering patients for their return to the community.

There are constant innovations in the field of occupational therapy. In some institutions, for example, there are occupational therapy apartments where patients with physical impairments learn adaptive methods of cooking and other home responsibilities and where the patient and his or her family may have an overnight trial living experience prior to hospital discharge. To determine if a patient has the potential for on-the-road driving, a sophisticated driving simulator, which assesses selected component skills, may be used.

Over 1,000 occupational therapists around the country and 1,000 volunteer magicians have joined forces in a special rehabilitation program called Project Magic. This program was begun by magician David Copperfield and inaugurated at Daniel Freeman Memorial Hospital in Inglewood, California. It teaches persons with disabilities how to perform magic tricks as a method of achieving improvement of gross motor skills, fine motor skills, problem-solving abilities, perception, higher cognitive skills, and psychosocial abilities. Project Magic not only works the patient's hands and minds, it gives the person with a disability a skill that most people do not have. The patient, in turn, teaches his or her magic tricks to a nonpatient. Both the learning of a unique and entertaining skill and the teaching role do much to enhance the patient's self-esteem.

Many OTs specialize, working with patients who are of a certain age group, such as children or the elderly, or who have a certain disability. Three out of five occupational therapists work primarily with persons who have physical disabilities.

SETTINGS, SALARIES, STATISTICS

Occupational therapists serve a wide population in a wide variety of settings. Some 20 percent of OTs work in hospitals, and 25 percent work in nursing homes. Jobs also exist in schools for children and adults who have physical and mental disabilities, community mental health centers, special camps, clinics, retirement communities, senior citizen centers, rehabilitation centers, and home care programs. Some occupational therapists who have graduate degrees carry out research and/or teach.

Most occupational therapists work standard forty-hour weeks. Depending on the setting, evening and weekend hours may be required. Occupational therapy is a career that also offers many part-time work arrangements.

Approximately 50,000 occupational therapists are now currently practicing. Earning potential for occupational therapists is very good. Salaries vary with the type of employer, the OT's experience, and the geographical location.

Median annual salaries for occupational therapists were $52,822 in 2004, with the lowest levels running at about $46,269 and the highest at $60,265. OTs who are in supervisory and administrative positions may earn salaries as high as $75,000 per year.

Advancement for occupational therapists usually comes in the form of promotion from staff therapist to senior therapist or specialized practitioner. Some therapists advance further to supervisory or administrative positions in occupational therapy programs, and other experienced occupational therapists become teachers and/or researchers in occupational therapy.

HOW TO BECOME AN OCCUPATIONAL THERAPIST

To become an occupational therapist, a student must graduate from one of the many occupational therapy educational programs offered by colleges and universities throughout the United States. Approximately 120 institutions offer educational programs that are accredited by the American Occupational Therapy Association (AOTA). OTs earn baccalaureate, master's, or doctoral degrees. Some baccalaureate programs admit students for a four-year occupational therapy curriculum. Others require two years of liberal arts and science courses prior to admittance to an occupational therapy curriculum for the junior and senior years.

Graduate study is often required for teaching, research, and administrative positions in this field. It is offered both to students with undergraduate degrees in occupational therapy, leading to a master's in occupational therapy, or M.O.T., and to students who have undergraduate degrees in majors other than occupational therapy, leading to a certificate or to an M.O.T.

Occupational therapy students learn about the structure and function of the human body and human systems; the structure and function of human personality and cognition; the human growth process; sociocultural systems and the interrelationship with individual development functioning; developmental tasks and needs in each period of life from birth to death; the development of human relationships, roles, and values; the impact of nonhuman environmental factors on normal growth and development; the meaning of activity in the development of human potential and competency; the meaning and impact of symbols and the symbolization process throughout the life cycle; and the concepts and modes of adaptation and their relationship to performance. They are taught how to observe, identify, and analyze tasks and activities performed by others and to relate the elements of these tasks to psychological, perceptual-motor, cognitive, physical, social, cultural, economic, and age-specific needs, capabilities, and roles.

Specifically, an accredited curriculum typically includes courses that cover anatomy; neuroanatomy; physiology; pathology; neurophysiology; kinesiology, which is the science and study of human muscular movements; general, educational, group, social, and developmental psychology; sociology; anthropology; psychoanalytic theory; neurobehavioral science; psychobiology; pediatrics; gerontology, which is the study of the aged; human relations; fine and applied arts; home economics; industrial and manual arts; self-care activities; physical education and recreation; vocational rehabilitation; public health; communication theory and principles; teaching/learning theory; and community resources.

Students are also required to spend six to nine months in a hospital, health agency, school, or other setting to gain experience in clinical practice.

In high school, interested students should take courses in biology, chemistry, health, art, and social studies. Admission to occupational therapy educational programs is highly competitive. A minimum grade of B in the science courses is usually necessary.

Personal qualifications for success and satisfaction in this career include patience, imagination, maturity, tact, stamina, manual and teaching skills, and a genuine love of people. Very important, too, is a balance of objectivity and empathy, professionalism and compassion. Occupational therapy is a career that provides almost constant patient contact and the opportunity to contribute to and follow the progress of patients over an extended period of time. The potential for deep personal satisfaction in this profession is great.

Graduates of accredited occupational therapy educational programs are eligible to sit for the certification examination administered by the National Board for Certification in Occupational Therapy. Upon passing this examination, a candidate becomes a registered occupational therapist and may use the designation OTR after his or her name. The vast majority of states regulate the practice of occupational therapy, most by licensure. Applicants for licensure must have a degree or certificate from an accredited educational program and satisfy the requirements of the state's licensing program. Successful completion of the National Board for Certification in

Occupational Therapy examination generally satisfies the licensing requirements.

THE FUTURE

The employment outlook for occupational therapists is favorable. The growing number of older Americans and the ever-expanding application of occupational therapy to various disabilities should contribute to an increase in demand.

For more information about occupational therapists, contact:

American Occupational Therapy Association (AOTA)
4720 Montgomery Lane
Bethesda, MD 20814
aota.org

OCCUPATIONAL THERAPY ASSISTANT

The approximately 20,000 occupational therapy assistants in the United States work under the supervision of occupational therapists and perform much of the routine work that an occupational therapy program entails. Like occupational therapists, they select and construct equipment that helps patients function more independently; help plan and implement treatment activities for individuals and groups of patients; and, under supervision, perform most of the other functions inherent to occupational therapy. Occupational therapy assistants may also be expected to order, prepare, and lay out materials and maintain equipment.

SETTINGS, SALARIES, STATISTICS

Occupational therapy assistants work in the same settings as occupational therapists. Openings for occupational therapy assistants are particularly prevalent in nursing homes and mental health facilities. According to the American Medical Association, the annual starting salary for occupational therapy assistants is $26,000. According to Salary.com, in 2004, the median annual salary for all certified occupational therapy assistants was quoted at $36,562.

HOW TO BECOME AN OCCUPATIONAL THERAPY ASSISTANT

There are two routes to get the preparation necessary to work as an occupational therapy assistant: two-year associate's degree programs that are offered by community colleges, which are the majority of programs, or one-year certificate programs offered by junior/community colleges and vocational/technical schools. Occupational therapy assistant educational programs are accredited by the American Occupational Therapy Association.

The curriculum typically includes classroom study of the history and philosophy of occupational therapy; occupational therapy theory and skills; and human anatomy, physiology, and development. There is also supervised practical experience lasting several months. A high school diploma or its equivalent is required for admission to an occupational therapy assistant program. In high school, classes in health, the sciences, and arts and crafts are useful.

Graduates of approved occupational therapy assistant educational programs are eligible to sit for a certification examination administered by the National Board for Certification in Occupational Therapy. Candidates who pass this examination are designated certified occupational therapy assistants, and they may use the abbreviation COTA after their names.

THE FUTURE

The employment picture for occupational therapy assistants should be favorable.

For more information about occupational therapy assistants, contact:

American Occupational Therapy Association (AOTA)
4720 Montgomery Lane
Bethesda, MD 20814
aota.org

OPHTHALMIC LABORATORY TECHNICIAN (OLT)

Also Known as Optical Mechanic, Optical Goods Worker, Manufacturing Optician, and Precision Optical Manufacturing Technicians

Ophthalmic laboratory technicians (OLTs) make the lenses that are used in prescription eyeglasses. Working from specifications written by the customer's ophthalmologist, or eye doctor; optometrist, or licensed, nonmedical eye practitioner; and/or optician, the technician selects the appropriate lens blanks, then cuts, grinds, and finishes lenses according to the prescription by using various specialized equipment and machines such as grinders, polishers, and lensometers. He or she then assembles them in the frames selected by the customer.

In smaller ophthalmic laboratories, the same technician may perform all of these procedures. In larger laboratories, these processes may be broken down, and technicians may specialize as surfacers who grind the lenses and bench technicians who finish the glasses. In some laboratories, these two functions are even further specialized.

An OLT must safely, effectively, and consistently operate and maintain the equipment in the lab; perform mathematical and algebraic calculations as required to transpose a prescription; tint and coat lenses; perform minor frame repairs; and provide follow-up services, such as adjustments, repairs, or replacement, to the customer.

SETTINGS, SALARIES, STATISTICS

Ophthalmic laboratory technicians work in ophthalmic laboratories, in the offices of ophthalmologists and optometrists who dispense glasses directly to patients, and in opticians' shops and other retail outlets that sell eyewear, such as department stores or drugstores. Some ophthalmic laboratory technicians own their own laboratories. Most job opportunities in this field are in or near large cities.

The workweek for an OLT is typically forty hours long, much of which is spent standing. Part-time positions in this field also exist.

According to the U.S. Bureau of Labor Statistics, the median annual income for ophthalmic lab technicians in 2002 was $10.46 an hour, or about $21,757 per year. The lowest-paid 10 percent earned less than $7.56 per hour, and the highest-paid 10 percent earned more than $16.40 per hour.

HOW TO BECOME AN OPHTHALMIC LABORATORY TECHNICIAN

Both formal and informal education and training options exist for students interested in this field. Most ophthalmic laboratory technicians learn their skills on the job in small and medium-size laboratories. Students learn procedures gradually, and it usually takes about three years before a student has the experience and expertise to work as an all-around technician. A high school diploma is usually required for on-the-job training.

Of the formal educational routes, many optical goods companies offer three- to four-year formal apprenticeships in optical technology. Students who have superior ability may progress through an apprenticeship in less time. These programs are considered an excellent method of preparation. A high school diploma is almost always required for acceptance into an apprenticeship. Many community colleges around the country offer two-year associate's degree programs in optic technology; for admittance, a high school diploma is usually necessary. In addition, many vocational/technical institutes and trade schools offer shorter certificate or diploma programs in this field for which a high school diploma is also necessary. Students who learn their skills in these shorter programs usually need additional on-the-job training.

In high school, students interested in ophthalmic laboratory technology should take courses in physics, algebra, geometry, and mechanical drawing.

Abilities and personal qualities that are important to effective performance in optical technology include good or good corrected vision, manual dexterity, and an appreciation for precision.

THE FUTURE

According to the U.S. Bureau of Labor Statistics, overall employment for OLTs is expected to grow more slowly than average through 2012. Job opportunities will be affected by the aging population, which will need more vision care, and by fashion demands for more stylish glasses, but these gains may be offset by the use of more automated machinery for manufacturing the lenses. Most jobs are expected to be created to replace retiring and transferring workers, rather than to supply the workforce for an expanding industry.

For more information about ophthalmic laboratory technicians, contact:

Optical Laboratories Association (OLA)
P.O. Box 2000
Merrifield, VA 22116-2000
ola-labs.org

Commission on Opticianry Accreditation (COA)
P.O. Box 3073
Merrifield, VA 22116-3073
coaccreditation.com

National Academy of Opticianry (NAO)
8401 Corporate Drive, Suite 605
Landover, MD 20785
nao.org

CHAPTER 39

OPHTHALMIC MEDICAL PERSONNEL

Including Ophthalmic Assistant,
Ophthalmic Technician, and
Ophthalmic Technologist

Ophthalmic medical personnel of all types work directly with patients, to assist opthalmologists—the physicians who treat eye defects, diseases, and injuries by prescribing medications, performing eye surgery, fitting contact lenses, and providing other types of treatments. These ophthalmic assistants, ophthalmic technicians, and ophthalmic technologists are skilled persons qualified by academic and clinical training to render support services to ophthalmologists. They are always dependent practitioners and do not have independent practices of any kind.

Working under the supervision, direction, and responsibility of the ophthalmologist, the ophthalmic medical personnel carry out various diagnostic and therapeutic procedures inherent to the practice of ophthalmology. Depending on the worker's experience and level of education, the specific functions may include taking the patient's medical history; administering diagnostic tests; making anatomical and functional ocular, or eye, measurements; testing visual acuity, visual fields, and sensorimotor function; administering topical ophthalmic medication; instructing the patient about home care and the use of contact lenses; the care and maintenance of optical instruments; the care, maintenance, and sterilization of surgical instruments; the maintenance of ophthalmological office equipment; assisting in ophthalmic surgery in the ophthalmologist's office or in the hospital; making optical measurements; administering orthoptic procedures; performing ocular electroneurological procedures; assisting in the fitting of contact lenses; fitting, adjusting, and making simple repairs on glasses; and clinical photography.

The term *ophthalmic medical personnel* includes specialists of three levels of skill and preparation.

- An *ophthalmic assistant* is qualified by education and training to perform an entire range of tasks required to provide continuous assistance to the physician. Ophthalmic assistants typically take detailed medical histories, administer eye drops, change dressings, and give simple vision tests.
- An *ophthalmic technician* is qualified to do everything an ophthalmic assistant can do, only in greater detail, plus certain special, more complex tasks.
- An *ophthalmic technologist* has the most education and assists the ophthalmologist in advanced areas of microbiology, advanced color vision, ophthalmic photography, and surgery, using the most sophisticated instruments and diagnostic techniques.

SETTINGS, SALARIES, STATISTICS

Ophthalmic medical personnel may be involved with patients of an ophthalmologist in any setting for which the ophthalmologist is responsible. Most ophthalmic medical assistants, technicians, and technologists work in ophthalmologists' offices. Opportunities also exist in hospitals, clinics, medical centers, and research settings. The workweek is usually forty hours long, and those hours tend to be predictable. There are more than 14,000 certified ophthalmic assistants, technicians, and technologists in the United States, Canada, and some foreign countries combined.

Median annual earnings for all medical assistants in 2002 was $23,940. The lowest-paid 10 percent were earning less than $17,640 and the highest-paid 10 percent were earning more than $34,130. Salaries varied by setting, and ophthalmic assistants working in hospitals and in doctors' offices earned median incomes of $24,460 and $24,260 respectively, compared to the median of $23,440 in smaller health-care services.

HOW TO BECOME AN OPHTHALMIC ASSISTANT, TECHNICIAN, OR TECHNOLOGIST

There are more than thirty educational programs in the United States, Canada, and India for ophthalmic medical personnel. These programs are located in universities, colleges, and hospitals. All of these programs require a high school diploma. Two years of college and experience working with the public are useful, however.

For many years, the accrediting body for these programs was the American Medical Association's Committee on Allied Health Education Accreditation (CAHEA). Since 1994, accreditation of educational programs in this and seventeen other allied health professions has been granted by CAHEA's successor, the Commission on Accreditation of Allied Health Education Programs (CAAHEP), which is an independent body.

The ophthalmic technology curriculum typically covers anatomy and physiology; medical terminology; medical law and ethics; psychology; ocular anatomy and physiology; ophthalmic optics; microbiology; ophthalmic pharmacology and toxicology; ocular motility, or eye movement; diseases of the eye; and diagnostic and treatment procedures, including ophthalmic surgery, contact lens fitting, visual field testing, and the care and maintenance of ophthalmic instruments and equipment. Supervised clinical practice is also part of the program of instruction.

Personal qualifications for a career in ophthalmic medical work include good vision, manual dexterity, good communication skills, maturity, common sense, and concern for accuracy and neatness. In addition, ophthalmic medical personnel have a lot of patient contact, so they must enjoy working with and helping a wide variety of people.

Certification in this field is available through the Joint Commission on Allied Health Personnel in Ophthalmology (JCAHPO). Although voluntary, certification has become an important credential documenting competence. Certification is awarded upon successful completion of a computer-based examination plus a practical test at the technician and technologist levels. To qualify for the computer-based examination, candidates must fulfill a basic educational requirement and a work experience requirement.

THE FUTURE

The job outlook for all medical assistants is expected to be the highest of any job in the United States. There are currently more positions available than there are applicants to fill them. Older individuals are traditionally major consumers of ophthalmic care, and as the surge in the over-sixty-five population continues, the demand for ophthalmic medical personnel should increase. Individuals with the best academic credentials will have the widest range of opportunities.

For more information about careers in ophthalmic medical assisting and technology, contact:

Joint Commission on Allied Health Personnel in Ophthalmology
  (JCAHPO)
2025 Woodlane Drive
St. Paul, MN 55125-2995
jcahpo.org

C H A P T E R

OPTICIAN

Also Known as Dispensing Optician

Opticians work directly with patients, and they also work at the direction of an optometrist or ophthalmologist. They fit, adjust, and dispense glasses and other optical devices according to the written prescription of an ophthalmologist or optometrist.

The optician interprets the prescription, assists the customer in selecting frames that complement the customer's facial features and hairstyle and that can accommodate the thickness and weight of the lenses prescribed, and measures the distance between the centers of the customer's pupils to determine where the lenses should be positioned in relation to them. The optician then writes the orders—containing the lens prescription, lens size, frame style, and lens tint—from which an ophthalmic laboratory technician will work. When the glasses are ready, the optician adjusts them with optical pliers, files, and screwdrivers so that they fit comfortably and properly.

In some states, opticians may also fit contact lenses, a process that is more demanding than fitting conventional glasses. Again, the optician works from a prescription written by the customer's ophthalmologist or optometrist. He or she examines and measure the customer's corneas and then writes specific orders from which the contact lens manufacturer will work. After the lenses are made, the optician teaches the customer how to insert, remove, and care for them.

Some opticians also specialize in the fitting of optic prostheses—artificial eyes—or cosmetic shells that conceal defects in the appearance of the eye.

SETTINGS, SALARIES, STATISTICS

Opticians work in retail optical stores, ophthalmologists' and optometrists' offices, hospital eye clinics, and optical laboratories. Many opticians open their own retail optical shops. The average workweek is forty-five hours long. If the optician works in a retail situation, weekend and evening hours can be expected. Part-time positions in this field are also available.

There were approximately 63,000 jobs held by dispensing opticians in 2002. This number was down from 68,000 opticians in 1999, due primarily to the recession and downsizing in all areas and to the loss of the full or partial payment for glasses as job benefits for thousands of workers.

Beginning and more experienced opticians' salaries ranged from $16,310 to $43,490 annually. Opticians working in physicians' offices made the most, averaging $28,250, while those working in health- and personal-care stores made $25,860.

HOW TO BECOME AN OPTICIAN

Most opticians learn their skills on the job, a process that may last up to four years. Instruction typically includes optical mathematics, optical physics, the use of precision measuring instruments and other optical tools, sales, and office management. In small establishments, this training may be conducted informally. In large optometric dispensing companies, the on-the-job training is usually a structured apprenticeship lasting from two to four years. To prepare for such on-the-job training, applicants usually need a high school diploma. In high school, a student should take courses in physics, algebra, geometry, and mechanical drawing.

More than thirty community colleges in the United States offer two-year associate's degree programs in optical fabricating and dispensing, half of which are accredited by the Commission on Opticianry Accreditation. Other formal programs in this field are offered by vocational/technical institutes, trade schools, and manufacturers; these programs, which vary in length from six months to one year, award certificates or diplomas. In addition, short, nondegree courses in contact lens fitting are offered by some medical schools, contact lens manufacturers, and professional societies.

In approximately half of the United States, opticians must be licensed. To obtain a license, an optician must meet certain educational and training criteria established by the state and pass a written and/or practical examination. In many states, to maintain this license, the optician must accumulate a specific number of continuing education credits in this field.

Although voluntary, certification is an important enhancement to employment. Certification is offered by the American Board of Opticianry, which administers two examinations. The National Opticianry Competency Examination attests to entry-level competence, and candidates who pass this examination are awarded a certified optician certificate, the advanced certification in ophthalmic dispensing. The Master in Ophthalmic Optics Program is for advanced certified opticians, and a master in ophthalmic optics certificate is awarded. The American Board of Opticianry's National Commission of Contact Lens Examiners (NCLE) administers the Contact Lens Registry Examination, which tests basic competency in the fitting of contact lenses, and the Contact Lens Registry Advanced Level Examination, which awards the designation of advanced certified contact lens technician.

Abilities and personal qualities that can enhance performance in this career include manual dexterity, sharp vision, mathematical aptitude, patience, tact, good communication skills, and a pleasant personality.

THE FUTURE

Job opportunities for opticians are projected to increase about as fast as the average occupation in the years through 2012. With more than half of all Americans already wearing glasses or contact lenses to correct their vision and with the American population aging, and therefore requiring more vision care, the demand for opticians—and particularly for opticians who have an associate's degree—should be as good as average. Because of its retail nature, opticianry is an occupation easily affected by fluctuations in the general economy.

For more information about opticians, training, education, certification, and licensing, contact:

Commission on Opticianry Accreditation
P.O. Box 3073
Merrifield, VA 22116-3073
coaccreditation.com

Opticians Association of America (OAA)

10341 Democracy Lane

Fairfax, VA 22030-2521

opticians.org

National Academy of Opticianry (NAO)

8401 Corporate Drive, #605

Landover, MD 20785

nao.org

American Board of Opticianry and

National Commission of Contact Lens Examiners (NCLE)

6506 Loisdale Road, Suite 209

Springfield, VA 22150

abo.org

OPTOMETRIC TECHNICIAN AND OPTOMETRIC ASSISTANT

Also Known as Paraoptometric

Optometric technicians and optometric assistants provide assistance to optometrists in taking care of patient's vision problems. They perform a variety of functions, such as testing, helping patients with glasses frames, providing some types of therapy, and instructing patients about procedures and about caring for their glasses and contact lenses. They sometimes do laboratory and administrative tasks as well.

Details of their duties may include taking preliminary medical histories, preparing patients for eye examinations, conducting simple vision tests, recording the results of eye examinations, measuring patients for the correct and comfortable fit of glasses, suggesting appropriate eyeglass shapes and sizes, making adjustments and repairs on finished eyeglasses, assisting the optometrist in teaching the patient how to use and maintain contact lenses and how to carry out programs of vision therapy exercises, and cleaning and caring for optometric instruments. The technicians and assistants handle these routine functions so that the optometrist is free to carry out the more technical aspects of the practice.

Optometric assistants and technicians may also be expected to carry out certain clerical duties, including keeping patient records; maintaining the schedule book; handling bookkeeping, correspondence, and filing; and maintaining the inventory of optometric materials. In theory, optometric technicians have more extensive training and handle the more complex duties, such as conducting the more technical basic vision tests and recording pressures in the eye, while optometric assistants have less preparation and perform the less-demanding tasks. In reality, the specific division of labor may not be sharply defined and will vary according to the setting, the employer, and the size of the practice for which the paraoptometric works.

SETTINGS, SALARIES, STATISTICS

There are approximately 60,000 paraoptometrics in the United States, and most of these are female. Most optometric assistants and technicians work in optometrists' offices. Opportunities also exist in health clinics, health maintenance organizations, government agencies, the armed forces, and optical companies. A forty-hour workweek is common, with Saturday and evening hours often expected. Part-time positions also exist.

The average salary for optometric assistants is approximately $19,500 per year. For experienced optometric technicians, the average is approximately $27,500 per year.

HOW TO BECOME AN OPTOMETRIC ASSISTANT OR TECHNICIAN

Many optometric assistants are trained on the job by the optometrists for whom they work, but optometric technicians usually have some formal training. For prospective optometric assistants, there are one-year courses offered by community colleges and technical institutes. For prospective optometric technicians, there are two-year associate's degree programs offered by community colleges and colleges of optometry. The Council on Optometric Education of the American Optometric Association (AOA) has accredited several of the technician programs, and many employers give preference to graduates of accredited programs.

Courses for these programs usually include ocular, or eye, anatomy and physiology; vision training; and contact lens theory and practice. Course work may also include such administrative tasks as medical forms and front-desk procedures. Students learn in the classroom, in the laboratory, and in supervised clinical settings, such as clinics and private offices.

Though voluntary, registration can be an important advantage in seeking employment. Registration of paraoptometrics is available through the

National Paraoptometric Registry. An optometric assistant who satisfies certain training and experience criteria may become a registered optometric assistant (Opt.A.R.). An optometric technician who meets the appropriate criteria may become a registered optometric technician (Opt.T.R.).

Abilities and personal qualities that can contribute to success as a paraoptometric include accuracy, neatness, the ability to put patients at ease, good eyesight, manual dexterity, and good verbal and written communication skills.

THE FUTURE

The job outlook for optometric assistants and technicians is expected to increase at an average rate for the rest of this decade. Two factors in particular should contribute to an increased demand for paraoptometrics. First, the demand for eye-care services should increase. The population, in general, is growing larger; the senior citizen population, which traditionally accounts for a major segment of all optical service consumers, is growing disproportionately larger. Second, optometry students today are taught to work with paraoptometrics, so when they open their offices, they tend to hire assistants and technicians. Delegating certain responsibilities is a fairly recent development. The employment outlook for all assistants and technicians is good, and for those paraoptometrics who graduate from formal training programs, opportunities should be even better. Currently, the only major deterrents to job growth are the uncertain nature of the economy and the trend toward increasingly tighter cost containment by medical insurance companies and health-care providers in general.

For more information about optometric assistants and optometric technicians, contact:

American Optometric Association (AOA)
Paraoptometric Section
243 North Lindbergh Boulevard
St. Louis, MO 63141
aoanet.org

CHAPTER 42

ORIENTATION AND MOBILITY SPECIALIST FOR THE BLIND OR VISUALLY IMPAIRED

Also Known as Orientation and Mobility Instructor, O & M Instructor, O & M Specialist, Mobility Instructor, and Peripatologist

Guide dogs, audio aids, mental maps, white canes, and more are all part of the tools available to the orientation and mobility (or O & M) specialist, a professional who is especially trained to help visually impaired persons learn to navigate their homes, neighborhoods, and cities. In the course of the education and training necessary to become an orientation and mobility specialist, students spend time blindfolded and/or wearing low-vision simulation goggles so as to better appreciate the physiological changes that visual impairment can bring and to better understand the implications of travel with no or reduced vision.

Each year an estimated 50,000 Americans lose their sight, and hundreds of thousands of others suffer serious vision impairment. Orientation and mobility specialists help the visually impaired, such as young children who have never seen, newly blinded adults, and people with multiple disabilities, to achieve independence with regard to traveling. The O & M specialist evaluates the nature and extent of the patient's visual impairment and plans and implements an individualized program of instruction.

In real or practice travel situations, the patient is taught how to become oriented to physical surroundings so that eventually he or she can safely and effectively travel alone, with or without a cane, in familiar and unfamiliar environments. Gradually, the world in which the patient can safely travel independently expands from his or her own neighborhood to a larger area and from quiet residential streets to urban situations and the use of mass transit.

Communication skills are stressed during training. The instructor teaches the patient how to maximize his or her unaffected senses, particularly hearing and touch. The patient is taught how to be an especially effective listener.

Depending on the patient's needs, an orientation and mobility specialist may collaborate with other health-care professionals and educators—teachers of the visually impaired, occupational therapists, physical therapists, ophthalmologists, optometrists, and rehabilitation counselors—to help that patient become more competent and independent. Clearly, helping the visually impaired toward full and happy lives is very important and potentially very satisfying work.

SETTINGS, SALARIES, STATISTICS

Orientation and mobility is mostly taught on a one-to-one basis. O & M specialists teach about thirty individuals per year. They work in hospitals—mostly Department of Veterans Affairs facilities—residential and public schools, rehabilitation centers, public and private community-based agencies, nursing homes, and the homes of their students. A forty-hour workweek is typical.

As of 2004, there were 2,317 certified orientation and mobility specialist members of the AERBVI in the United States. Until twenty years ago, this was a male-dominated profession. Today, more than half of all practicing O & M specialists are women. As a group, O & M specialists are paid on a scale that is roughly equivalent to the pay scale for teachers in the United States; however, salaries range widely depending on the setting and the specialist's education. The average salary earned is approximately $39,500 per year. Generally, salaries paid by private agencies are not as competitive as those offered by public institutions.

HOW TO BECOME AN ORIENTATION AND MOBILITY SPECIALIST FOR THE BLIND OR VISUALLY IMPAIRED

A master's degree in orientation and mobility is the standard level of education, although in some settings a bachelor's degree is sufficient for employment. Master's degree programs combine academic and clinical training with an internship in a clinical setting. As of 2004, there were forty-five O & M college training programs in the United States.

O & M specialists who satisfy certain education and experience requirements may become certified by the Academy for Certification of Vision Rehabilitation and Education Professionals.

Abilities and personal qualities that can enhance performance and satisfaction in this career include patience, compassion, excellent verbal communication skill, warmth, and perseverance.

THE FUTURE

The employment picture for orientation and mobility specialists is excellent. Currently, there is a shortage of qualified O & M specialists and this shortage will most likely grow as the number of older Americans grows.

For information about a career as an orientation and mobility specialist, contact:

Association for the Education and Rehabilitation of the Blind and
    Visually Impaired
1703 North Beauregard Street, Suite 440
Alexandria, VA 22311
aerbvi.org

American Foundation for the Blind
11 Penn Plaza, Suite 300
New York, NY 10001
afb.org

The Academy for Certification of Vision Rehabilitation and Education
    Professionals
330 North Commerce Park Loop, Suite 200
Tucson, AZ 85754
acvrep.org

CHAPTER 43

ORTHOPTIST

Orthoptics comes from *ortho*, meaning "straight," and *optics*, meaning "eyes."

An orthoptist is an eye muscle specialist who, working under the supervision of an ophthalmologist, diagnoses and treats conditions affecting ocular motility, or eye movement, and binocular vision, or vision using both eyes at the same time. The work of orthoptists is therapeutic, and they do not perform surgery. They work with people of all kinds and all ages.

Orthoptics is still a relatively new health-care profession in the United States. During the late nineteenth and early twentieth centuries, orthoptic treatments were carried out in Europe and Great Britain, and the first orthoptic clinic was opened in England in 1930. Although the first orthoptic clinic in America opened in 1932, this field has become a recognized and organized auxiliary to ophthalmology only in the past sixty years.

Most patients seen by orthoptists are children who have an ocular defect known as strabismus, which is the misalignment of the eyes. In other words, the eyes do not work in tandem. The patient's vision is not fused; one eye will focus properly, but the other strays, sometimes creating a cross-eyed appearance. As the patient strains to use both eyes together, he or she may experience discomfort. Strabismus is often psychologically uncomfortable as well. Of all children, 2 to 4 percent suffer from some degree of this problem, which is typically present and detected early in the first few years of life. In addition to children, many adults have uncorrected strabismus, which may require treatment.

Corrective surgery is performed to repair most cases of strabismus. Eyeglasses are frequently prescribed to correct focusing errors and to improve eye alignment. Orthoptic therapy is a third, less common option.

Orthoptists teach patients special exercises that gradually improve the control of eye movement so that their vision, comfort, and appearance are improved. Treatment of strabismus improves not only patients' ability to see the world, but also the way they see themselves.

In addition to diagnosing and treating eye coordination defects, an orthoptist may, under the supervision of an ophthalmologist, conduct visual field and other ancillary ophthalmic tests. A new and exciting development in this field is the Preferential Looking Test, or PLT, which is a simple method of testing visual acuity in children under the age of three. An orthoptist presents to the child cards that are part blank and part striped and then observes the child's reaction. Most young children being tested will display a preference for the patterned portion. Their eyes become fixed on the stripes, suggesting that they can detect them and that normal infant vision includes a preference for pattern. Because the PLT requires neither verbal reliability nor verbal response on the part of the child, it is possible to assess younger children.

Although most orthoptists work in pediatric eye care, others work or specialize in general ophthalmology, ocular plastic surgery, rehabilitation medicine, or neurological eye care.

SETTINGS, SALARIES, STATISTICS

Opportunities for orthoptists exist nationwide. Orthoptists work in clinical settings, in the private offices of ophthalmologists, in hospitals, in eye clinics, and in the departments of ophthalmology of teaching hospitals. Some orthoptists work for more than one private practice. Many orthoptists teach and conduct research in their particular settings, in addition to their patient-care activities.

Orthoptics is a relatively small profession, with only 400 certified orthoptists in the United States. It is interesting that Australia, with a population about one-fourteenth the size of America's, also has approximately 400 practicing orthoptists. Orthoptics is also practiced extensively in Europe.

According to the American Medical Association website in 2004, the average salary for orthoptists was found to range from $45,000 to $50,000. Salaries for certified orthoptists tend to be at the high end of that earned by other allied health professionals, and upper-end salaries for experienced orthoptists can be up to $80,000 per year.

HOW TO BECOME AN ORTHOPTIST

College, plus a two-year professional program, is needed to prepare as an orthoptist. The college graduate, with a bachelor of science degree, must successfully complete a twenty-four-month orthoptics educational program. These programs, located in hospitals, in universities, and at training centers, combine practical and theoretical training.

As of 2004, there were only twelve orthoptic educational programs in the United States and Canada. These are accredited by the American Orthoptic Council. Primary subject areas include anatomy, neuroanatomy, physiology, pharmacology, ophthalmic optics, diagnostic testing and measurement, orthoptic treatment, systemic disease and ocular motor disorders, principles of surgery, basic ophthalmic examination techniques, genetics, child development, learning disabilities, clinical research methods, and medical writing. At this time, there are no graduate programs in orthoptics, but there are graduate-level courses offered in this field.

To qualify for admission to an educational program, a candidate must have successfully completed a baccalaureate degree. (It should be noted, however, that admission criteria vary from school to school, and exceptions may be considered on an individual basis.) High school and college courses in biology, physics, psychology, and anatomy provide a useful background for the study of orthoptics.

Personal qualities that can enhance performance and enjoyment as an orthoptist include patience, kindness, sound judgment, emotional maturity, and scientific curiosity. And, because they often work with young children, orthoptists should like children and be able to relate well to them. A good rapport with the patient is essential. Good vision and good health are also necessary.

In order to practice in the United States, orthoptists must be certified. Candidates who have successfully completed an accredited orthoptic education program and who pass written, oral, and practical examinations administered by the American Orthoptic Council, are awarded national certification and may use the inititals "CO" following their names. The American Orthoptic Council also annually offers continuing education credits, which are required for renewal of certification.

One-third of all ophthalmic technologists are orthoptists.

THE FUTURE

At present, the number of job openings for orthoptists is far greater than the number of orthoptists available to fill them. In some parts of the country, there are as many as five job openings for every available applicant. Because there are so few educational programs for orthoptists and because they graduate so few new orthoptists each year—not even enough to fill the openings created by retirement—this trend is expected to continue well through this decade.

For more information about a career as an orthoptist, contact:

American Association of Certified Orthoptists and American
    Orthoptic Council
3914 Nakoma Road
Madison, WI 53711
orthoptics.org

CHAPTER 44

ORTHOTIST (CO), PROSTHETIST (CP), AND ORTHOTIC-PROSTHETIC TECHNICIAN (OPT)

Orthotists design, fabricate, and fit braces and strengthening devices for patients who have disabling conditions of the limbs or spine. Such a device is called an orthosis, from the Greek word *orthos*, meaning "straight." Prosthetists make artificial limbs and help patients to learn to use them.

ORTHOTISTS

Orthoses support weakened body parts and help to correct skeletal problems. Persons requiring orthoses include those whose limbs or spines have been affected by stroke, polio, muscular dystrophy, spinal cord injury, congenital musculoskeletal disorders, fracture, or other orthopedic impairment. The back brace worn by some adolescents to manage severe scoliosis, or curvature of the spine, is a common example of an orthosis.

The trained orthotist actually formulates the design of the orthosis; selects the appropriate materials, predominantly thermoplastics, fabric, and aluminum; makes the necessary casts, measurements, model modifications, and layouts; performs fittings; evaluates the fit and function of the orthosis; and teaches the patient how to use and care for the device. The orthotist usually follows a prescription for the orthosis that has been written by a physician. In some cases, however, the orthotist may be called in by the physician to examine and evaluate the patient's orthotic needs and to consult on the formulation of the prescription.

Maintaining accurate patient records and keeping abreast of new developments in the field are also major parts of the orthotist's responsibilities. In addition, they supervise the tasks of support personnel as well as laboratory activities related to the development of orthoses. Some orthotists also teach and conduct research.

Computerized technology and other inventions make this an ever-changing field. There are always new and exciting developments. Just a few years ago, research orthotists developed the first all-carbon fiber knee-ankle-foot-orthosis (KAFO). This revolutionary brace, intended for patients with postpolio syndrome, spina bifida, cerebral palsy, and other lower-extremity disorders, is one-third the weight of traditional KAFOs. This sophisticated orthosis is also more cosmetically pleasing and less cumbersome for the patient to wear because it is contoured to the entire length of the affected leg. Experts expect this development to lead to other advancements in carbon-graphited orthotics.

The title of Certified Orthotist, or CO, is awarded to practitioners who satisfy specific educational, training, and examination requirements established by the American Board for Certification in Orthotics and Prosthetics (ABC).

PROSTHETISTS

Prosthetists design, fabricate, and fit artificial limbs for patients who, because of illness, accident, or congenital condition, are missing part or all of their own limbs. These artificial limbs are called prostheses, and they are made out of various plastics, metals, woods, and fiberglass. The prosthetist's goal is a prosthesis that the patient finds functional, comfortable, and aesthetically acceptable.

In prosthetics, the most advanced technology is myoelectrics, the technical term for electromechanical prostheses. Myoelectric technology utilizes electronic sensors, or electrodes, to detect small electric signals emitted during the contraction of muscles in the residual limb. These signals are electronically processed and used to control a motor within the prosthesis. The prosthesis, in turn, activates a simulated body part, such as an arm, wrist, or hand.

Another new development in prostheses is the use of computers to design and manufacture artificial limbs. The patient's body measurements are fed into a computer, which then produces a detailed, three-dimensional blueprint of the prosthetic joint needed. This blueprint, in turn, is fed into a manufacturing machine that sculpts the prosthesis.

Prosthetists formulate the design of the artificial limb; select the best materials; make the necessary casts, measurements, models, and alignments; evaluate the prosthesis on the patient; and instruct the patient on its use. In some cases, the prosthetist fills a prescription for the artificial limb that has been written by the attending physician. In other cases, the prosthetist is called in to consult on the formulation of the prescription, and he or she will examine the patient and personally evaluate his or her prosthetic needs.

Like orthotists, prosthetists are also expected to maintain patient records, supervise the functions of technicians and other support personnel, and keep up to date on new developments in the field. Prosthetists also engage in teaching and research.

The title Certified Prosthetist, or CP, is awarded to practitioners who satisfy specific educational, training, and examination requirements established by the American Board for Certification in Orthotics and Prosthetics (ABC).

Because the fields of orthotics and prosthetics are so closely related, many prosthetists study orthotics and vice versa. When sufficient additional education, training, and examination requirements are achieved in the complementary discipline, the professional designation certified prosthetist/orthotist, or CPO, is used.

SETTINGS, SALARIES, STATISTICS

Orthotists and prosthetists work in privately owned facilities and laboratories, hospitals, rehabilitation centers, university teaching and research programs, and government agencies. The U.S. Bureau of Labor Statistics reports that in 2002, approximately 4,600 orthotists and prosthetists held jobs in the United States.

In 2003, the average starting salary for orthotists and prosthetists holding bachelor's degrees was $50,319 per year. The median salary for practitioners with substantial experience was $57,323 per year, and individuals in private practice earned well beyond that figure—the highest incomes averaged $66,668. Advancement in these fields may come in the form of promotion to supervisory and administrative positions. A significant number of orthotists become owners or managers of private facilities.

In 2004, the ABC reported 7,000 members, and the Board for Orthotist/Prosthetist Certification (BOC) reported 5,000. The majority of these are men, but in recent years an increasing number of women are entering this field.

HOW TO BECOME AN ORTHOTIST OR A PROSTHETIST

There are three major educational routes to a career in orthotics and prosthetics. One route is to receive a bachelor's degree with the major emphasis in orthotics or prosthetics from a college or university that has a program accredited by the National Commission on Orthotic and Prosthetic Education (NCOPE) in conjunction with the Commission on Accreditation of Allied Health Education Programs (CAAHEP). In addition, the successful completion of an approved residency of at least one year in length is required. The candidate is then eligible to take the American Board for Certification in Orthotics and Prosthetics (or ABC) Practitioners Certification Examination, which is a three-part, written, clinical, and written simulation test of competence in the field. At this time, three colleges and universities across the country offer accredited bachelor's degrees in orthotics and/or prosthetics.

Undergraduate preparation in prosthetics and orthotics typically includes courses in psychology, and specifically, the psychology of the physically disabled; chemistry; physics; biology; anatomy; physiology; mathematics; biostatistics; mechanics; biomechanics; properties of materials; mechanical drawing; metalworking; prosthetic and orthotic techniques; orthopedic and neuromuscular conditions; lower and upper limb prosthetics; lower and upper limb orthotics; and spinal orthotics. This preparation also includes extensive clinical training.

The second route is that graduate students holding bachelor's degrees in majors other than orthotics or prosthetics can prepare for these careers by successfully completing a CAAHEP-accredited program. These are one to two years in length, at the end of which a certificate is awarded. A one-year residency is also required before the candidate may take the ABC Practitioners Certification Examination for a postgraduate certificate program in orthotics and/or prosthetics.

Beginning in 2005, the ABC is adding the requirement of a written examination for certification.

The third route is that candidates possessing qualifications that may not comply with the specific requirements set forth but that demonstrate a unique combination of education, clinical experience, and professional training at least equivalent to the specific requirements set forth are also eligible to apply to take the ABC Practitioners Certification Examination.

To keep orthotists' and prosthetists' certification current, the ABC also has specific requirements for continuing education. There are also many orthotists, prosthetists, and prosthetist/orthotists who are not certified. However, salaries and opportunities tend to be greater for certified practitioners.

High school preparation should include classes in biology, physics, chemistry, and mathematics. Shop courses in metal, wood, and plastics are recommended.

ORTHOTIC-PROSTHETIC TECHNICIANS

Also working in these fields are orthotic-prosthetic technicians. Orthotic-prosthetic technicians work in a laboratory fabricating, preparing, and maintaining braces, surgical supports, artificial limbs, and other orthotic and prosthetic devices under the supervision of a prosthetist or orthotist. They work directly with the materials and are responsible for ensuring that the workmanship is of high quality. Using precision measuring instruments and various tools, they shape and assemble the plastic, wood, and metal to meet the specifications of the prescription.

Registration of orthotic-prosthetic technicians who meet specific requirements is also handled by the ABC. Students must (1) complete a formal education program in orthotics or prosthetics that is approved by NCOPE, and then pass the ABC's Technical Examination, or (2) possess at least a high school education and accumulate a minimum of two years of work experience in the making of orthoses and/or prostheses under the supervision of a certified orthotist, certified prosthetist, or certified prosthetist/orthotist and then pass the ABC's Technical Examination. A registered technician (orthotics), or RT(O), is a person who has passed the technical examination in orthotics; a registered technician (prosthetics), or RT(P), is one who has passed the Prosthetic Technician Examination; and a registered technician (orthotics-prosthetics), or RT(OP), is someone who has passed the combined exam for orthotic-prosthetic technicians. Many junior and community colleges across the country offer technical training. There are many orthotic-prosthetic technicians who are not registered, but salaries for registered orthotic-prosthetic technicians are higher and job opportunities are greater.

An orthotist-prothetist technician needs skillful hands, mechanical ability, concern for detail, patience, good communication skills, and a genuine desire to help individuals who are disabled in order to succeed.

THE FUTURE

Technological and medical advances make this an exciting time to be working in the area of orthotics and prosthetics. New technology and materials allow prosthetists and orthotists to design and fabricate devices that provide greater comfort, safety, and freedom than ever before possible. The use of myoelectrics, hydraulics, and biofeedback to provide mobility are just a few of the new directions being pursued.

According to the U.S. Bureau of Labor Statistics, the demand for professionally trained and experienced prosthetists, orthotists, prosthetist/ orthotists, and orthotic-prosthetic technicians will grow from now through 2012. Actual employment, however, will depend largely upon the availability of funding, which will depend upon hospitals, rehabilitation clinics, and insurance companies as well as the overall economic conditions in the United States and the industrial world.

For more information about orthotists, prosthetists, prosthetist/orthotists, and orthotic-prosthetic technicians, contact:

Board for Orthotist/Prosthetist Certification (BOC)
515 West Lombard Street, First Floor
Baltimore, MD 21201
bocusa.org

American Board for Certification in Orthotics and
    Prosthetics (ABC)
330 John Carlisle Street, Suite 210
Alexandria, VA 22314
abcorp.org

PERFUSIONIST

Also Known as Cardiovascular
Perfusionist, Clinical Perfusionist,
Extracorporeal Perfusionist,
Perfusion Technologist/Technician,
and Pump Technician

A perfusionist, the preferred occupational title now in wide use, is a skilled specialist, qualified by academic and clinical education, who operates extracorporeal—outside the body—circulation equipment.

Perfusionists provide consultation to the physician in the selection of the appropriate equipment and techniques to be used during extracorporeal circulation. During cardiopulmonary bypass surgery, the perfusionist may, on prescription, administer blood products, anesthetic agents, and drugs through the extracorporeal circuit.

Perfusionists are also involved in the blood salvaging, or blood conservation, techniques that are often critical in light of today's diminishing blood bank supplies and the fear of AIDS. Blood salvaging is the effort to use as much of a patient's own blood and as little bagged, or donated, blood as possible during and after surgery. Depositing a person's own blood several weeks prior to the person's surgery is an example of one procedure for blood salvaging.

A heart-lung machine is the crucial piece of biomedical equipment that temporarily maintains proper oxygen and carbon dioxide levels and blood circulation extracorporeally during heart-lung bypass procedures, such as open-heart surgery and surgery of the large blood vessels, and during respiratory failure and other medical situations where it is necessary to support or temporarily replace the patient's circulatory or respiratory functions. The heart-lung machine continuously drains blood by gravity from the patient's venous system, reoxygenates it, and pumps it back into the patient's arterial system.

Mary Gibbon was the first extracorporeal perfusionist. The revolutionary heart-lung machine was developed by Dr. John H. Gibbon, Jr., who used it in 1953 in the first successful human open-heart surgery. Assisting Dr. Gibbon in that landmark operation was a nurse, Dr. Gibbon's wife, Mary, who had been specially trained to operate the new heart-lung machine and also to monitor the critical oxygenation of the patient's blood during the operation.

Today, other biomedically engineered devices are available to the critical, lifesaving work of the perfusionist. Perfusion technology helps to conserve blood in the cases of preoperative and intraoperative phlebotomies performed on bypass patients. After anesthesia is administered, before or during the operation, one or two units of the patient's blood are drained and stored to be given back—through the heart-lung pump—to the patient at the end of the procedure when blood volume is needed.

Cell-Savers are another essential tool used by perfusionists. These machines use centrifugal force to separate, from any blood left in the pump after surgery, all of the plasma, damaged platelets, and saline that should not be returned to the patient's body. After washing the clotting inhibitor heparin and other drugs from the reclaimed red blood cells, the perfusionist can then return the patient's own blood, via the pump. In both these situations, the need for bagged blood can be radically reduced, if not eliminated.

A perfusionist must also be in attendance when extracorporeal membrane oxygenation (ECMO) is being carried out. ECMO is a procedure for premature infants who are experiencing respiratory distress, certain post-op heart patients, heart patients awaiting transplant organs, and others needing extra heart and respiratory support. The surgeon places the patient on a heart-lung pump, which is then operated and monitored by a perfusionist. The pump buys the patient the time needed for additional development, for healing, or, in the case of the transplant recipient, until a donor can be matched.

Today, perfusionists can also be found in the operating room when liver transplants, orthopedic surgery, and cancer surgery are being performed, using rapid infusion techniques to quickly replace lost or lowered blood volume with warmed blood, thereby minimizing trauma and maximizing the opportunity for healing. New applications for perfusion techniques are developing constantly.

Perfusion procedures involve specialized instrumentation and/or advanced life-support techniques and may include a variety of related functions. The perfusionist is educated to conduct extracorporeal circulation and to ensure the safe management of physiologic functions by monitoring the necessary variables.

Final medical responsibility for extracorporeal perfusion rests with the surgeon in charge, but the perfusionist is a vital member of the surgical team. He or she may also be involved in monitoring the patient's heart and lung functions for extended periods of up to several weeks, both before and after the surgery. This job requires physical stamina as well as intelligence and a steady personality, because the work with patients is carried out on twenty-four hours a day, seven days a week.

SETTINGS, SALARIES, STATISTICS

Perfusionists usually work in a hospital setting, and the vast majority are employed directly by hospitals. Perfusionists also work outside of their hospitals when they are engaged in efforts to procure and transport organs for transplant. Specifically, in heart-lung transplant cases, a perfusionist will travel to the donor's hospital and maintain the donor's respiration and heart rates until the optimal time for removal of the organs prior to transport or throughout the trip if the donor's body is transported. The perfusionist maintains respiration by placing the donor on the coronary bypass machine; on the receiving end, the perfusionist puts the patient who is to be the recipient on the machine during surgery.

Some perfusionists work for individual surgeons or surgical groups, and health-care corporations also employ perfusionists. Perfusionists work long hours. Emergencies frequently necessitate working back-to-back shifts. Eighty-hour workweeks have not been uncommon, although some states have begun to limit the number of hours medical personnel can work without adequate rest breaks.

Most job openings for perfusionists are in large cities and other high-population areas.

According to the American Society of Extra-Corporeal Technology (AmSECT), there were approximately 3,700 perfusionists holding jobs in the United States in 2004. Starting salaries were estimated at $58,000 to $61,000, and those for perfusionists with ten or more years of experience were estimated to be approximately $85,000 to $100,000 per year.

HOW TO BECOME A PERFUSIONIST

Until about thirty years ago, most perfusionists came to the field from other disciplines, such as nursing, respiratory therapy, biomedical engineering, surgical technology, and the laboratory, and trained on the job. About one-fourth of the perfusionists in current practice were educated this way. Today, students embarking on a career in cardiovascular perfusion are encouraged to attend one of the formal educational programs in perfusion, which are accredited by the Commission on Accreditation of Allied Health Education Programs (CAAHEP).

Perfusionist educational programs are generally one to two years in length, depending on the program design, its objectives and prerequisites, and the student's qualifications and prior experience. Because there are not many perfusionist educational programs, admission is highly competitive. Almost all of the programs require a bachelor's degree as a prerequisite. Several of the programs also require candidates to have backgrounds in medical technology, respiratory therapy, nursing, or another medical discipline.

In the early years of development of this field, most perfusionist educational programs were offered by community colleges or were hospital based. Today, as is the case with other allied health professions, larger universities have initiated educational programs. A perfusionist's education typically includes classroom work in anatomy, physiology, pathology, chemistry, and pharmacology as well as courses covering heart-lung bypass for adults, heart surgery for pediatric and infant patients, long-term supportive extracorporeal circulation, and special applications of perfusion technology. Clinical experience incorporating performance of an adequate number and variety of circulation procedures is also a required part of the formal education.

A perfusionist should have high intelligence, physical stamina, a stable personality, the ability to communicate well, skillful hands, and mechanical aptitude. He or she must also be able to think calmly but quickly under pressure and to concentrate intensely for long periods of time. Other important personal qualities include a strong sense of responsibility, the ability to work well, and, especially, the ability to work correctly and quickly in emergency situations. Perfusionists work under very stressful conditions.

The hours are long, and the situations are life-and-death. A perfusionist must be emotionally stable and—mentally and physically—to react efficiently, reliably, and effectively to all situations within the hospital.

Certification in this field is available through the American Board of Cardiovascular Perfusion (ABCP). To become certified, a candidate must satisfy the ABCP's education and clinical experience requirements and pass a rigorous oral and written examination. A perfusionist who satisfies all of these requirements is known as a certified clinical perfusionist and may use the letters CCP after his or her name.

THE FUTURE

The demand for experienced certified perfusionists exceeds the present supply, and several studies have identified cardiovascular perfusion as an occupation that should experience better-than-average growth in the near future. The high earnings potential in this allied health profession makes it especially attractive, and interest in this field is high. The significant number of bypass procedures performed annually plus the many new applications for perfusion technology discussed earlier in this chapter, such as blood salvage techniques, ECMO, should cause continued demand for perfusionists in the coming decade.

For more information about perfusionists, contact:

The American Society of Extra-Corporeal Technology (AmSECT)
503 Carlisle Drive
Herndon, VA 20170
amsect.org

American Academy of Cardiovascular Perfusion (AACP)
P.O. Box 3596
Allentown, PA 18106-0596
aacp.org

For information about perfusionist certification, contact:

The American Board of Cardiovascular Perfusion (ABCP)
207 North 25th Avenue
Hattiesburg, MS 39401
abcp.org

For a list of accredited educational programs for perfusionists, contact:

The Accreditation Committee for Perfusion Education
6654 South Sycamore Street
Littleton, CO 80120
ac-pe.org

PHARMACIST

Pharmacists are the health-care professionals who serve patients, as well as other health-care professionals, in assuring the appropriate use of medications and in achieving optimal therapeutic results from their use.

Specifically, pharmacists are responsible for the professional interpretation and review of the prescription orders written by physicians, dentists, and other authorized prescribers and for the accurate dispensing of the medications ordered. The principal goal of pharmaceutical care is improvement in the quality of patients' lives through the use of medications that have been developed and prescribed to achieve definite outcomes.

Pharmacists are educated in the composition, uses, and interactions of medicines and in how those medicines change biological functions. They maintain detailed patient medication profiles listing vital health information, such as allergies and other medications the patient is taking; advise people on the use of prescription and nonprescription, or over-the-counter, medications; and act as an information resource to physicians and other health-care professionals.

As opposed to the early days of pharmacy, when the pharmacist measured, mixed, and assembled ingredients to form the capsules, solutions, and ointments prescribed, most medications today are mass-manufactured in the form in which they will be used by the patient. For this reason, the majority of the community pharmacist's activity is in maintaining and dispensing—counting, decanting, packaging, and carefully labeling—medications, not in compounding them.

SETTINGS, SALARIES, STATISTICS

There were approximately 230,000 pharmacists in the United States as of 2002. The number of women enrolling in pharmacy schools has grown dramatically in the past decade, now accounting for about 60 percent of all pharmacy students.

Community pharmacies are still the largest employer of pharmacists, but today that includes independently owned drugstores, chain drugstores, chain grocery and department stores, and mass merchandisers. About 22 percent of pharmacists work in hospitals. Others work for the government, pharmaceutical wholesalers and mail-order companies, clinics, and home health-care companies. Pharmacists who work in community pharmacies average forty-five-hour workweeks, including evening and weekend hours. According to the U.S. Bureau of Labor Statistics, about 19 percent of pharmacists worked part-time in 2002.

The median annual salary for a full-time pharmacist in 2002 was $77,050. The lowest-paid 10 percent earned less than $54,110, and the highest-paid 10 percent earned more than $94,570 per year.

The median salary for those employed in grocery stores was $78,270; the median in health- and personal-care stores was $76,800, and the median in general medical and surgical hospitals was $76,620.

HOW TO BECOME A PHARMACIST

Because of the critical nature of the work, a license to practice pharmacy is required in all fifty states, the District of Columbia, and Puerto Rico. To become a licensed pharmacist, a student must graduate from one of the pharmacy programs that are accredited by the American Council on Pharmaceutical Education; pass a state board examination; and either serve as an intern under the supervision of a licensed pharmacist for a specific period of time, usually in a community or hospital pharmacy, or accumulate a specific amount of practical experience, which varies from state to state.

Most states accept licenses granted by other states, and many pharmacists are licensed in more than one state.

The initial educational preparation of the pharmacist is accomplished through professional degree programs offered by the nation's colleges and schools of pharmacy. Those programs are accredited by the American Council on Pharmaceutical Education. Completion of an accredited program makes the graduate eligible to take state licensure examinations to practice pharmacy.

Approximately two-thirds of all students currently enrolled in professional programs in pharmacy are enrolled in Pharm.D. programs. The doctor of pharmacy curriculum is usually a four-year professional degree program, preceded by a minimum of two years of preprofessional collegiate course work, often referred to as a "two-four" curricular design. A small number of institutions use alternative curricular designs for their Pharm.D. programs.

A single set of accreditation standards and guidelines for professional degree programs in pharmacy has been adopted by the profession, effective in July 2000. These standards and guidelines address only the doctor of pharmacy degree program.

A pharmacist who wishes to do administrative work, teach, or carry out research in this field may go on to study in an advanced professional program leading to a master of science or a doctor of philosophy (Ph.D.) in pharmaceutical science. Although many pharmacists who seek advancement continue on to graduate study in pharmacy, some go on to medical or dental school; to law school, which leads to jobs as pharmaceutical patent attorneys or consultants on pharmaceutical and drug laws; or to graduate education in pharmacology, toxicology, pharmaceutical bacteriology, or other related fields.

In the professional curriculum, pharmacy students study medicinal chemistry. or the study of all aspects of chemicals used as medicinal agents; pharmacology, or the medicine science that involves all of the actions of drugs on living systems and their constituent parts, including the intermolecular reactions of chemical compounds in a cell with drugs, the evaluation of a drug's effectiveness, and the effects of chemicals in our environment on entire populations; pharmaceutics, or the physical and chemical properties of medicinal agents with respect to dosage forms and their impact on pharmacological activity; clinical pharmacy, or drug management problems in the care of patients; pharmacy practice, or the skills involved in compounding and dispensing prescriptions and professional ethics; and pharmacy administration. From six months to one year of the curriculum is spent in clinical experience rotations in various pharmacy practice settings.

Personal qualifications for a career in pharmacy include accuracy, orderliness, honesty, and, for the majority of pharmacists who are self-employed, good business sense. A pharmacist must be the kind of person the public can trust. Patients want more from their pharmacist than just having their prescriptions properly filled; they want a reliable, thoughtful, and pleasant explanation of the medication's use and of any side effects. To be effective in a patient-care setting, a pharmacist must have good communication skills and be patient, friendly, and considerate.

THE FUTURE

The employment outlook for pharmacists is good. In some areas of the country, competition for positions has developed. Older individuals are major consumers of medical services and medicines, and as the percentage of older Americans in the population grows, the demand for the services of pharmacists will grow as well. One factor that may cause some job reduction, however, is the trend toward automation by mail-order houses.

For more information about a career in pharmacy, contact:

American Association of Colleges of Pharmacy
1426 Prince Street
Alexandria, VA 22314
aacp.org

National Association of Boards of Pharmacy
700 Busse Highway
Park Ridge, IL 60068
nabp.net

PHYSICAL THERAPIST (PT) AND PHYSICAL THERAPIST ASSISTANT (PTA)

$\mathbf{P}$atients often feel that their physical therapist was the person who got them back on the road to normal life. The primary purpose of physical therapy is the promotion of optimal health and function, helping patients to regain as much normal movement as possible after surgery, accidents, illnesses, and other problems that have reduced normal function.

PHYSICAL THERAPIST

Physical therapists (PTs) provide services to people who have impairments, functional limitations, disabilities, or changes in physical function and health status resulting from injury, disease, or other causes. The physical therapist applies scientific principles to the processes of examination, i.e., the history, systems review, and tests and measures; evaluation; diagnosis; prognosis; intervention, including anticipated goals; reexamination; outcomes; and criteria for discharge. PTs interact and practice in collaboration with a variety of health-care professionals, including physicians, dentists, nurses, educators, social workers, occupational therapists, speech-language pathologists, and audiologists.

Some of the more common conditions for which physical therapists examine and provide intervention are: orthopedic conditions, such as low back and neck pain, headaches, and osteoporosis; joint and soft-tissue injuries, such as sprains and strains, hand injuries, fractures and dislocations, and pre- and postsurgical conditions; neurologic conditions, such as stroke, traumatic brain injury, Parkinson's disease, cerebral palsy, peripheral nerve injury, and multiple sclerosis; connective tissue conditions, such as burns, ulcers, wounds, and collagenous disorders; arthritis conditions, including osteoarthritis and rheumatoid arthritis; systemic diseases, such as cancer and HIV/AIDS infection; cardiopulmonary and circulatory conditions, such as congestive heart failure, emphysema, chronic obstructive pulmonary disease, lymphedema, and peripheral vascular disease; workplace injuries, such as carpal tunnel syndrome, cumulative trauma, and stress disorders; and sports injuries, such as overuse injuries and trauma.

During an examination, the PT performs tests and measurements that provide information about the status of the patient's musculoskeletal, neurological, pulmonary, and cardiovascular systems as well as his or her functional independence. The PT administers a breadth of examinations, including the following:

- Motor function examinations to assess an individual's ability to learn or to demonstrate the skillful and efficient assumption, maintenance, modification, and control of voluntary postures and movement patterns
- Muscle performance examinations to assess strength, power, and endurance and to determine an individual's ability to produce movements that are prerequisites for functional activity
- Gait and balance examinations to assess disturbances in gait and balance that may lead to a decline in mobility and functional independence or an increased incidence of falls
- Neuromotor development and sensory integration examinations to assess motor capabilities, including the acquisition and evolution of movement skills and abilities across the life span
- Aerobic capacity or endurance examinations to measure the ability to perform work or participate in activities over time and to indicate the degree and severity of impairment and functional limitation
- Ventilation, respiration, and circulation examinations to assess whether the individual has an adequate ventilatory pump, oxygen uptake, and oxygen delivery system to perform the activities of daily living, ambulation, and aerobic exercise

PTs use various interventions to achieve patient treatment goals, including therapeutic exercises, such as aerobic conditioning; functional training in self-care and home management, including the activities of daily living; the prescription, fabrication, and application of assistive, adaptive, supportive, and protective devices and equipment; manual therapy techniques, including joint mobilization and manipulation; airway clearance techniques; debridement and wound care; physical agents and mechanical and thermal modalities; electrotherapeutic modalities; and patient-related instruction.

Today's physical therapists play a dynamic, comprehensive role in health care—improving and maintaining the quality of life for millions of Americans. Some of the most surprising and awe-inspiring miracles in medicine happen in the physical therapy room.

SETTINGS, SALARIES, STATISTICS

The diversity of settings in which physical therapists practice reflects the versatility of the physical therapist's knowledge and skills. Most PTs in the United States work in the rehabilitation departments of hospitals; in fact, 90 percent of all hospitals with 100 or more beds provide physical therapy services. Opportunities also exist in nursing homes, schools for children who have physical disabilities, private offices, rehabilitation centers, community health centers, hospices, corporate or industrial health centers, work or occupational environments, sports injury treatment centers, fitness centers, and research centers.

Approximately one in four physical therapists are in private practice. Others are physical therapy educators and consultants to public schools and community and government agencies. In 2002, approximately 137,000 physical therapists held jobs in the United States, most of whom are women.

Median annual salaries in 2002 were approximately $57,330, with the lowest-paid 10 percent earning below $40,200 and the highest-paid 10 percent earning above $86,260. Salaries vary considerably, depending on the type of setting and the sector of the health-care industry. Median annual salaries in different areas of physical therapy were as follows:

- Home health-care services—$62,480
- Offices of other health-care practitioners—$58,510
- Physicians' offices—$57,640
- Nursing care facilities—$57,570
- General and surgical hospitals—$57,200

Advancement in this field can come in the form of elevation to therapy positions of greater responsibility, such as senior therapist or department supervisor, or to administrative positions, such as coordinator of rehabilitation services or facility administrator.

HOW TO BECOME A PHYSICAL THERAPIST

Licensing is required for physical therapists in all fifty states, the District of Columbia, and Puerto Rico. To become licensed, a PT must have a degree or certificate from an accredited physical therapy education program and pass the licensure examination of the state(s) in which he or she intends to practice. To maintain a current license, most states and jurisdictions also require continuing education.

Since January 1, 2002, postbaccalaureate degrees have been required. According to the American Physical Therapy Association (APTA), there were about 203 accredited programs in 2003. Accreditation is handled by the Commission on Accreditation in Physical Therapy Education.

Prerequisites for physical therapist education programs generally include courses in biology, chemistry, physics, pharmacology, mathematics, and the social sciences. A physical therapist curriculum typically includes courses in human anatomy, histology, physiology, neuroanatomy, neuroscience, biomechanics of motion, pathology, human growth and development, manifestations of diseases and trauma, behavioral sciences, applied sciences, tests and measurements, therapeutic exercise and assistive devices, and physical agents. The curriculum will also include supervised clinical experience applying physical therapy theory in a variety of practice settings.

In high school, prospective physical therapy students should take courses in health, biology, chemistry, physics, mathematics, and social studies. There is strong competition for admission to most physical therapy educational programs. A very good grade average in high school and in any post–high school courses is also required. Students may be able to learn what physical therapists do and whether they have the personal qualities necessary to work in this field, by serving as summer or part-time volunteers in a physical therapy practice setting.

Personal qualities and abilities that are important to career-long success and satisfaction as a physical therapist include optimism, tact, manual dexterity, good communication skills, imagination, patience, persistence and compassion, and stamina. Physical therapy can be a long, slow process. The personal rewards of the work are frequently delayed but may eventually be very satisfying.

THE FUTURE

Job growth in this area is expected to be faster than average through the rest of this decade and into 2012. It must be remembered, however, that federal legislation imposing limits on reimbursement for therapy services may affect employment and job openings. In addition, the economy will have a profound effect, as will the policies and practices of third-party payers, such as insurance companies, Medicare, and Medicaid.

Predictions about physical therapy's prospects in the last decade or so have met with some surprises as time went by. In 1995, for example, physical therapy was expected to be one of the "hottest" occupations of the coming decade. A spectacular 52 percent growth was projected between 1995 and 2005, which would have meant almost 50,000 new job openings. As we now know, the employment picture has changed drastically in the health-care fields.

Physical therapists will still find employment, but the positions may not be ideal in terms of setting or location. Economics may have discouraged some prospective students from this profession. Managed care's emphasis on cost containment has been a major factor. Still, with America's elderly population growing, with the bulge of the Baby Boom generation turning sixty-five, and with medical advances expanding treatment opportunities, physical therapy is still expected to be among the faster-growing occupations through 2012.

For more information about physical therapists, contact:

American Physical Therapy Association (APTA)
1111 North Fairfax Street
Alexandria, VA 22314-1488
apta.org

PHYSICAL THERAPIST ASSISTANT

Physical therapist assistants (PTAs) are educated health-care providers who, functioning under the direct supervision of licensed physical therapists, assist in patients' treatment programs. The scope of a PTA's responsibilities is defined by state law, rules, and regulations as well as by the policies of the practice setting in which he or she works. These duties may include training patients in exercises and the activities of daily care, such as dressing, undressing, and moving about; preparing for and carrying out treatments utilizing special equipment; assisting in the carrying out of tests, evaluations, and more complex treatment procedures; observing and reporting patients' progress; and cleaning and preparing the work area for the next activity and/or patient. The PTA also teaches patients how to use and care for orthoses, prostheses, and assistive apparatuses.

SETTINGS, SALARIES, STATISTICS

Physical therapist assistants held approximately 50,000 jobs in the United States in 2002, and nearly three-fourths of these were in hospitals and the offices of physical therapists. PTAs must have an associate's degree and supervised clinical practice.

Median annual income in 2002 was reported at $36,080, with the lowest 10 percent of salaries being below $23,530 and the highest 10 percent of salaries being above $48,910.

HOW TO BECOME A PHYSICAL THERAPY ASSISTANT

In 2002, there were 245 accredited programs in schools in the United States, according to the APTA. The program is a two-year preparation, which includes academic and hands-on experience. Courses include algebra, anatomy, biology, chemistry, physiology, and psychology. Basic first aid and CPR training is also usually required.

Most states license physical therapist assistants; in these states, PTAs must be graduates of accredited associate's degree programs and pass a state examination. The physical therapist assistant educational programs are accredited by the Commission on Accreditation in Physical Therapy Education (CAPTE), and most of them are offered by community colleges.

It is important to note that the career transition from physical therapist assistant to physical therapist may not automatically be an easy one to make. Very little of the assistant education is convertible to therapist course credit, and therapist courses are academically much more complex and difficult. For this reason, it is very important for a person to assess his or her career goals before deciding to embark on the training and education necessary for practice in this field.

THE FUTURE

As with physical therapists, employment for physical therapist assistants is projected to grow faster than the average over the next ten years as more Americans reach retirement age and as new developments in treatment expand opportunities for therapy.

For more information about physical therapist assistants, contact:

American Physical Therapy Association (APTA)
1111 North Fairfax Street
Alexandria, VA 22314-1488
apta.org

CHAPTER 48

PHYSICIAN ASSISTANT (PA)

The physician assistant is a health-care professional who, having successfully completed an accredited program of academic and clinical training, is qualified to work under the supervision of a physician performing certain diagnostic, therapeutic, and preventive activities and services that until the mid-1960s were carried out almost exclusively by physicians themselves. The physician assistant is a dependent practitioner working with the supervision of a doctor of medicine (M.D.) or doctor of osteopathy (D.O.) who is responsible for the PA's performance. Various laws, regulations, and rules specifically define the functions a PA may carry out. These limits have been developed by the medical community and by the various states. The physician assistant is also subject to the limitations established by his or her supervising physician.

Most physician assistants (PAs) have a bachelor's or a master's degree in addition to about two years of study for their particular specialty. Physician assistants are not the same as medical assistants, whose duties are more involved with routine clinical, administrative, and clerical tasks.

The physician assistant can be expected to carry out duties directly with patients, including interviewing patients and taking detailed medical histories; conducting physical examinations; ordering and/or interpreting selected diagnostic studies, such as common laboratory procedures and radiologic studies; making tentative diagnoses; performing certain therapeutic procedures, such as administering injections and immunizations, applying casts, and suturing wounds; following up on patient care; teaching and counseling patients regarding nutrition, disease prevention, and family planning; assisting the physician by conducting rounds and recording patient progress in inpatient settings; and responding to emergencies, from severe drug reactions to psychiatric crises to heart attacks to uncomplicated deliveries—but always under the supervision of a physician.

In most states, the District of Columbia, and Guam, PAs may prescribe medications. PAs also assist in delivering health services to patients requiring continuing care at home, in nursing homes, or in other extended-care facilities.

Professional studies have shown that PAs have the training to care for the needs of approximately eight of every ten types of patients who visit a family physician's office in any one day.

Physician assistants came into being during the 1960s when there was a critical doctor shortage. This shortage was most acute in rural areas and in the low-income areas of the inner cities. (Today, about 20 percent of all Americans live in counties with less than 50,000 people, but only 8 percent of all actively practicing physicians are located in these areas.) Almost everywhere in the nation, primary care physicians—general practitioners, general internists, and general pediatricians—were struggling to deliver medical services to large patient loads. Primary care physicians and their patients particularly felt the crunch because of the nature of the primary care practice.

Primary care physicians are the doctors that patients usually turn to first when they have health concerns. They are very different from the specialists who deal with only one part or system of the body or one particular type of health problem, such as gastroenterologists or gynecologists. Primary care physicians deal with the whole body. They are expected to handle a wide range of medical situations, from treating injuries and illnesses to handling emergencies and emotional problems. The primary care physician traditionally has a heavy workload. Passing through his or her office are patients suffering from everything from the sniffles and minor sprains to serious physiological and emotional disorders.

Until the advent of the physician assistant profession, the primary care physician was the first line of defense in coping with health situations, with referral to a specialist as a subsequent course of action when necessary. Today, in many health-care situations in many states, the PA is the first line of defense. He or she is often the first health professional with whom many

Americans now come in contact when they seek medical attention. But again, in all cases, the supervising physician is ultimately in charge of the patient's care.

During the doctor shortage of the 1960s, nurses were also in short supply because of a pattern of high turnover. Coinciding with this demand for health practitioners was the influx of former medical corps members, trained during the Vietnam War, who were returning to civilian life and seeking employment. Many of them hoped to utilize their military medical training in their new civilian careers. The physician assistant profession developed from the hope that, with additional training, these ex-medics and others with patient-care experience, such as nurses, might be able to fill the health-care gap.

In 1965, at the Duke University Medical Center, the first physician assistant educational program began with a student body consisting of four ex-military corpsmen. In 2002, physician assistants held approximately 63,000 jobs in the United States.

The physician and the physician assistant form a health-care team that offers benefits all around. The diagnostic and therapeutic patient care provided by PAs frees supervising physicians to devote more time to patients with the most serious illnesses. PAs are providing more health care than has ever before been available in rural areas and the inner city. In rural and remote areas, a PA usually keeps in contact with his or her supervising physician via telephone, radio, or beeper, and the doctor visits the rural clinic one or two days a week.

About one-third of all PAs practice in towns of fewer than 50,000 people, and between one-third and one-half practice in cities of more than 500,000. Other traditionally underserved geographical areas are benefiting from the presence of these new health-care practitioners. In many cases, patient waiting times have been reduced, examinations are less hurried, and there is more time for the patient to ask questions and have them answered. Sixty percent of all doctors responding to a recent national survey stated that they felt delegation of certain responsibilities to PAs would increase the quality of health care.

As was hoped when the PA concept was begun, PAs provide strong support to primary care physicians. Most PAs in clinical practice assist physicians who are in primary care practices, such as family and general internal medicine, emergency medicine, pediatrics, and obstetrics and gynecology. PAs also work wherever doctors work, in a full spectrum of specialties— allergy, dermatology, endocrinology, gastroenterology, hematology, psychiatry, public health, physical rehabilitation, radiology, anesthesiology, infectious diseases, geriatrics, preventive medicine, and neurology. In addition, about one-fifth of all PAs work in surgical specialties, including general surgery, orthopedic surgery, thoracic surgery, cardiovascular surgery, urologic surgery, neurosurgery, plastic surgery, otolaryngology, and ophthalmic surgery.

PAs do important and respected work in our society. That work is well remunerated both financially and emotionally. As with other medical paraprofessions, by virtue of the shorter training time, lesser educational preparation, and smaller dollar commitments required, the PA field is attractive to many people who are interested in serving in a medical profession but who are unable or unwilling to attend medical school.

SETTINGS, SALARIES, STATISTICS

Because physician assistants help physicians, they can be found in private practices, comprehensive health clinics, hospitals, satellite clinics, prisons, the military, nursing homes, health maintenance organizations, industrial clinics, student health services, and urban community centers.

A normal workweek for a physician assistant ranges between forty and forty-five hours. Depending on the specific nature of the practice and the duties assumed, a PA can be expected to be on call or to work additional and evening hours. About one-third of all PAs now spend some hours on call per week.

According to the American Academy of Physician Assistants (AAPA), approximately 90 percent of certified PAs were in clinical practice in 2003. Of the approximately 63,000 PAs who held jobs in the United States in 2002, more than half were women.

Salaries for PAs vary because of state, specialty, and practice differences. The median income in 2003 was $72,457, according to the AAPA, with the median income for first-year graduates being approximately $63,437.

HOW TO BECOME A PHYSICIAN ASSISTANT

Requirements for admission to physician assistant educational programs are set by the programs. A minimum of two years of undergraduate study in a science or health profession program is the common prerequisite today. Some work experience in personal health care is preferred. The typical PA student has a bachelor's degree and more than four years of healthcare experience before being accepted into a program. Competition for admission to PA educational programs is strong.

The typical PA educational program is approximately two years long, and the curriculum is broken into two segments. The first segment requires students to complete classroom studies covering anatomy, physiology, biochemistry, clinical laboratory sciences, pharmacology, microbiology, pathology, physical diagnosis, pathophysiology, differential diagnosis, medical ethics, and behavioral sciences.

The second segment includes more than 2,000 hours of working closely with physicians to treat patients in settings such as teaching and community hospitals, rural clinics, long-term care facilities, and physicians' offices. These clinical rotations cover a wide variety of medical specialties, including family medicine, internal medicine, surgery, pediatrics, psychiatry, emergency medicine, geriatrics, and obstetrics and gynecology.

In recent years, as the physician assistant concept and physician assistant programs have become more accepted and popular, a number of postgraduate PA programs have been developed. These include fellowships and residencies, and they provide additional clinical experience in such areas as emergency medicine, surgery, and neonatology—the care of newborns.

Among the personal qualities important to success in this very people-oriented occupation are intelligence, compassion, patience, and the capacity for calm and good judgment when confronted with emergency situations. The willingness to carry out instructions and the ability to work with others are essential.

In all states, PAs must be certified by the National Commission on Certification of Physician Assistants (NCCPA). To become certified, a PA must pass the Physician Assistant National Certification Examination, developed jointly by the NCCPA and the National Board of Medical Examiners. This day-long examination is administered nationwide. To take the certifying examination, a student must graduate from a physician assistant program that is accredited by the Commission on Accreditation of Allied Health Education Programs (CAAHEP), which in 1994 succeeded the Committee on Allied Health Education and Accreditation (CAHEA) of the American Medical Association and which accredits education programs for many allied health professions. Candidates who successfully satisfy the certification requirements may use the title physician assistant–certified or the designation PA-C after their names. To maintain certification, a PA must complete 100 continuing medical education credits every two years and retake the national certification exam every six years.

State licensure requirements include proof of graduation from an accredited educational program, proof of NCCPA certification, and letters of reference.

THE FUTURE

The employment outlook for PAs is excellent. The validity and effectiveness of PAs' contributions to health care have been clearly demonstrated, and patient acceptance of this health profession has been growing. PAs did, in fact, help to alleviate the strains on both physicians and patients created by the doctor shortage, and they have succeeded as well in providing more health care and health education than ever before.

This profession has grown very quickly. In 1970, there were fewer than 100 PAs nationwide. As of 2003, there were approximately 63,000, and they are practicing in every state, the District of Columbia, and several foreign countries. Most certified PAs have several employment offers from which to choose. Securing a satisfactory position sometimes requires relocating to a medically underserved area, but a large percentage of PA students have expressed a preference for a small-town setting.

One long-standing barrier to major expansion in this field fell in the mid-1980s. While almost every study has shown that the use of PAs lowers medical costs without compromising medical care—not an insignificant factor considering the staggering medical bills that the United States annually rings up—until recently this advantage was largely lost because most health insurance plans, including Medicare and Medicaid, would not provide reimbursement for treatment performed solely by a PA. Today, reimbursement by third-party payers exists for many patients, and physicians can bill Medicare for services provided to their hospital and nursing-home patients by their PAs. This change in Medicare policy has spurred the increased use of PAs by office-based physicians.

Opportunities have also opened up in hospitals and health maintenance organizations. These attitudinal and economic changes, set against a backdrop of an aging population needing more health care, may create a job situation where the demand for PAs outstrips the supply. The U.S. Department of Labor expects a faster-than-average growth rate in this profession through 2012.

For more information on physician assistants, contact:

American Academy of Physician Assistants (AAPA)
950 North Washington Street
Alexandria, VA 22314-1552
aapa.org

The academy's book, *Physician Assistant Programs Directory*, gives listings of accredited educational programs and information about application and financial aid.

National Commission on Certification of Physician Assistants (NCCPA)
6849-B Peachtree Dunwoody Road
Atlanta, GA 30328
nccpa.net

CHAPTER 49

PULMONARY FUNCTION TECHNOLOGIST

Also Known as Pulmonary Technologist, Pulmonary Function Technician, Pulmonary Physiology Technologist, and Cardiopulmonary Technologist

Pulmonary function technologists conduct diagnostic evaluations of lung conditions, at the direction and under the supervision of a physician.

Pulmonary means "pertaining to the lungs," and pulmonary disease includes lung cancer, emphysema, asthma, and environmental damage. Pulmonary disease is a leading cause of death and disability in America today. The use of new and sophisticated medical instruments to screen for medical problems related to pulmonary function has become an integral part of modem preventive medicine and comprehensive health care. Operating these machines and evaluating the diagnostic data they produce are specially trained, credentialed, and recognized allied health professionals called pulmonary function technologists. The support service that they perform is called pulmonary technology.

Working under the supervision of a physician, a pulmonary function technologist conducts diagnostic evaluations of normal and abnormal pulmonary parameters by administering a variety of tests to the patient. These tests include spirometry, lung volume studies, gas diffusion studies, arterial blood gas studies, bronchial challenge, and exercise studies. Microprocessor-assisted gas analyzers and other devices are used by the technologist to measure various aspects of the patient's lung function. Some of these tests are invasive, others are noninvasive. Some use video apparatus, scans, and computerized interpretation.

The cardiovascular—heart and arterial—and pulmonary systems are closely related in the human body, and the functions of a pulmonary function technologist often overlap with or call upon the functions of another health-care professional, the cardiovascular technologist (see Chapter 7). In pulmonary exercise testing, for example, an electrocardiograph monitor is used to observe the patient's heart activity while his or her lung function is being studied. Other tests call for the administering of certain medications that help in evaluating the patient's pulmonary status.

The pulmonary function technologist is responsible for selecting, setting up, maintaining, and calibrating the various testing devices; explaining the procedure to the patient and eliciting his or her cooperation; carrying out the test; supervising other personnel who are assisting; monitoring the patient's response; calculating the test results and evaluating their reliability; and evaluating the patient's performance and its clinical implications. From the data gathered from these various tests, a picture of the patient's pulmonary health emerges. Using this picture, the physician can make a diagnosis and determine a course of treatment.

SETTINGS, SALARIES, STATISTICS

The work setting for pulmonary function technologists is usually in a hospital, but some jobs are in clinics, private practice offices, home-care facilities, environmental institutions, diagnostic centers, rehabilitation centers, mobile units, research facilities, and government facilities. As with many other health-care professions, moderate exposure to infectious diseases exists.

Work hours are usually a standard of forty hours a week. Longer hours can be expected at peak emergency times, such as a severe flu season, and some jobs may occasionally require irregular hours.

Salaries depend on the level of training, the location, and the type of facility in which the specialist works. A range of from $27,000 to $40,000 can be expected. The national average salary for a pulmonary function technologist was approximately $32,860 annually.

HOW TO BECOME A PULMONARY FUNCTION TECHNOLOGIST

A nursing background or a background as a respiratory therapist is often the preliminary stage of a pulmonary function technologist's career. Many people go into pulmonary function technology through respiratory therapy, adding on-the-job training in pulmonary function therapy to the formal education and experience they have acquired in respiratory therapy (see Chapter 53). Therefore, prerequisite to this specialized training is often the successful completion of one of the approximately 360 respiratory therapy educational programs accredited by the Commission on Accreditation of Allied Health Education Programs (CAAHEP), which typically are two years in length and award an associate's degree or certificate.

Currently 48 states require pulmonary function technologists to be licensed in respiratory care. All states that require licensure accept the National Board of Respiratory Care (NBRC) certification and registry credentials. Certification is the entry level; registration is the advanced level. Even if a particular state does not require licensure, a particular hospital in that state may require technologists to pass the NBRC certification examination. The credentials in this profession are CPFT (certified pulmonary function technologist), and the more advanced RPFT (registered pulmonary function technologist). Since its inception, the NBRC has issued credentials to more than 150,000 individuals.

Personal qualities important for this field include mathematical and analytical aptitude, precision, dexterity, dependability, and good communication skills.

THE FUTURE

The U.S. Bureau of Labor Statistics has said that jobs in this field are expected to grow faster than the average through the year 2010. A shortage of trained, qualified personnel currently exists. As more hospitals and other health-care institutions establish cardiopulmonary laboratories, the demand should grow for these specialists.

For more information about pulmonary function technologists, contact:

American Association for Respiratory Care
11030 Ables Lane
Dallas, TX 75229
aarc.org

For certification information, contact:

National Board for Respiratory Care (NBRC)
8310 Nieman Road
Lenexa, KS 66214
nbrc.org

CHAPTER

50

RADIATION THERAPIST

Radiation therapists treat patients with radiation therapy. They use high-energy x-rays, gamma rays, electron beams, and other forms of radiation in the treatment of diseases, especially certain forms of cancer. They work in coordination with radiologists and at the direction of a physician, usually an oncologist—a medical doctor who specializes in the treatment of cancer.

Radiation therapy is one of the most sophisticated tools of modern medicine. Radiation can kill cells, but it is indiscriminate, killing normal as well as abnormal cells. Radiation therapy uses careful and controlled application of radiation to cancerous cells while shielding the adjacent normal cells from exposure and possible damage. Radiation is directed to the patient's malignant tumor for just a few seconds from the outside, through the skin and other tissues overlying the tumor.

Because of the potential for damage to normal cells, the exact location of the tumor must be pinpointed. Physical examinations and diagnostic x-rays as well as computed tomography (CT scans), magnetic resonance imaging (MRI), ultrasound, and the use of radioisotopes may be required to determine its exact position and dimensions. The frequency of the treatments, duration of the therapy, dosages, and the type of radiation therapy must be carefully planned and the treatment skillfully administered. Depending on the nature and extent of the cancer, radiation therapy treatment—used alone or in combination with chemotherapy and/or surgery—can ease the pain caused by this disease, prolong life, and, in a growing number of cases, bring about a permanent cure.

In most hospitals, a team of health-care professionals plans and carries out radiation therapy. The radiation oncologist is a physician who has specialized training in the use of radiation; he or she evaluates the patient and writes the radiation therapy prescription and instructions for its administration. The radiation physicist has extensive experience in planning radiation treatments as well as in calibrating and maintaining the equipment. The dosimetrist is an expert in designing specialized treatment plans for each patient. Computers are used to produce the elaborate plan necessary for a course of treatment. The radiation therapy nurse is trained to care for the cancer patient as he or she undergoes and recuperates from therapy.

Using sophisticated therapeutic equipment, such as high-energy linear accelerators and x-ray machines, the radiation therapist exposes specific areas of the body to the prescribed doses of ionizing radiation, accurately delivering, with a minimum of supervision, the planned course of radiotherapy. The therapist checks the physician's prescription, helps the radiation physicist to calibrate and prepare the equipment, assists in tumor localization and dosimetric procedures, helps to maintain the equipment so that it will function effectively and safely, and assists in the preparation and handling of the various radioactive materials used in the procedures.

In addition, the radiation therapist observes the clinical progress of the patient undergoing radiotherapy; watches for any signs of complications; keeps accurate, detailed records of the specifics of the treatment administered and the patient's reactions to that treatment; provides psychological support to the patient and family at what can be a very stressful time; applies surgical dressings as required; assists in minor surgical procedures related to the therapy; and cares for any surgical instruments used, following the principles of aseptic technique. And because radiation can have dangerous effects on the patient and the user when mishandled, the radiation therapist carries out all of these duties while strictly adhering to the principles of radiation protection. Lead blocks are used to "shape" the treatment field and protect adjacent tissues and the controls on the machinery are carefully maintained and used so that only the specific area is exposed and only the designated amount of radiation is administered. The radiation therapist knows how to detect any defects in the equipment that might become a radiation hazard and what steps to take should a radiation accident occur.

Radiation therapists do very important, responsible, exacting work. They routinely deal with patients who are experiencing pain and anxiety, and the treatment they provide offers hope, relief from pain, and, for many millions of these patients, a cure.

SETTINGS, SALARIES, STATISTICS

The work setting for most radiation therapists is in the radiology department of hospitals. Radiation therapists also work in clinics, in research laboratories, in veterinary clinics, in commercial sales applications, for government agencies, and in education and management settings. There are approximately 12,000 radiation therapists in jobs in the United States.

The Mayo Clinic College of Medicine reported in 2004 that starting salaries for radiation therapists were between $40,000 and $50,000, depending on the employer and the location. Additional sources report that an experienced radiation therapist can earn between $45,000 and $100,000, depending upon the therapist's specialization, experience, responsibilities, location, and employer. Salaries are significantly higher on the West Coast.

HOW TO BECOME A RADIATION THERAPIST

Four educational routes to a career in radiation therapy are possible, but they vary in level of preparation. There are one-year, hospital-based certificate or diploma programs; two-year, hospital-based certificate programs; two-year associate's degree programs; and baccalaureate degree programs. Within each of these options, specific prerequisites and program lengths vary. Each of these options is sufficient for employment, but in a competitive job market, the better prepared candidates will be preferred. Administrators, instructors, and researchers often obtain their bachelor's degrees and then go on to graduate study.

The Joint Review Committee on Education in Radiologic Technology (JRCERT), an independent accrediting agency for radiation therapists and radiographers that is recognized by the U.S. Department of Education, currently accredits educational programs for radiation therapy technologists. Accredited programs are offered by hospitals, universities, four-year colleges, and community colleges throughout the country. Several institutions offer more than one program. The one-year, hospital-based certificate programs are open only to graduates of accredited radiography programs and, in some cases, to registered nurses and students holding bachelor's degrees in certain areas or specialties. The two-year, hospital-based certificate programs usually require only a high school diploma or its equivalent. In high school, courses in the basic sciences and mathematics are strongly advised. Two-year associate's degree programs also typically require a high school diploma, and eleven programs offer a bachelor of science degree. The bachelor's degree programs vary somewhat in length and requirements, but all entail a minimum of approximately four years of post–high school education.

The professional curriculum typically includes courses in medical ethics and law, methods of patient care and health education, medical terminology, human structure and function, pathology, clinical radiation oncology, radiobiology, mathematics, radiation physics, radiation protection, technical radiation oncology, medical imaging, brachytherapy, quality assurance, computers, introduction to hyperthermia and venipuncture, and clinical dosimetry.

Personal qualities that are important to success and satisfaction as a radiation therapist include a genuine desire and willingness to help others, compassion, a mechanical inclination, aptitude in math, aptitude in the physical sciences, and attention to detail.

Almost all employers today require their radiation therapists to be certified by the American Registry of Radiologic Technologists (ARRT). To be certified, a candidate must be a graduate of an accredited radiation therapy educational program and must pass a four-hour competency examination.

The certification examination is a computer-based test offered throughout the year at numerous locations throughout the United States. Graduates of accredited programs who pass the ARRT examination and are of good moral character may call themselves registered radiation therapists and use the letters RT(T)(ARRT), for registered technologist in therapy certified by the American Registry of Radiologic Technologists, after their names.

At this time, most states require radiation therapists to be licensed. Other states are currently considering adopting licensure. In some of these states, certification by the ARRT is accepted in lieu of satisfactory completion of the state's licensure examination.

THE FUTURE

The American Society of Radiologic Technologists (ASRT), which is the professional association for radiation therapists, radiographers, nuclear medicine technologists, and sonographers, estimates that there are several thousand more openings than there are therapists. Cost-containment efforts have resulted in the closing of many academic departments. Radiation therapy programs are by nature expensive to operate. The high cost of the sophisticated equipment and the clinical aspect of the education, plus the small class sizes—ten to twelve students per year—of these programs, have resulted in these closings.

The strong demand for radiation therapists should continue, further spurred by such factors as a growing American population, longer life spans, the growing number of older Americans, and the widening application of new radiological technologies to an expanding range of conditions. The U.S. Department of Labor projects a steady increase in the number of job openings in this profession through 2012.

For more information about radiation therapists, contact:

American Society of Radiologic Technologists (ASRT)
15000 Central Avenue SE
Albuquerque, NM 87123-3917
asrt.org

American Registry of Radiologic Technologists (ARRT)
1255 Northland Drive
St. Paul, MN 55120-1155
arrt.org

For information about accredited educational programs, contact:

Joint Review Committee on Educational Programs in Radiation Therapy
    (JRCERT)
20 North Wacker Drive, Suite 900
Chicago, IL 60606-2901
jrcert.org

RADIOGRAPHER

Also Known as Radiology
Technologist and X-Ray
Technologist

Radiographers, formerly called x-ray technologists, use radiation to perform examinations. Unlike radiation therapists, their primary role is to use x-rays and other radiographic technology, such as computed tomography (CT scans) and magnetic resonance imaging (MRI), to produce radiographic images for use in patient diagnoses.

Radiography is the use of radiation to provide images of various body parts, such as bones, organs, tissues, and vessels, and of various body functions, such as digestion, circulation, and the action of the heart's valves, to facilitate the diagnosis and, in some cases, the treatment of certain injuries and illnesses. These images are recorded on sheets of film—the black-and-white translucent images with which most of us are familiar—videotape, or motion picture film, or they are displayed on a video monitor.

Radiography is an invaluable diagnostic tool that is used by almost every medical specialty. Using radiography, fractures and other orthopedic problems, tumors, ulcers, deposits and foreign matter in the body, and diseased and malfunctioning organs and vessels can be uncovered and assessed without having to perform surgery on the patient.

More than 200 million medical diagnostic x-rays and other radiologic examinations are performed in the United States each year. Chest x-rays continue to be the most common, accounting for 50 percent of all x-rays. Approximately 70 percent of all Americans have radiologic examinations of one kind or another each year. When a physician must know what is happening inside a patient's body, he or she orders x-rays or one of their sophisticated cousins—computed tomography (CT scans), mammography, and digital subtraction angiography.

Perhaps the most revolutionary breakthrough in this profession has been magnetic resonance imaging. This imaging modality uses magnetic impulses instead of radiation; among other things, it allows a physician to observe the course of a disease at the cellular level. Using MRI, the physician is able to see and evaluate the effect a therapeutic drug has on a diseased cell so that he or she can modify or eliminate the therapy accordingly. As these new technologies make visible conditions in the body that until recently were inaccessible, earlier and better diagnoses are becoming possible, often with less discomfort, inconvenience, and cost to the patient, and new perspectives on the body and its workings are opening up.

When radiographic examinations are ordered by a physician, radiographers are primarily responsible for the operation of the radiologic equipment and for the preparation of the patient. The radiographer positions the patient, adjusts the equipment to the correct setting for the particular examination, administers any chemical tracing mixtures that are needed (to make an organ or other body part visible for radiological examination, liquids are often swallowed by or injected into the patient), and makes the required number of radiographs, all the while adhering to the principles of radiation safety so as to protect the patient, him- or herself, and others.

If used by persons uneducated in its characteristics and potential hazards, radiation can be dangerous to the patient and to the user. The trained radiographer understands radiation and can carefully position the part of the body being imaged, protect other body parts with lead aprons and other coverings, and use only the amount of radiation necessary to produce a quality image.

A radiographer can also be expected to maintain the equipment, process the film, and keep patient records as well as recognize emergency patient conditions and initiate lifesaving measures.

SETTINGS, SALARIES, STATISTICS

Most radiographers work in the radiology departments of hospitals and, when necessary, bring mobile equipment to the patient's bedside or into the operating room.

Radiographers also work in clinics, in private offices, in industrial and experimental laboratories, in commercial sales and applications, and on the teaching staffs of hospitals, colleges, and universities. About 5 percent of all radiographers are employed by the federal government, primarily in the Department of Veterans Affairs.

Radiographers usually work forty hours per week, some of which may be weekend or evening hours. Radiographers are sometimes expected to be on call. Part-time opportunities exist, particularly in clinics and physicians' offices.

According to the Mayo Clinic College of Medicine, in 2004, there were more than 180,000 radiographers in the United States. This was down from an estimated 200,000 just five years before. The drop was due to cost-cutting measures in the health-care and health insurance industries and to the economic downturn in general. In addition, large numbers of laid-off workers who lost their health insurance often went without medical care.

As of 2004, the starting salary for a radiographer was approximately $30,000 to $35,000 a year, nationwide. At large hospitals, however, it was higher, reported at $40,000.

This career offers a great deal of mobility and flexibility. Radiologists are needed in all fifty states. With additional educational preparation, a radiologist can build his or her career upward to a number of related, higher-level jobs. These may include such positions as senior radiographer, ultrasonographer (see Chapter 15), diagnostic supervisor, cardiac echo technologist (see related information in Chapter 7), and nuclear medicine supervisor (see related information in Chapter 33), to name just a few.

HOW TO BECOME A RADIOGRAPHER

There are several routes to a career as a radiographer. All begin with a minimum of a high school diploma or its equivalent. In high school, courses in physics, chemistry, biology, algebra, and geometry are strongly recommended. Almost all radiography students receive their education at institutions offering programs accredited by the Joint Review Committee on Education in Radiologic Technology (JRCERT), an independent accrediting agency for radiographers and radiation therapists that is recognized by the U.S. Department of Education. At this time, most of the JRCERT-accredited educational programs for radiographers are offered by hospitals and clinics. Radiographer educational programs are also located in junior and community colleges, vocational/technical schools, medical schools, four-year colleges and universities, and the military.

Accredited programs vary in specific requirements, length, and the credentials awarded upon successful completion. Of the baccalaureate programs, several offer a specific bachelor of science in radiologic technology degree, or B.S.R.T. Some of the institutions offer more than one of these educational options for radiography students. Certain degree programs require one or two years of college credit. All three levels of educational preparation are sufficient for employment as a radiographer. Educators and administrators in this profession, however, usually have their bachelor's or master's degrees.

The education for radiographers is rigorous and entails classroom study, laboratory work, and clinical experience. The professional curriculum for an accredited program includes introduction to radiography, ethics in the radiological sciences, introductory law in the radiological sciences, medical terminology, radiologic science patient care, human structure and function, radiographic procedures, medical imaging and processing, imaging equipment, evaluation of radiographs, radiation physics, radiation protection, radiation biology, radiographic pathology, introduction to quality improvement, computers in radiologic science, and pharmacology and drug administration.

Most institutions consider certification a requirement of employment. Only graduates of accredited programs are eligible to take the American Registry of Radiologic Technologists' (ARRT) certification examination. This is a computer-based test offered throughout the year at various locations throughout the country. Passing this examination entitles a radiographer to use the credential RT(R)(ARRT), for registered technologist in radiography certified by the American Registry of Radiologic Technologists, after his or her name. Certification is recognized in all fifty states. The ARRT also offers advanced qualification examinations in cardiovascular-interventional technology, mammography, computed tomography, magnetic resonance, and quality management.

Personal qualities that are important to the successful and satisfying execution of this job include physical and mental stamina, intelligence, compassion, emotional stability, good overall health, strong attention to detail and accuracy, and the ability to communicate well. A radiographer must also have a genuine interest in helping people with all kinds of medical conditions.

Employment opportunities in radiography are expected to grow in the coming decade. One factor influencing this growth is the spreading use of new x-ray and related equipment in diagnosing and treating an ever-expanding range of health conditions. Another factor affecting this growth is the American population growing larger and older and, therefore, demanding more medical care.

It should also be noted that over the last decade, the number of accredited educational programs available in this profession has declined. The high cost of providing an education—including expensive equipment and clinical experience—in this field is causing some programs to close.

Nevertheless, the ARRT reports more than 235,000 registrants and, in 2004, their postprimary examination volume was up more than 8 percent over 2003.

For more information about a career in radiography, contact:

American Society of Radiologic Technologists (ASRT)
15000 Central Avenue SE
Albuquerque, NM 87123-3917
asrt.org

For information about certification, contact:

American Registry of Radiologic Technologists (ARRT)
1255 Northland Drive
St. Paul, MN 55120-1155
arrt.org

For information about accredited programs, contact:

Joint Review Committee on Education in Radiologic Technology
    (JRCERT)
20 North Wacker Drive, Suite 900
Chicago, IL 60606-2901
jcert.org

REHABILITATION COUNSELOR

Also Known as Vocational Rehabilitation Counselor, Including Psychiatric Rehabilitation Counselor and Vocational Rehabilitation Therapist

Rehabilitation counselors are experts at putting men and women whose lives have been sidetracked by physical and/or mental disabilities back on track as functioning, working members of society. Where a medical doctor rehabilitates a patient with treatment, medication, or surgery, a rehabilitation counselor restores a patient to functioning life with personalized counseling, emotional support, and instructional therapy that typically entails learning useful work activities.

Disability can take many forms. Patients include men and women with psychiatric or mental disabilities who have histories of institutionalization; workers disabled by disease or accident who, as a result, can no longer perform their old jobs; veterans; and individuals recovering from alcohol and drug abuse.

As soon as the injury or illness is stabilized, the patient is referred to the rehabilitation counselor, who observes the patient and tests his or her motor ability, skill level, interests, and psychological makeup. Hundreds of different batteries of tests are available for these purposes, and the counselor is educated to know which tests are most appropriate for particular patients. Sometimes new interests and talents are uncovered in the process.

Over a period of several months, the counselor develops a profile of the patient, especially noting how the patient adapts to the disability. The counselor looks at the "whole person" and learns about what the patient's life was like prior to the disabling trauma. The rehabilitation counselor consults with the patient's family, physicians, psychologists, and other therapists. Then, using all of this information, the counselor formulates a rehabilitation plan.

Sometimes this program entails retraining the patient in a new vocation. For individuals who have physical and/or mental disabilities and who have never worked, rehabilitation may entail learning vocational and social skills that are necessary to function in a work setting. Training typically takes place in a sheltered workshop, where the trainee may learn a new occupation and test his or her new abilities and social skills in a controlled, noncompetitive environment. When the training is completed, for many patients a job in the community, which is often arranged by the rehabilitation counselor, is possible.

Psychiatric rehabilitation counselors specialize in helping psychiatric patients prepare for greater participation in the community. They also help the community prepare for the rehabilitated patient. Psychiatric rehabilitation counselors test and evaluate psychiatric patients, and, on the basis of the results, they teach the patient how to perform suitable, productive activities that can be used in the marketplace. Patients who have been institutionalized for many years are often out of touch with society and can easily be frightened by the daily demands of life in a noninstitutional, nonstructured setting.

Years of psychological progress can quickly unravel if the patient is unprepared to reenter the community. The psychiatric rehabilitation counselor acts as the patient's supervisor, helping him or her to adjust gradually. Patients are slowly eased from the institutional setting to a less-protected, dormitory setting. The patient's new skills are gradually put to use in an actual work situation—perhaps first in a sheltered work setting and then in private industry. Counselors teach the patient the rules of society and offer practical lessons in how to handle money, use public transportation, and complete other everyday tasks required to function in the community.

Simultaneously, the psychiatric rehabilitation counselor works to educate the community about rehabilitated psychiatric patients. To dispel any misconceptions, calm any fears, and counter any prejudices that might exist regarding former psychiatric patients, the counselor may conduct community meetings and send out educational literature in the community in which the patient will be living and working. The counselor also works with local and national companies, educating them about the productivity and societal benefits of hiring men and women with physical and psychological disabilities who have been rehabilitated.

After the patient is placed in a vocation, either in the community or in a long-term sheltered situation, the rehabilitation counselor provides follow-up counseling and support.

Manual arts therapy programs, which formally began at the end of World War II in response to the large number of returning soldiers who needed rehabilitation, are important providers of vocational rehabilitation counseling. In addition to the traditional manual arts vocations, such as woodworking, photography, appliance repair, graphic arts, welding, sheet metal work, drafting, gardening, automobile repair, and jewelry making, other skills, such as clerical work, accounting, and general office skills, are often introduced in these rehabilitation programs. Manual arts therapy is also known as industrial therapy, industrial arts therapy, industrial rehabilitation therapy, compensated work therapy, incentive therapy, sheltered workshop programs, and vocational rehabilitation therapy.

There is no set list of functions that rehabilitation patients are taught. The goal of rehabilitation counseling is to work with each specific patient's mental and physical abilities, interests, education, and experiences and then to tailor the training program to meet the needs of the whole person.

Education therapists also take part in the nonmedical assessment and rehabilitation of individuals who are disabled. They use educational activities, such as typing, shorthand, computer skills, bookkeeping, painting, and the study of mathematics, science, and English, to evaluate and treat patients. In educational therapy, mastering the subject matter is not as important as mastering one's emotions. Acquiring knowledge of the course work is subordinate to acquiring a growing knowledge of one's own potential. Rehabilitation therapy is the "umbrella" profession in nonmedical rehabilitation, providing counseling, vocational assessment, psychiatric assessment, and job placement in all the areas of rehabilitation.

SETTINGS, SALARIES, STATISTICS

Rehabilitation counselors work in rehabilitation centers; in mental hospitals; in federal, state, and local government agencies; in private agencies; and in public schools where they counsel troubled and disabled youths.

Rehabilitation counselors' salaries vary depending on their experience, education, agency, and function. Rehabilitation counselors start between $16,000 and $32,000 per year, and the average salary is estimated at more than $30,000 per year, according to the *Health Career and Education Directory, 2004–2005 Edition*. Generally, private, nonprofit agencies pay the least, and private, for-profit agencies pay the most. Government salaries for rehabilitation counselors fall in between. Across the board, salaries tend to be higher on the East and West coasts than elsewhere in the United States. Starting salaries as high as $40,000 per year have been reported for master's degree holders working for private, for-profit agencies in southern California.

HOW TO BECOME A REHABILITATION COUNSELOR

The minimum educational requirement for most entry-level rehabilitation counseling jobs is a bachelor's degree. Many rehabilitation counselors go on to obtain their master's degree, which entails eighteen months to two years of additional study, or their doctorate degree, which entails four to six years of postgraduate study. Gradually, the master's degree is becoming the minimum standard preferred by most employers, and the National Rehabilitation Counseling Association (NRCA) encourages counselors to pursue the master's degree. Rehabilitation counseling students study psychiatric rehabilitation problems, techniques of counseling, vocational guidance, testing and statistics, public relations, public speaking, community resources, and occupational and medical subjects.

Certification in this field, although voluntary, is an important and respected indication of proficiency. Certification is offered by the Commission on Rehabilitation Counselor Certification (CRCC). There are several combinations of education and experience that qualify a counselor to sit for the CRCC competency examination. The first option requires candidates to hold a master's degree in rehabilitation counseling from an educational program that is accredited by the Commission on Rehabilitation Education (CORE) and to complete 600 semester hours of internship under the supervision of a certified rehabilitation counselor. The second option requires a candidate holding a master's degree from a rehabilitation education program not accredited by CORE to accumulate 600 semester hours of supervised, on-site internship plus twelve months of acceptable employment is this field. The third option is for holders of master's degrees in rehabilitation counseling from nonaccredited educational programs that have no internship semesters. These candidates for the examination must have two years of work experience, one of which has been appropriately supervised.

In addition, there are certification options for doctorate holders. These options similarly call for additional course work, internship, and/or acceptable employment experience, as needed, to supplement the doctorate.

CORE accredits the educational programs for rehabilitation counselors. Students who satisfy the eligibility requirements may sit for the CRCC examination; those who pass the examination are designated certified rehabilitation counselors and may use the letters CRC after their names. CORE also offers specific certification for rehabilitation counselors who have the education, experience, and other requirements to be case managers—the formal designation is certified case manager, or CCM—and for rehab counselors who are specially educated and experienced in substance abuse counseling—the formal designation is certified rehabilitation counselor in substance abuse counseling, or CRCSAC.

Almost all of the states, plus the District of Columbia, require some form of licensing for rehabilitation counselors. Requirements vary from state to state, and the trend toward licensure is strong.

Qualifications for a successful career in rehabilitation counseling include the personal qualities of empathy, clear thinking, good mental and physical health and energy, patience, impeccable honesty, sincerity, good listening skills, good observing skills, warmth, and imagination as well as a genuine interest in people and the willingness to help them.

THE FUTURE

At present, the employment outlook for rehabilitation counselors is good. The current supply of counselors is not adequate to meet the needs of the disabled, and as rehabilitation services expand, this shortage will intensify. In addition, the ranks of returning veterans from the Afghanistan and Iraq war areas will require increasing services. Opportunities in this profession should grow about as fast as average through 2012.

Some experts in this field see state licensing as a step toward the assumption of ever-greater responsibilities for rehabilitation counselors. Because of cost-containment efforts by insurance companies and other third-party payers of health-care expenses, under some health-care reform proposals, rehabilitation counselors would eventually do some of the work of doctorate-level psychologists and master's-level social workers.

Although the employment outlook is favorable for most rehabilitation counselors, for two professions under this umbrella—educational therapy and manual arts therapy—the future is questionable. Those who are especially interested in one of these areas should monitor the job market closely and stay in touch with the professional associations on an ongoing basis to keep current on the changes occurring in the field. The very effective and valid work performed by educational therapists is still being carried out in Veterans Administration and other public and private hospitals, residential facilities, schools, adult learning centers, and prisons, but the specific job title is slowly disappearing. The educational therapist's functions are gradually being absorbed by other related rehabilitation professionals—psychologists, occupational therapists, and vocational rehabilitation therapists, from substance abuse therapist to manual arts therapist to case manager. The specific personnel at work in a given setting is usually in direct response to the needs of the community being served.

The fate of manual arts therapy as a specific rehabilitation profession is also clouded. Manual arts therapists have also seen their ranks dwindle. As the first generations of manual arts therapists, the oldest of whom were educated and trained to help the soldiers returning from World War II, retire, they are not being replaced. As with educational therapists, many of the therapeutic modalities once exclusive to this profession gradually have been adopted and assumed by other rehabilitation personnel, including vocational rehabilitation therapists. In the case of manual arts therapy, there is an additional limiting factor, and it is perhaps best described as "generational." It appears that perhaps the hands-on manual arts are not as relevant to younger patients as they were in the 1940s to 1960s. In settings serving older populations, the demand for manual arts therapists is still solid, but in other settings, these programs are often being phased out. However, innovations such as the introduction of computers to the manual arts—for drafting, woodworking, and even for self-evaluation—may renew interest in this specialty, and the emphasis on preventive medicine and wellness may result in a positive reassessment of the very important work of the manual arts therapist.

For more information about rehabilitation counselors, contact:

National Rehabilitation Counseling Association (NRCA)
8807 Sudley Road, Suite 102
Manassas, VA 20110-4719
nrca.org

Commission on Rehabilitation Counselor Certification (CRCC)
1835 Rohlwing Road, Suite E
Rolling Meadows, IL 60008
crccertification.com

American Rehabilitation Counseling Association (ACA)
5999 Stevenson Avenue
Alexandria, VA 22304
counseling.org

International Association of Rehabilitation Professionals in the Private
    Sector (IARPPS)
P.O. Box 697
Brookline, MA 02146
narpps.org

RESPIRATORY THERAPIST

Also Known as
Respiratory Therapy Practitioners

Respiratory therapists care for patients with breathing or cardiopulmonary—heart-lung—problems. Respiratory therapy is the diagnostic evaluation, emergency, and long-term treatment of patients suffering from cardiorespiratory abnormalities and deficiencies, such as chronic asthma, pneumonia, bronchitis, emphysema, and breathing difficulties resulting from heart failure, drowning, drug poisoning, severe allergic reactions, stroke, shock, surgery, and head and chest injuries.

Respiratory therapists are the health-care specialists who, working under the supervision of a physician, perform the tests that aid in the diagnosis and evaluation of these respiratory problems. They treat patients with the respiratory apparatus, administer the various respiratory therapies, monitor patients' progress, teach patients how to use the prescribed respiratory treatment methods and aids, and provide emergency respiratory care. In some hospitals, respiratory personnel routinely visit surgical patients prior to their operations to teach them certain breathing exercises that can reduce the incidence of postoperative respiratory complications. Respiratory therapists are also responsible for the maintenance of the respiratory equipment.

Respiratory therapists use such specialized equipment as mechanical ventilators, resuscitators, heart monitors, and blood-gas analyzers and such respiratory treatments as intermittent positive pressure breathing (IPPB), humidity/aerosol therapy, medical gas administration, bronchopulmonary drainage, continuous ventilation, and airway management. Respiratory therapy also includes pulmonary function testing, cardiorespiratory rehabilitation, infection control, and cardiorespiratory drug administration.

Respiratory therapy patients range in age from very premature babies with underdeveloped lungs who are experiencing respiratory distress to the very old who are suffering from the cumulative effects of chronic lung disease. Respiratory therapists play a crucial role. If a patient stops breathing and his or her brain is deprived of oxygen for longer than three to five minutes, serious brain damage will almost certainly follow. If oxygen is cut off for more than nine minutes, death usually results. Respiratory therapists are among the first medical specialists on the scene in emergencies where head injuries or drug poisoning threaten respiration.

Performing emergency resuscitation accounts for only a small part of the respiratory therapist's functions. Respiratory therapy is mostly used to improve the quality of life of patients with chronic lung ailments. It can prevent or postpone certain complications as well as allow patients with respiratory conditions to feel better and function better longer.

Respiratory therapists' educations include courses in anatomy, physiology, pharmacology, and clinical medicine, which prepare them to exercise independent clinical judgment and to accept responsibility in performing therapeutic procedures based on their own observations of the patient. An experienced respiratory therapist is capable of serving as a technical resource person to the physician and other members of the hospital staff with regard to current practices and procedures in respiratory care. Some respiratory therapists also conduct research.

Until recently, respiratory workers were divided into three types: (1) respiratory therapists, (2) respiratory therapy technicians, and (3) respiratory therapy aides. Respiratory therapists and respiratory therapy technicians carried out many of the same functions, although therapists had more in-depth education and training and were expected to carry out more complicated respiratory procedures. Respiratory therapy aides differed from respiratory therapists and respiratory therapy technicians in that they had little patient contact; their major responsibilities included maintaining the respiratory equipment and record keeping. As of July 1999, however, there is only one certified level in this field—the respiratory therapist.

Most respiratory therapists work as members of teams along with physicians, nurses, and other health-care specialists in the respiratory therapy, anesthesiology, and pulmonary medicine departments of hospitals. Other respiratory therapy personnel work in physicians' offices, in nursing homes, in clinics, for ambulance services, and for commercial companies that provide emergency oxygen equipment and other services to home-care patients. Sometimes respiratory therapists go to patients' homes to provide treatment, check equipment, and instruct the patient and the patient's family.

Most respiratory therapists work forty hours per week. Because this lifesaving and life-supporting therapy may be needed at any hour of any day, there are evening, weekend, and holiday work hours on occasion.

Respiratory therapists held about 112,000 jobs in the United States in 2004, and most of those were held by women. More than four out of five jobs were in hospital departments of respiratory care, anesthesiology, or pulmonary medicine. Other jobs were in home health agencies, nursing homes, emergency services companies, and physicians' offices.

Salaries for respiratory therapy personnel vary according to the therapist's education and experience, the geographical location, and the place of employment. Median annual earnings for respiratory therapists in 2002 were $40,220, with the lowest-paid 10 percent earning less than $30,270 and the highest-paid 10 percent earning more than $54,030.

There is potential for advancement in this profession with increasing levels of education and professional credentialing. Respiratory therapists can not only increase their level of clinical responsibility, they can also advance to supervisory status—specifically, to assistant chief or chief of the respiratory therapy department. Therapists with graduate educations may also become instructors of respiratory therapy at the college level.

The American Association for Respiratory Care (AARC), the professional association for respiratory-care practitioners, reports that an increasing number of people are turning to respiratory therapy as a second career. Many of these individuals seek careers in the health field and find the educational requirements, work schedules, and nature of the work in respiratory therapy to be compatible with their needs and goals. These older students often bring to the job excellent life experiences in dealing with people, and this experience tends to enhance their performance.

HOW TO BECOME A RESPIRATORY THERAPIST

As respiratory equipment and treatments have become more sophisticated, the education necessary to become a respiratory therapist has become more formalized and demanding. To become a respiratory therapist, a candidate must graduate from a respiratory therapy training program. These programs range from two-year associate's degree programs to four-year bachelor's degree programs. Several hundred junior colleges, four-year colleges, and vocational/technical schools offer training programs. These programs are accredited by the Commission on Accreditation of Allied Health Education Programs (CAAHEP).

Typically, respiratory therapist programs contain course work and clinical work in general science, such as biology, chemistry, physics, and mathematics; general anatomy and physiology; cardiopulmonary-renal anatomy and physiology; microbiology; pharmacology; cardiovascular diseases; diseases of the respiratory system and disorders of breathing; general medicine and medical subspecialties; general surgery and surgical subspecialties; pediatrics; anesthesiology; patient psychology and communication; gas, humidity, and aerosol therapies; airway management; mechanical ventilation therapy; blood-gas analysis and interpretation; cardiopulmonary resuscitation; chest physiotherapy; general patient care; cardiovascular evaluation and testing; pulmonary function testing; pulmonary rehabilitation and home care; and the ethics of respiratory therapy and medical care.

In high school, interested students should take college preparatory courses, including biology, physics, chemistry, health, mathematics, English, and, where possible, psychology. The academic record necessary for acceptance into respiratory therapy educational programs varies from institution to institution. A high school diploma is usually required for employment as a respiratory therapy aide.

Personal qualities that are essential for a successful and satisfying career in respiratory therapy include an interest and aptitude in science, initiative, sound judgment, mechanical ability, physical stamina, compassion and sensitivity, and the ability to function effectively in extreme emergency situations and when working with the gravely sick and dying. Those interested in the field should keep in mind that some of the electronic equipment and high pressure gases with which respiratory therapy personnel routinely work can be dangerous. Therefore, respiratory therapists must adhere to strict safety measures and must perform regular equipment safety checks.

Certification in this field is voluntary but highly desirable. The National Board for Respiratory Care (NBRC) has established criteria for certified respiratory therapists (CRTs) and for registered respiratory therapists (RRTs). To become a certified respiratory therapist, a candidate must graduate from an accredited respiratory therapy educational program and pass a computer-based test. Upon satisfying these requirements, the candidate is eligible to use the designation CRT after his or her name. To become a registered respiratory therapist, a candidate must graduate from an accredited respiratory therapy educational program, satisfy the requirements for certified respiratory therapist, and then pass a two-part, computer-based, written and clinical simulation examination. Upon satisfying these requirements, the candidate is eligible to use the designation RRT after his or her name.

THE FUTURE

The employment outlook for respiratory therapists is expected to remain good. The Bureau of Labor Statistics of the U.S. Department of Labor projects a 46 percent increase in job opportunities by 2006. Job opportunities will be best for therapists who work with newborns and infants. Several other factors will affect the employment picture as well. The American population is not only growing, it is growing older; as this occurs, it is likely that more chronic lung disease will appear. Incidences of emphysema will increase along with those of stroke and heart failure.

More cases of chronic asthma are appearing in younger populations. And the spread of HIV/AIDS is contributing to the demand for respiratory therapy because lung disease is common among patients with HIV/AIDS. Advances in the diagnosis and treatment of cardiopulmonary disorders and in respiratory technology should further broaden the functions of respiratory-care practitioners. Greater health consciousness, accessibility of health care, and the ability to pay for health care through private and public health insurance will also contribute to keeping the demand for respiratory personnel high.

For more information about careers in respiratory therapy, contact:

American Association for Respiratory Care (AARC)
9425 North MacArthur Boulevard, Suite 100
Irving, TX 75063-4706
aarc.org

National Board for Respiratory Care (NBRC)
8310 Nieman Road
Lenexa, KS 66214-1579
nbrc.org

For information about accredited education for respiratory therapists, contact:

Committee on Accreditation for Respiratory Care (COARC)
1248 Harwood Road
Bedford, TX 76021-4244
coarc.com

SOCIAL AND HUMAN SERVICE ASSISTANT

Also Known as Mental Health
Associate/Assistant, Human Service Worker, Social Service
Assistant, Psychiatric Technician, Case Manager, Alcohol and Drug
Abuse Counselor, and Community Support Worker

The job title of social and human service assistant is applied to people who perform a wide variety of therapeutic, supportive, and preventive functions for persons who are mentally ill or developmentally disabled. These patients include individuals who are mentally disabled; children, adolescents, and adults who are psychotic and emotionally disturbed; the acutely and chronically ill; the elderly; and individuals who abuse alcohol and drugs.

Although programs for the mentally ill had declined for more than 25 years in many communities, the needs have grown, and national attention has been given to the problem. The New Freedom Commission on Mental Health was established in April 2002 to assess the needs of children and adults with serious mental and emotional problems and to identify policies that could be implemented to address these needs. The Commission received more than 2,500 direct communications, by telephone, letter, and e-mail, making suggestions for mental health policies. The work of the Commission has highlighted the importance of the mental health field and is expected to encourage job growth. Up-to-date information on current mental health initiatives can be accessed by going to the website for the National Mental Health Information Center, at mentalhealth.org.

Social and human service assistants are usually generalists who assume a wide variety of specific functions. Working under the supervision of a psychiatrist, psychologist, social worker, or registered nurse (RN), they interview and evaluate clients; provide behavior modification counseling; carry out therapeutic activities; keep client records; motivate clients and teach them new skills; advocate for clients; serve as community resources for clients and their families; help the transition to home for the client and the client's family; and follow up and report on the client's progress. They must also be skilled in such nursing techniques as taking temperature and blood pressure, counting pulse and respiration, and assisting in the administration of medications and physical treatments. Basically, their function is to work closely with the client, providing instruction; care, such as feeding and dressing; and comfort that will help the person achieve his or her maximum level of functioning.

In recent years there has been a trend toward specialization in this field. Social and human service assistants may specialize in the problems of children who are mentally disturbed, the clinical training of individuals who are developmentally disabled, drug abuse counseling, psychiatric emergencies, and crisis intervention.

In some states, another type of social and human service assistant, the case manager, is recognized. A case manager finds and negotiates for the various services, such as housing, food stamps, vocational rehabilitation, and transportation, that a patient who is about to be discharged from the hospital might need.

Social and human service assistants provide important one-to-one, day-to-day contact for the people they serve. The personalized nature of their role and the continuity they give to their clients make them important and very effective therapeutic and rehabilitative agents who are indispensable to the social service and mental health delivery system in America.

SETTINGS, SALARIES, STATISTICS

Most social and human service assistants are employed in inpatient mental health settings: state and private mental health hospitals, schools for the mentally disabled, community health centers, and mental health clinics. Opportunities also exist in after-care programs, emergency and crisis centers, alcohol and drug programs, sheltered workshops, halfway houses, social rehabilitation centers, child guidance clinics, nursing homes, and the offices of private psychiatrists. A small number function as administrators and mental health educators.

In 2002, there were approximately 305,000 paid social and human service assistants in the United States. About half worked in the health-care and social assistance industries, and a third were employed by government public welfare agencies and by organizations for the mentally and physically disabled and for the developmentally challenged.

Salaries vary greatly depending on the assistant's experience and degree of responsibility and the type of agency and its funding. Salary also depends on geographical location. In some parts of the country, the work of social and human service assistants is recognized as a career, with increased job performance matched by increased responsibility and pay. In other parts of the country, however, this work is considered a tightly defined job; to advance, assistants must acquire progressively higher academic credentials. Those who are employed in state mental health facilities are civil servants whose pay is based on the civil service scale.

Median salary level for all social and human service assistants in 2002 was approximately $23,370. Variations existed in different segments of the employer group, with government jobs paying the most, at $31,280. Residential facilities for mental health or for developmentally disabled persons and facilities for substance abusers paid the least, at about $20,010. Entry-level salaries are low, at about $14,000 in most cases, There are exceptions, however, and in some areas, a few entry-level salaries are in the $30,000 range.

HOW TO BECOME A SOCIAL AND HUMAN SERVICE ASSISTANT

Some states and some settings require only a high school diploma and on-the-job training for social and human service assistants. In most employment situations, however, some post–high school classroom time is necessary, and this preparation usually entails the awarding of an associate's degree in mental health, human services, or mental health/human services. Many community colleges offer such educational programs.

In California, where the more specialized level of mental health or psychiatric technician exists, course work in practical nursing is required. Increasingly, a bachelor of science degree in human services or mental health is required for many jobs across the United States.

The curriculum typically includes courses in basic and psychiatric nursing, general and abnormal psychology, mental health technology, sociology, personality and social development theory, group dynamics, and child development and growth. An opportunity for supervised experience working directly with clients in mental health and other settings is also provided.

Personal qualities that are important for effectiveness and satisfaction in this field include emotional stability, patience, compassion, tact, good humor, good physical health, and stamina as well as a genuine desire to help individuals who are emotionally ill or mentally impaired. The ability to relate well to these patients and their families is essential.

Licensure is currently required in only a few states, but more are adding the requirement each year.

THE FUTURE

Job openings are expected to be greater than average in this field through 2012. Several trends should contribute to a significant increase in the number of jobs for social and human service assistants. First, the mental health establishment, third-party insurers, the states, and the public are becoming increasingly aware of the cost-effectiveness and safety of this practice. Second, the population of mental health clients in community-based services and facilities is growing because of a trend toward earlier release of institutionalized patients and closure of large state facilities. This trend has created greater demand for social and human service assistants in transitional service agencies, such as sheltered workshops, halfway houses, and crisis centers. Third, as more Americans in need of help reach out for that help—or are reached out to—demands on our country's mental health and social service services should increase.

For more information about social and human service assistants, contact:

National Organization for Human Service Education (NOHSE)
375 Myrtle Avenue
Brooklyn, NY 11205
nohse.org

Council for Standards in Human Service Education (CSHSE)
Harrisburg Area Community College
Human Services Program
One HACC Drive
Harrisburg, PA 17110-2999
cshse.org

SPECIALIST IN BLOOD BANK (SBB) TECHNOLOGY

Including Blood Bank Technologist, Immunohematology Technologist, and Blood Bank Medical Technologist

A specialist in blood bank (SBB) technology is qualified by education and experience to perform all the functions of the blood bank and to serve as supervisor, educator, administrator, technical consultant, and/or research specialist in this field. An SBB demonstrates a superior level of technical proficiency and problem-solving ability in selecting donors; drawing blood; typing, or classifying, blood; running pretransfusion tests to ensure the safety of the patient; detecting and identifying any unexpected antibodies in the blood that might make transfusion dangerous or impossible; investigating hemolytic diseases in newborns; and supporting the physician in transfusion therapy.

An SBB may also study transfusion reactions, perform and evaluate quality assurance programs, establish programs to preserve and store blood by freezing, and operate reference laboratories to solve blood banking problems. A specialist in blood bank technology is skilled in all blood bank operations and may follow virtually any career path within this profession. Their importance in the health-care and emergency health-care teams can not be overestimated.

Human blood is made up of cellular elements—red blood cells, white blood cells, and platelets—that are suspended in a watery fluid called plasma. The red blood cells, or erythrocytes, carry oxygen from the lungs to the body's cells and then bring carbon dioxide back to the lungs, where it is exhaled. The white blood cells, or leukocytes, protect the body against disease and infection by surrounding and destroying invading bacteria and providing immunity. Platelets help blood to clot when a person bleeds. Approximately 7 percent of a person's weight is blood—the average male has about twelve pints of blood circulating through his body and the average female has about nine pints.

Blood—both as red blood cells and as whole blood—is transfused to replace blood in situations where blood has been lost during surgery or as a result of accident, in situations where the patient is in severe shock, and in the treatment of certain conditions and diseases, including anemia, low blood protein, hemophilia, leukemia, and cancer. The first successful transfusions of human blood were performed in 1818 by the English physician James Blundell, who used his new technique to control hemorrhaging in women who had just given birth. But success in transfusing was erratic; not until 1900 did the Austrian physiologist Karl Landsteiner discover why some transfusions helped the patient, while others were fatal. Dr. Landsteiner discovered that not all blood is the same; he identified three different types of human blood and observed that they are not always compatible.

To give a successful whole blood transfusion, the blood from the donor must be compatible with the blood of the recipient. Dr. Landsteiner determined that blood is incompatible when certain factors in the donor's red blood cells and plasma differ from those in the recipient's red blood cells and plasma. All living cells—including the cells, bacteria, and viruses in human bodies—have as part of their surfaces protein molecules that have their own unique characteristics. Dr. Landsteiner's Nobel Prize–winning discovery was that there are three different major blood types—A, B, and O. In 1902, a fourth major blood group, AB, was discovered and added to the ABO, or Landsteiner, Blood Group.

Today, many other blood systems and more than three hundred blood factors have been identified, the most common being the Rh factor. To ensure compatibility, when possible, the donor's blood is carefully cross-matched with the recipient's blood.

Approximately 14 million units—a unit is slightly less than a pint—of blood are collected to meet the transfusion needs of about 4 million Americans in a given year. Recruiting, collecting, processing, storing, testing, and typing that blood were various blood bank personnel working in public and private hospital blood banks, community blood banks, American Red Cross blood banks, and privately owned blood banks. These blood bank personnel include medical laboratory technicians, who perform daily tasks under supervision and who may also perform specialized tests that provide data for use in diagnosing diseases and evaluating treatment; medical technologists, who perform routine and certain specialized procedures in conjunction with the attending pathologist, physician, and/or scientist as well as supervising the laboratory and teaching other technologists; and specialists in blood bank technology, who are trained to collect, type, and prepare blood and its components for transfusions.

SETTINGS, SALARIES, STATISTICS

Specialists in blood bank technology work in public and private hospital blood banks and transfusion services; community blood banks; university-affiliated blood banks and transfusion services; independent laboratories; privately owned, profit-making blood banks; and university-, government-, and industry-related research laboratories. Some SBBs teach blood bank technology to medical students and medical technology students. The workweek often includes night duty, weekend hours, and emergency calls.

There are more than 4,300 certified specialists in blood bank technology in the United States, the majority of whom are female. In 2002, starting salaries ranged from $32,000 to $42,000. Advancement in this field to supervisory or administrative positions is possible, and qualified specialists may also move into teaching and/or research.

HOW TO BECOME A SPECIALIST IN BLOOD BANK TECHNOLOGY

To become an SBB, a person must first be certified as a medical technologist and hold a baccalaureate degree that includes a minimum of sixteen semester hours each of biology and chemistry, with one semester of organic or biochemistry and one semester of mathematics, or earn a baccalaureate degree in a biological or physical science and then acquire a minimum of one year of full-time acceptable clinical laboratory experience. Students satisfying these prerequisites may then apply to one of the eighteen year-long blood bank technology educational programs accredited by the Committee on Education of the American Association of Blood Banks (AABB) and by the Commission on Accreditation of Allied Health Education Programs (CAAHEP). Accredited programs are offered by hospital blood banks, community blood banks, universities, and American Red Cross facilities across the country.

A blood bank technology education consists of didactic activities covering all of the theoretical concepts of blood bank immunohematology plus practical experience in a blood bank setting. The curriculum typically contains courses and training in immunology, genetics, blood products, blood group systems, serology, physiology and pathophysiology, transfusion practices, and laboratory operations.

All of the accredited programs accept very limited numbers of students per class, and competition is stiff.

Certification in blood bank technology is offered by the American Society of Clinical Pathologists (ASCP) in conjunction with the AABB. The ASCP administers a written examination to eligible candidates. To be eligible for this examination, a candidate must (1) have a baccalaureate degree from a regionally accredited college or university and successfully complete an accredited specialist in blood bank technology program, (2) hold BB (ASCP) certification or be an ASCP-certified medical technologist and have a baccalaureate degree plus five years of full-time acceptable clinical laboratory experience in blood banking that has been appropriately supervised, or (3) hold a master's or doctorate in immunohematology or a related field and have three years of experience. Upon satisfying the requirements for certification, a candidate may use the designation SBB (ASCP), for specialist in blood bank who is certified by the Board of Registry of the American Society of Clinical Pathologists, after his or her name.

The Board of Registry of the ASCP has also established certification at the blood bank technologist level in response to a perceived need for credentialing, particularly for two groups of laboratory workers: (1) individuals employed in blood bank or transfusion services who have baccalaureate degrees but are not certified medical technologists, and (2) medical laboratory technicians who work in blood banks or transfusion services who have completed a baccalaureate degree. The test consists of a written section only and is administered in numerous test centers throughout the United States. Upon passing this competency examination, a candidate is designated as a BB (ASCP), for blood bank technologist certified by the American Society of Clinical Pathologists. Although this level of certification is new, great interest has been shown in it.

Personal qualities and aptitudes that can contribute to success and career-long satisfaction as a specialist in blood bank technology include intelligence, a strong interest and ability in the sciences, dependability and a sense of duty, good organizational skills, good psychomotor skills, good health, and a genuine desire to help the ill. Also, blood bank work is hectic, and SBBs must be willing and able to function effectively at that hectic pace.

THE FUTURE

The demand for specialists in blood bank technology and other blood bank personnel currently exceeds the supply, and job growth in this field is expected to grow steadily through 2012. Special needs caused by the war in Iraq, other military actions, and violence in other areas creates special needs for blood supply. The government, the American Red Cross, and other organizations all need more blood technologists in such times of critically increased need.

For more information about a career in blood bank technology, contact:

American Association of Blood Banks (AABB)
8101 Glenbrook Road
Bethesda, MD 20814
aabb.org

The AABB website maintains a job line that emphasizes jobs in blood banking, transfusion medicine, and cellular therapy.

For information regarding certification, contact:

Board of Registry
American Society for Clinical Pathology (ASCP)
2100 West Harrison Street
Chicago, IL 60612
ascp.org

SPEECH-LANGUAGE PATHOLOGIST AND AUDIOLOGIST

Speech-language pathologists and audiologists are health professionals who provide specialized help to children and adults who have communication disorders.

Approximately 47 million people in the United States of all ages, races, and gender experience or live with some type of communication disorder. According to the National Health Statistics Center, 28 million people in the United States have a hearing impairment and 14 million have a voice, speech, or language disorder. Twenty-one of every thousand children under the age of eighteen have some degree of hearing loss. Six million children have a speech or language disorder. Every day, about thirty infants are born with hearing loss. Speech and hearing disabilities can affect more than a person's ability to communicate effectively—they can imperil the ability to learn, to play, to work, and to relate to others. Left untreated, they can seriously reduce the person's quality of life and cause behavioral and other emotional problems.

Speech-language pathologists are health professionals who are concerned with the identification, prevention, assessment, and treatment of speech, language, and voice disorders caused by total or partial hearing loss, a cleft palate or other anatomical anomaly, mental retardation, cerebral palsy, brain trauma, or emotional problems. Children who fail to learn to talk at the usual age, those who improperly pronounce certain letters or combinations of letters, individuals who stutter, people recovering from strokes, those suffering from partial or temporary aphasia—the loss of the power to use or understand words—and other patients whose ability to communicate verbally is impaired are helped by this form of treatment. In addition to the traditionally recognized role, the speech-language pathologist may also be available to provide elective clinical services to nonstandard-English speakers who do not present a disorder.

Speech-language pathologists and audiologists are autonomous professionals and do not work under direct medical supervision. In diagnosing and evaluating the patient's speech and language abilities and in planning and implementing a treatment program to restore and/or develop the patient's verbal communication skills, the speech-language pathologist may work closely with audiologists; physicians; psychologists; social workers; counselors; and educational, physical, and occupational therapists. Speech-language pathologists may also engage in research relating to human communication.

Audiologists are health professionals who specialize in the identification, assessment, and nonmedical treatment of hearing problems caused by certain otological or neurological disorders. Their goals are the prevention of hearing disability and the conservation of hearing in children and adults.

The audiologist assesses the type and extent of the hearing disability and supplements his or her findings with medical, educational, social, behavioral, and other data supplied by the patient's physician and other health professionals. The audiologist will then plan and implement a program of aural rehabilitation designed to meet the patient's needs. When necessary, a hearing aid is dispensed to the patient.

Because speech and hearing are so interrelated, competency in one field necessitates knowledge of the other.

Speech-language pathologists and audiologists do very important "people work." Because of their skills, insights, and dedication, many hearing- and speech-impaired individuals who have felt isolated by their disabilities can at last understand and be understood. Whole worlds of information are suddenly opened to them, and their ideas, dreams, personalities, and futures are freed.

SETTINGS, SALARIES, STATISTICS

Audiologists and speech-language pathologists work in hospitals and medical centers, public and private schools, rehabilitation centers, nursing care facilities, adult day-care centers, colleges and universities, and state and federal government agencies. Some are in private practice. Speech-language pathologists are also often employed by long-term health-care facilities and home health programs.

Speech-language pathologists held about 94,000 jobs in 2002, according to the U.S. Department of Labor. Most of those were in schools, and others were in hospitals, medical offices, nursing homes, home health services, family services, childcare facilities, and others. A few speech-language pathologists were in private practice and contracted their services or work as consultants.

Median annual earnings for speech-language consultants in 2002 were $49,450, with the lowest-paid 10 percent earning less than $32,580 and the highest-paid 10 percent earning more than $74,010. Starting salaries were approximately $37,000 for those working an academic year and $42,000 for those on a full calendar year.

The median annual income for audiologists was comparable, at $48,400 in 2002. The median starting salary level was approximately $43,000 on a calendar-year basis.

HOW TO BECOME AN AUDIOLOGIST OR SPEECH-LANGUAGE PATHOLOGIST

To practice as a speech-language pathologist or audiologist, a master's degree in speech-language pathology or audiology is necessary. The undergraduate program is considered preprofessional and prepares students only to function as technicians or aides. As an undergraduate, the student learns anatomy; biology; physiology; physics; sociology; linguistics, which is the science of language; semantics, which is the branch of linguistics concerned with the nature, structure, and, especially, the development and evolution of speech forms; phonetics, or speech sounds; and psychology.

After obtaining a bachelor's degree in speech-language pathology or audiology, the candidate proceeds to graduate school. The master's degree program, which typically entails two years of study, provides advanced course work in anatomy; physics; acoustics; the normal development and function of speech, language, and hearing; the nature of speech, language, and hearing disorders; the psychological aspects of communication; the mechanisms and processes of hearing and speech; and the evaluation and correction of speech, language, and hearing disorders. These programs also include supervised clinical experience.

A master's degree is an important enhancement to employment because Medicare and Medicaid will pay only for the services of audiologists and speech-language pathologists who hold a master's degree in these fields. In addition, a master's degree is necessary for certification. Speech-language pathologists and audiologists who hold a master's degree in these fields and who have completed a minimum of one year as an intern in an approved setting are eligible for the certification examination administered by the American Speech-Language Hearing Association (ASHA).

Upon passing this national examination, the candidate earns a certificate of clinical competence, or CCC. Some people hold a certificate in both audiology and speech-language pathology. Although voluntary, certification is usually necessary for professional advancement. Most speech-language pathologists and audiologists who work in public schools must have a state-issued practice certificate, and, in many states, a CCC is necessary to obtain this state certificate. In many states, all audiologists and speech-language pathologists must be licensed to work.

Personal qualities that are essential to career-long success and satisfaction in the fields of audiology and speech-language pathology include the ability to concentrate intensely; a warm, friendly personality that inspires trust and confidence; and a genuine desire to help. And, because audiology and speech-language pathology are often slow processes that produce gradual results and moments of frustration as well as of deep satisfaction, large helpings of patience and perseverance are required.

THE FUTURE

Job growth is expected to be much faster than average in both of these fields through 2012. Contributing to the increase in demand for audiologists and speech-language pathologists are two major factors: first, the population is expanding and the number of older Americans—who tend to comprise a large percentage of persons with communication disorders—is expanding even faster; second, awareness of the importance of early detection of hearing and language problems has resulted in legislation mandating the creation of elementary school speech-language-hearing programs.

For more information about audiologists and speech-language pathologists, contact:

American Speech-Language Hearing Association (ASHA)
10801 Rockville Pike
Rockville, MD 20852
asha.org

American Academy of Audiology
11730 Plaza America Drive, Suite 300
Reston, VA 20190
audiology.org

CHAPTER 57

SURGICAL TECHNOLOGIST

Also Known as Operating Room Specialist, OR Technician, Operating Room Technician, and Scrub Technologist

Surgical technologists are members of the surgical team who work primarily in the operating room, performing tasks that provide a clean, safe surgical environment; contribute to the efficiency of the operating room team; and support the surgeons, surgeon assistants, anesthesiologists, nurse anesthetists, registered nurses (RNs), licensed practical nurses (LPNs), and any other personnel who may be involved in the operative procedure.

This allied health professional provides these services under the supervision and responsibility of the operating room supervisor, who is an RN, or under a surgical technology supervisor.

A *scrub technologist* is the surgical technologist who checks supplies, equipment, sterile linens, and fluids needed for the procedure; sets up the sterile table with instruments, sutures, blades, cautery, suction, and any prostheses and solutions needed for the procedure; helps drape the sterile field; gowns and gloves the surgeons and assistants; and counts sponges, needles, and instruments prior to surgery and after the incision is closed. During surgery, he or she passes instruments and other sterile supplies to the surgeons and surgeon assistants; holds retractors; cuts sutures; prepares sterile dressings; cleans and prepares instruments for sterilization; operates sterilizers, lights, suction machines, and EKG monitors; and assists in the use of electrosurgical equipment, pacemaker equipment, and sophisticated endoscopic equipment. The scrub technologist may also help in cleaning the operating room and readying it for the next patient. He or she must be able to anticipate the surgeons' needs, understand the procedures being performed, and be constantly vigilant that sterile technique is maintained.

A *circulating surgical technologist* is the surgical technologist who is the primary unsterile member of the surgical team who obtains additional instruments, supplies, and equipment required while the surgical procedure is in progress. The circulating surgical technologist checks the patient's chart; identifies the patient and brings him or her to the operating room; transfers the patient to the operating table; positions the patient; prepares the incision site; and otherwise prepares the patient. This technologist also applies electrosurgical pads and tourniquets before the procedure begins; opens the sterile field, or the packages of sterilized instruments; supplies the sterile field with anything necessary during the procedure; keeps accurate records throughout the procedure; assists the anesthesia personnel; handles specimens; takes the sponge, needle, and instrument count; makes certain that dressings are secure after surgery; transports the patient to the recovery room; and assists in the cleaning and preparation of the operating room for the next patient.

Surgical technologists with additional specialized education and training may also act in the role of the *surgical first assistant*. The surgical first assistant provides aid in exposure, hemostasis, and other technical functions under the supervision of the surgeon.

From region to region, institution to institution, and operation to operation, there is, of course, variation in the specific functions carried out by a surgical technologist. Some surgical technologists become highly trained and specialize in one or several related areas of surgery. A private scrub is a surgical technologist who is employed directly by a surgeon or group of surgeons to assist them during all of their operations.

SETTINGS, SALARIES, STATISTICS

Surgical technologists held about 72,000 jobs in 2002. Approximately 85 percent work in hospitals—usually in the operating room but also in the emergency room and the delivery room. Surgical technologists also work in outpatient surgicenters as instructors and as private-duty scrubs for physicians.

The median annual salary for surgical technologists was approximately $31,210 in 2002, with a range of approximately $21,500 to $44,000. Surgical technologists working on the East and West coasts tend to earn more than average, and private scrubs also earn higher salaries. Surgical technologists usually work five-day, forty-hour workweeks and must spend some time on call.

Advancement to the positions of assistant operating room administrator—the manager of the operating room who orders supplies and arranges work schedules—or assistant operating room supervisor—the supervisor who directs the other surgical technologists in the operating room—is possible with experience. Other career options include materials manager, central service manager, educator, medical sales representative, and organ transplantation technician.

HOW TO BECOME A SURGICAL TECHNOLOGIST

Most technologists today receive their education at vocational/technical schools and colleges. Surgical technologist educational programs offered by these institutions are typically nine months to one year in length. Some of the community college programs entail two years of study and award an associate's degree.

All of these programs entail both classroom instruction and supervised clinical experience. Almost all require a high school diploma or its equivalent. In high school, courses in health and biology provide good background instruction.

Surgical technologists are educated in asepsis—maintaining a sterile environment—and also study anatomy, physiology, medical terminology, microbiology, pathology, operating room procedure, environmental dangers, surgical complications, pharmacology, suturing, instrumentation, prosthetics, anesthesia, and transporting and positioning patients. In the supervised clinical phase of their educations, they will learn about the surgical procedures common to general surgery and to the surgical specialties, namely obstetric, gynecologic, plastic, thoracic, vascular, orthopedic, ophthalmologic, otorhinolaryngologic, pediatric, urologic, cardiovascular, oral, and neurosurgery.

Educational programs are accredited by the Commission on Accreditation of Allied Health Education Programs (CAAHEP), which is an independent body that accredits education programs for this and seventeen other allied health professions. Students in these programs spend between 500 and 1,000 hours in clinical training in the operating room.

Some surgical technologists are trained on the job over a period of six weeks to one year, depending on the institution and the student's previous experience. Often such trainees are nursing aides, practical nurses, or other hospital personnel who have transferred to their institution's department of surgery. However, surgical technologists who are trained on the job are not eligible to take the certification examination this profession offers.

The U.S. Army, Navy, and Air Force also train surgical technologists, designated as operating room specialists, OR technicians, and operating room technicians.

Personal qualities that are important for success as a surgical technologist include intelligence, integrity, stamina, manual dexterity, the ability to work as a member of a team, an orientation toward service to people, respect for the patient's privacy, the capacity for calm and reasoned judgment particularly in stressful situations, attention to detail, and accuracy.

The Liaison Council on Certification, which is an independent certifying body affiliated with the Association of Surgical Technologists (AST), offers a certification examination for surgical technologists. Since March 2000, only graduates of CAAHEP-accredited surgical technology programs are eligible for this exam.

This multiple-choice examination, which is administered nationwide each month, tests the candidate's knowledge of the basic sciences, safe patient care, aseptic technique and environmental control, supplies and equipment, and surgical procedures. A passing score (which ranges from 65 percent to 75 percent, depending on the difficulty level of each exam) entitles the candidate to use the letters CST, for certified surgical technologist, after his or her name. Although not required for employment, certification is accepted by most employers as a measure of ability, and being certified definitely expands the number of job possibilities and enhances earnings.

To maintain certification, technologists must accumulate eighty continuing education credits every six years or must retake the certifying examination.

The Liaison Council on Certification of AST also offers an advanced certifying examination for certified surgical technologists who are practicing surgical first assistants. Upon passing this examination, a surgical technologist may use the letters CST/CFA, for CST-certified first assistant, after his or her name.

Licensure for surgical technologists currently is not required anywhere in the United States. Several states, however, require registration with the state in order to practice.

THE FUTURE

The occupational outlook for surgical technologists—and especially for certified surgical technologists—is good, with growth in the field expected to exceed 30 percent in the next ten years. It is estimated that an additional 25,000 jobs will be created for surgical technologists by the year 2010.

Several factors should contribute to this strong demand. They include the growing American population, the aging American population, the ability of more Americans than ever before to afford surgery because of public and private health insurance plans, greater health-consciousness, the ever-increasing variety of surgical procedures available, and the expanded role of the surgical technologist. Cost-containment considerations on the part of hospitals and third-party insurers have resulted in the greater use of surgical technologists and their assignment to a wider range of responsibilities in the operating room, depending on the technologist's level of education and experience.

Surgical technologists do important work. Their days are fast paced, and both the technical and the human sides of their work are fascinating and rewarding.

For more information about surgical technologists, certification, and accredited programs, contact:

Association of Surgical Technologists (AST)
7108-C South Alton Way
Centennial, CO 80112-2106
ast.org

Liaison Council on Certification for the Surgical Technologist
128 South Tejon Street, Suite 301
Colorado Springs, CO 80903
lcc-st.org

CHAPTER 58

THERAPEUTIC RECREATION SPECIALIST (TRS)

Also Known as Recreational Therapist and Activities Director

Therapeutic recreation specialists (TRSs) provide recreation services to people who are ill or who have disabilities. The TRS is a member of the medical treatment team that works with people who have mental, physical, and/or emotional disabilities by creating and implementing medically approved activities.

Recreational therapy programs help individuals build confidence, socialize effectively, and remediate the effects of illness or disability. The goals of recreational therapy are the relief of emotional and physical tension, increased physical and mental health, increased independence, improved quality of life, and the establishment of a lifestyle that promotes a person's sense of self-worth within a community.

The therapeutic recreation specialist uses a variety of treatment modalities that include life skills, leisure activities, recreation, and play—adaptive sports, dancing, arts and crafts, music, gardening, camping, dramatics, and various social activities—combined with individual and group counseling techniques. The TRS promotes health, wellness, and a level of functioning that maximizes the patient's ability to lead a full life.

The goal is for the patient to not only experience the immediate excitement, fun, satisfaction, and social interaction of the recreational activity, but also to gain the longer-range benefits of enhanced self-esteem, greater independence, and a sense of involvement, all leading, ideally, to a minimizing of symptoms and a maximizing of potential.

Nursing homes and hospitals are the leading employers of therapeutic recreation specialists. In these settings, they are sometimes called activities directors. TRSs also work in public and private facilities for the mentally ill or mentally disabled; general, pediatric, and psychiatric hospitals; senior centers; group homes; community recreation centers; correctional facilities; juvenile detention homes; schools for persons who are visually impaired; rehabilitation centers; day-care centers; camps; and private community agencies. A few therapeutic recreation specialists are self-employed and provide therapeutic recreation services on a contract basis to institutions or groups of institutions.

The primary populations served by recreational therapists are older adults and individuals with psychiatric impairments.

Approximately 27,000 recreational therapists held jobs in 2002—a drop from 38,000 just a few years before. This job loss was due to the general recession in the economy and to cost-containment policies by hospitals, nursing homes, and other institutions as well as by third-party payers, such as insurance companies and governmental agencies.

It is expected that the increased needs of senior citizens, returning veterans, and others will contribute to job growth, but, in general, this field is not expected to grow as fast as the average through 2012.

Median annual earnings of recreational therapists were $30,540 in 2002, with a range from less than $18,130 to higher than $47,180. The median annual salary for those working in nursing homes was about $25,000 a year. Therapists working in small nursing homes tend to have salaries at the low end of the scale, and experienced therapists working in large institutions tend to have earnings at the high end.

HOW TO BECOME A THERAPEUTIC RECREATION SPECIALIST

Prospective therapeutic recreation specialists can enter the profession through education and experience. A student must obtain a minimum of a bachelor's degree in recreation with course work in therapeutic recreation, general education, supportive course work, and an internship in therapeutic recreation. Administrative, research, and teaching positions in this field usually require a master's degree in therapeutic recreation.

Certification in this field is offered by the National Council for Therapeutic Recreation Certification (NCTRC). While voluntary, certification is increasingly important because many states have already adopted or are considering adopting laws requiring certification for employment.

To become a CTRS, or certified therapeutic recreation specialist, a candidate must meet eligibility requirements and then pass the National Exam for Therapeutic Recreation Specialists. The eligibility requirements to take the CTRS exam include either (1) a baccalaureate degree or higher with a major in therapeutic recreation or recreation with therapeutic recreation course work; general recreation course work; supportive course work in anatomy, physiology, abnormal psychology, and human growth and development; and a field placement experience in therapeutic recreation services under a CTRS supervisor; *or* (2) a baccalaureate degree or higher with upper-division therapeutic recreation course work, upper-division general recreation course work, supportive course work, and work experience in therapeutic recreation.

Men and women who are interested in becoming therapeutic recreation specialists should be healthy mentally and physically, imaginative, enthusiastic, and warm. They should also have a good speaking ability, a sense of humor, and a genuine desire to help others.

THE FUTURE

Employment opportunities in this field are not expected to grow as fast as the average over the next decade. Recreation therapy is still a relatively new profession; as rehabilitation programs and facilities expand to meet the demands of the growing and aging population and as recognition of the validity of this therapy grows, opportunities for therapeutic recreation specialists should increase. Unfortunately, however, as is the case with other support therapies, recreation therapy programs are very often subject to shifts in the economic picture.

For more information about therapeutic recreation specialists, contact:

American Therapeutic Recreation Association (ATRA)
1414 Prince Street, Suite 204
Alexandria, VA 22314-2853
atra-tr.org

National Therapeutic Recreation Society (NTRS)
22377 Belmont Ridge Road
Ashburn, VA 20148-4501
ntrs.org

National Council for Therapeutic Recreation Certification (NCTRC)
7 Elmwood Drive
New City, NY 10956
nctrc.org

ABOUT THE AUTHOR

Barbara Mardinly Swanson is a professional writer with a lifelong interest in health care and an extensive knowledge of the American health-care system and the services it provides. Her abiding respect for medical professionals motivated her to write this book.

Previous books by Barbara Swanson include *Tax Shelters: A Guide for Investors and Their Advisors* (Dow Jones-Irwin, 1982), which she coauthored with her husband, Robert E. Swanson. Her essays and poetry have appeared nationally. She is a graduate of Smith College.